Walking the
MW00774593
Everywhere I look, memories that aren't mine creep in from the corners, creep out of the shadows.
I've always known about the beauty and magic that is concealed within the crevices of everyday life, but this...
I don't deserve this.
POP WILL EAT ITSELF
SOUNDGARDEN
STORY: JIM COMER
ART: JOE CORRONEY
LETTERING: AILEEN E. MILES

The Wyrm had caught me in its poisonous trap. It seems so long ago now...
I had gone to the Amazon, pretending to be there to fight the Dissolver when what I really wanted was to find a cure.
I found the Mokolé, and they gave me the memory to find the cure. And more.

It was the "more" part that brought me to find these two.
COFFEE $1
SANDWICHES
OPEN
HEY, PETE, YOU READY?
ARE YOU SURE THAT IT'S OKAY TO DO THIS IN PUBLIC? AREN'T PEOPLE GOING TO WONDER?
YOU WANTED TO SEE IF DRAGON LIKES YOU! IF I TOO YOU HOME, YOU'D BE PUPPY CHOW NOW PUT YOUR LIPS ON THE DREAMSTICK AND BLOW.

My head's exploding.
My lungs are bursting.
WHOOO
Is it the drugs or oxygen deprivation?
Oh, Gaia, I'm falling.
I am not just Peter Ward.
I am not just my parents.
I am not just the Garou.
I am all there was, all there is, and all there shall be again.

We are all there is. The Bunyip are nearly destroyed and the Dissolver is corrupting the Dreamtime. Now, as these blood drinkers come for us, it seems as if there is no hope left for the land.
tek
BLAM BLAM BLAM
BLAM BLAM BLAM
KRAK
Why the Rainbow Serpent chose me to guard her sacred stone is a mystery. I am not Mokolé. I am not Bunyip. Born in eclipse, yes, but still nothing more than Kin. How can I possibly save the stone from these creatures?
My brethren are all exhausted, their Rage nearly spent on just keeping us from being overtaken by the ship. They can't save me either.
PLIP
PLIP

I have to get away with the stone...

EVERYONE, FOLLOW ME INTO THE JUNGLE. STANDING STONE AND TEETH OF KINGS, WAIT HERE TO AMBUSH. WE NEED TIME TO GET AWAY.

BLAM BLAM BLAM
tik
tik
tek
KRAK

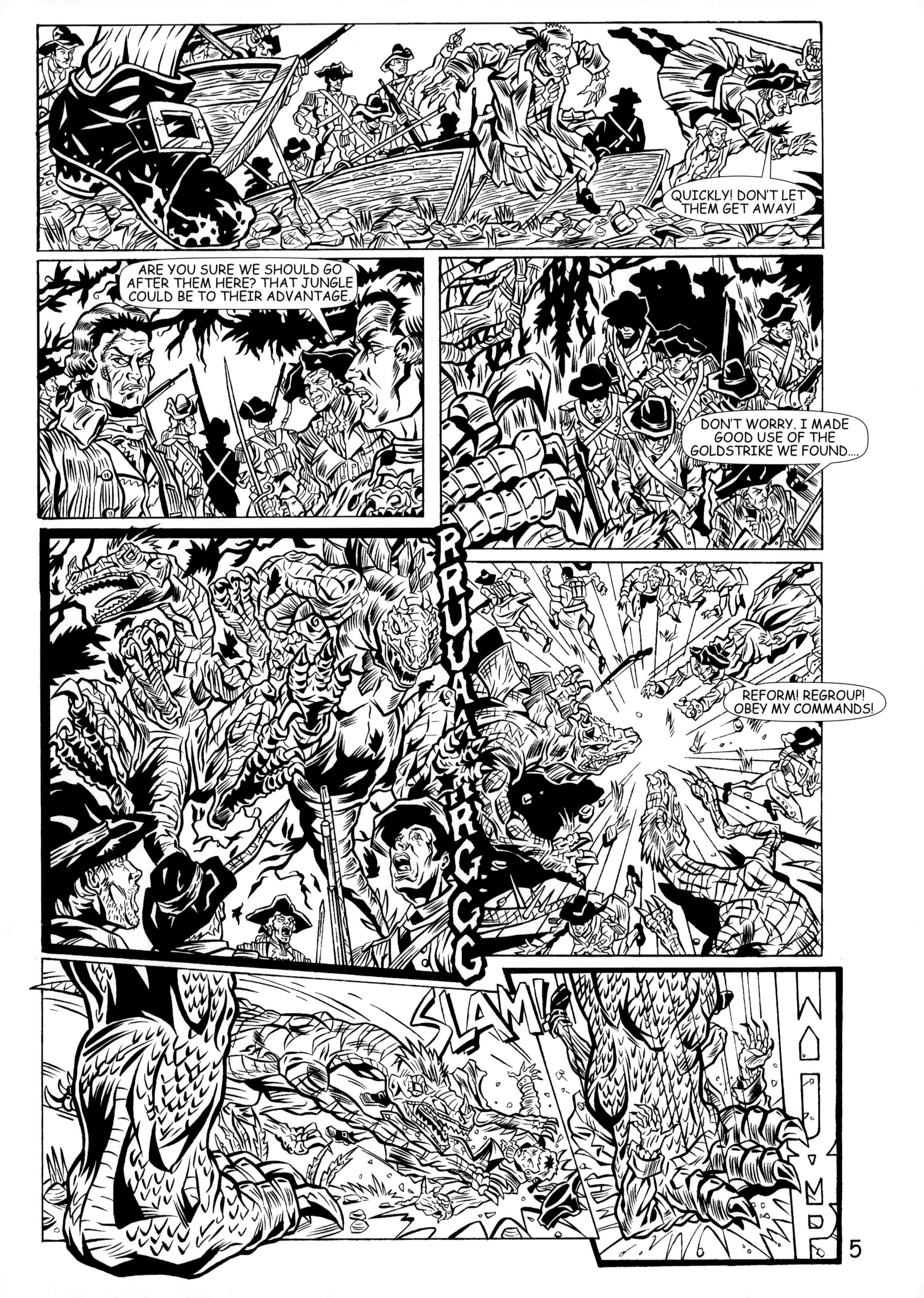
QUICKLY! DON'T LET THEM GET AWAY!
ARE YOU SURE WE SHOULD GO AFTER THEM HERE? THAT JUNGLE COULD BE TO THEIR ADVANTAGE.
DON'T WORRY. I MADE GOOD USE OF THE GOLDSTRIKE WE FOUND....
RRUAARRGGG
REFORM! REGROUP! OBEY MY COMMANDS!
SLAM!
WOOOMP

FIRE!
BLAM
BLAM
BLAM

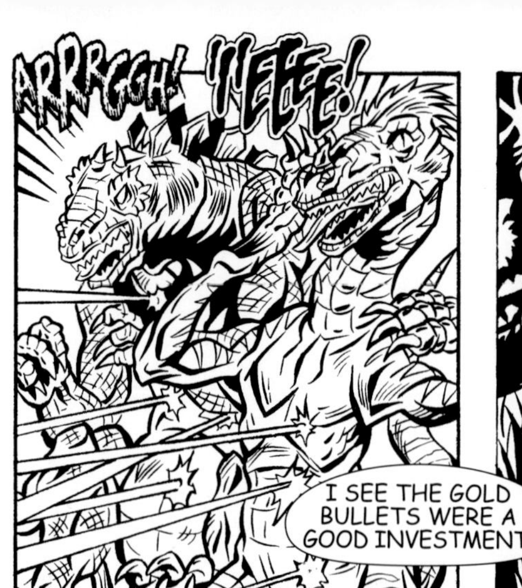
ARRRGGH!
I SEE THE GOLD BULLETS WERE A GOOD INVESTMENT.

OF COURSE THEY WERE! I TOLD YOU THE YOUNGLING WASN'T LYING!

CROWNED, STANDING STONE AND TEETH OF KINGS ARE DEAD! THEY'RE USING GOLD!

PLEASE, I'M NOT YOUR CROWNED! I'M ONLY KIN. WHY MUST I MAKE ALL THE DECISIONS?

BECAUSE DRAGON SAID YOU ARE TO BE TREATED AS ONE OF US. BECAUSE RAINBOW SERPENT SAID YOU'RE SUPPOSED TO CARRY HER TO SAFETY.
BECAUSE THAT'S HOW IT IS.

FINE. I NEED TO GET THE STONE TO SAFETY. I THINK THERE WILL BE A PLACE AT THE CENTER OF THE ISLAND. GIVE ME THE TIME.

DRAGON, PLEASE, WHAT AM I TO **DO**?

I am not Mokolé, though they say that you've chosen me.
I have no powers to guard the great spirit you have entrusted me with.
Is this a gift or a curse you have granted me?
Please, give me a sign!
KRRIK
PETE! WHAT HAPPENED, MAN? DID DRAGON GIVE YOU AN ANSWER?

J.C.

Mokolé™

Keepers of Sun's Wisdom

By Jim Comer

Credits

Author: Jim Comer
Additional writing: Rick Russell, Chad Imbrogno, Conrad Hubbard
Developer: Ethan Skemp
Editor: Aileen E. Miles
Art Director: Aileen E. Miles
Comic Book Art: Joe Corroney
Art: Jeff Holt, Larry MacDougall, Steve Prescott, Ron Spencer, James Stowe
Layout & Typesetting: Aileen E. Miles
Cover Design: Aileen E. Miles

Special Thanks

Not a lot of jokes this time, just a fond farewell to two of the greatest gentlemen who ever edited or developed a White Wolf book (and they write a mean Changing Breed or two as well), and who have made the office a genuinely better place to be during the time they stayed here:

Ed "El Tiburon Gigante" **Hall**, for making damn sure that *any* book he worked on, particularly those stupid ol' **Werewolf** books, was going to be done *right*.

Richard E. "Eye-Drinkin', Black-Wearing, Wisecrackin' Raven" **Dansky**, for just about everything, including movie reviews, Seder hospitality and the killer cat.

All our best, fellas. You know where to find us if you ever get nostalgic for the old grind, and want to stop and laugh at the rest of us still doing this for a living.

To Mark and Chris.

Thanks to the clutch: Chad, Mike, Meegan, Dean, Liz, Steve, Troy and Christopher; thanks to Patrick and Gregg for encouragement; thanks to Conrad for India, and to John C. McLoughlin for the Kings. The dragons in this book are yours; the errors are all mine.

735 PARK NORTH BLVD.
SUITE 128
CLARKSTON, GA 30021
USA

Mokolé™

Contents

These dragons grow exceeding big, and from their mouths cast forth a most pestilential breath, like unto thick smoke rising from a fire. At their destined time they gather together, and developing wings they begin to raise themselves into the air. Then, by God's good judgment, being too heavy they fall into a certain river which springs from Paradise, and therein they perish wholly. All those who dwell round about attend the season of the dragons, and when they see that one has fallen they yet wait seventy days. Then they go down and discover the bare bones of the dragon, that they may take the carbuncle that is rooted in the forehead thereof.

— Jordanus, The Wonders of the East.

Coils.

They filled his mind's eye as glass crunched beneath his Pumas. How much glass, how many nights, how many cities? His head felt heavy as he shook it, heavy with horns and crests, heavy with the Was. Sun reddened the glass and steel of Sydney's skyscrapers as he paced along trying to make up his mind. Should he take Jeffo and Morwangu's offer? Would he still be Peter if he did?

He was full of time. Christmas dinner didn't compare to the way it bloated him. There were days when the mammalian heat of his own body felt wrong. He dreamed of jungle swamps older than the Amazon. The fetish cellphone he carried was silent now, its technospirit angered. He saw tropical plants in corporate lobbies, and felt a longing for the Sun.

Why, Mother? Why?

Dragon had called him, with Jeffo and Morwangu as His agents, and done more to Peter than Nyi and Trees Dream could hope to. Dragon had steered him to the airport, bags packed for he knew not where, half dazed. In the Pacific night he had shaken awake and realized that this was a flight to Australia. On a street corner two Aboriginal musicians had known his name, told him why he was here. They had said that they had the answer, the way he should go, and had completed the gift of their Amazon cousins. Now the bequest was more than a flood of unwanted memories. It was the training manual for an army of dreams, the scripture for a church millions of years old. It was the creed of his deadliest enemies.

Garou had fought Mokolé for ten thousand years. Since before there were Glass Walkers, before there were even tribes at all, packs had taught their cubs to fear and hate the great reptiles. In the Wars of Rage, Garou had killed so many

Mokolé that the Crescent Moons had finally declared the crocodile-shapeshifters extinct.

That belief had betrayed them in the Amazon. Both the Garou and their enemies had been ambushed, trapped, destroyed without quarter by hidden foes mightier than them by far. Only Peter's friends, the Ghost Raptors, had managed to communicate with the Dragon Breed at all, and then only imperfectly. Nyi Feathered-Thunder and her grandson Trees Dream had saved them from the deadly snow plague, filling Peter's head with memories, the ancient Mnesis of the Mokolé. He had remembered things he never could, that no one could. He was more than himself, more than any Garou since the beginning of time.

He wasn't happy with it.

Peter turned another corner and saw them again.

"Took y' long enough, dinnit?" The younger Aborigine took another swig of cane spirit and offered the bottle to Peter, who shook his head. "Y'wanna hear more, then?"

"Yeah. Uh, yeah, I think I better."

Morwangu quickened the beat of the click sticks and began to chant, not Lardil or Pitjantjara but an older language, one Peter had heard half a world away. His words were impossible to understand, then impossible to mistake, and Peter's eyes blurred. *I know what he's saying. I learned it... Within.*

Was and Is were one.

Where Are All the Dragons?

Everyone knows that there are dragons. And, if you think about it, you always knew. Remember? Lurking in the corners of folklore and fairy tales; every creature in your dinosaur books. Under your bed, under the pond, under the surface of your mind? They were there.

You started to ask questions and the grownups told you there weren't any such things. You didn't believe them and looked for yourself. Looked into yourself for the coils and scales. The dragons were real.

You were a dragon.

The Mokolé are shapeshifters: beings with three forms who can change between them at will. One form is human. One is reptilian: crocodile, alligator, perhaps monitor lizard. The one in between is a beast out of time — dinosaur, dragon, sea-serpent, or some other living fossil, an amalgam of dreamed-of power. But the Mokolé are more than just shapeshifters. They are the Memory of Gaia, the living record of "all that's past," and they carry within them millions of years of history. Memory is the ocean wherein they swim and the wilderness they explore; they are living treasures of wisdom and power. This book will help you bring Mokolé into a role-playing game. It is a players' guide, a book of rules, and a book about the Dragon Breed.

The Mokolé are immensely powerful creatures, but they are more than just living battle tanks who rampage over the bloody World of Darkness. Their true work is memory, the Last Art, and they remember like no others. However, the Wars of Rage have slain so many of them and so damaged their "great work of time" that, according to them, Gaia is now almost mindless. If the decay is not halted, the Memory will be destroyed, and even saving Gaia will not be worth it.

The Dragon Breed

For I am a brother to dragons, and a companion to owls.

— Job 30:29

The Mokolé are the oldest of the Changing Breeds. Paradoxically, they are at once the most unified and the most divided. Unlike their old enemies, the Garou, who are one wolf species worldwide, they are many species and many genera: monitors, gavials, alligators, crocodiles and Gila monsters. Their human forms are divided likewise among the human peoples of the tropics. Each Mokolé lives by the "moment of the sun" which marked the time of her birth in the day or year. The absence of Sun at night means that some Mokolé follow Luna instead; in all, they are the only Changing Breed to revere both Helios and Luna. Complicating things further, the Mokolé are further divided into streams (the four great regional alliances of their kind) and individual clutches (local groups). Unifying forces, however, are stronger. All Mokolé speak the Dragon's Tongue, and all share Mnesis, memories inherited from ancestors which connect them to the distant past when dinosaurs walked the Earth.

There are no "tribes" to command the loyalty of Mokolé. Mokolé are neither pack creatures like the Garou, nor solitary like the Bastet. Instead, they are united into clutches, family-like groups of Mokolé and Kin. The clutches are localized and preserve the Memory of a certain area. Wanderers pass between them to unite what remains of Gaia's Memory. Clutches ally into streams, the four great "rivers out of Eden" which are the Mokolé. The four streams are:

The **Gumagan**, the Stream of the Forerunners, are the ancient Mokolé of Australia and Oceania. Now few in number, they are more adept than others at entering the Umbra and at deep Mnesis voyaging. They are Aborigines and Melanesians in their Homid forms, and saltwater crocodiles or perenty monitors in their Suchid forms.

The **Makara**, the Stream of the Folk, are the complex patchwork of Mokolé lineage and clutches native to the Indian subcontinent. They are skillful at negotiating the turbulent waters of Indian politics, religion and mysticism, and are Indian natives in their human forms. Their Suchid forms are gavials, mugger crocodiles and saltwater crocodiles. They use the motions of the Sun through the year, not through the day, to distinguish their auspices.

The **Mokolé-mbembe**, the Stream of the Fighters, are the largest and best known stream. They are the stream famous for their deeds and sufferings in the Wars of Rage. They are the Mokolé of Africa and the Americas, who are Native Americans and Africans in their Homid forms, and crocodiles, alligators, caimans, or even Gila monsters in

their Suchid forms. Among them there have been many heroes, and they are the greatest warriors among the Mokolé.

The **Zhong Lung**, the Stream of the Philosophers, are the scholars and teachers of the Dragon Breed, the stream least harmed by the ravages of the Garou. They are the Mokolé of the Middle Kingdom, including China, Korea, Japan, Vietnam and surrounding areas. They have great learning and share it with the other shapeshifters of the East, the hengeyokai. In their Homid forms, they are Asians of various kinds, and in their Suchid forms, they are Chinese alligators, saltwater crocodiles and monitor lizards. Like their kin the Makara, they count their auspices by the seasons of the year, not by the times of day.

But every stream has a spring, and all four streams of the Mokolé remember their source in the Dinosaur Kings. According to the most ancient of Mokolé lore, these reptilian toolmakers walked Gaia's Face two hundred million years ago, and were Her original guardians. Their living cities and tools surpassed any work of human hands, and their Memory served them in place of written record or schooling. Among them the Mokolé of that age were scholars, teachers, soldiers, workers, hunters and priests of Sun. Their reign endured for over one hundred and fifty million years, until a mysterious catastrophe called the Great Dying or the WonderWork of the Wyrm laid them low. No Mokolé who saw this disaster lived to speak of it, but in time, surviving Kin produced more shapeshifters. The next sixty million years were an Age of Sleep, from which the Mokolé awakened when human beings evolved. In the Wars of Rage the Garou savaged the Mokolé, and the memory of the slaughter remains fresh today. The Mokolé are the Memory of Gaia, and each one carries within him a myriad of ancestral names and faces. This tumult of inner voices makes it a wonder that the Mokolé ever get anything done at all, but in fact they have a complex social order, one traditional since the time of the Kings.

Dragon Society

The past ain't dead. It ain't even past.

— William Faulkner

Mokolé are anything but tribal. Their concerns are at once more global and more local. Their society, embracing both Changers and Kin, is one of strict roles and close community.

Mokolé live among humans when they must, but prefer the company of Kin and other weresaurians. They realize this by grouping into wallows — homes for the human and reptile shapes that they take. A wallow can be a traditional village, an apartment building (hopefully with a pool!), a remote jungle mudhole, or a high-tech alligator refuge with tourist shows. Visitors can be admitted (or eaten), but the wallow belongs to the clutch. Clutches can be rivals to one another, competing for lands, mates and treasures through courtship, games, ridicule and even dueling. But as the

Mokolé dwindle in number, their main concern is the struggle for survival against the encroaching forces of the human despoilers. The forces of a market economy are cutting forests, damming streams, and scattering Kin to the winds. Like their enemies, the Garou, the Mokolé see and fear the death of Mother Gaia. This has moved Mokolé all over the earth from thought to action.

A Mokolé's role in his society is determined by his sun sign. The Rising Suns are hunters, explorers and soldiers. The Noonday Suns are judges, lawmakers and executioners. The Setting Suns protect and defend, while the Midnight Suns are clowns, poets and doers of the impossible. The Shrouded Suns perform the mysteries, while Mokolé born beneath a haloed or Decorated Sun organize. Finally, the rare Mokolé born under an eclipse are rulers and priests.

Mokolé are born either human or reptile, and live as such, having no special powers, until adolescence. At maturity, the ancestral memories of the Mokolé emerge, and the young Mokolé falls into a trance. At that time, a new shape is born: the battle-form, the dinosaur or dragon forms of the Kings. When the trance ends, a true Mokolé awakens. This experience binds all Mokolé together and teaches them the course of life upon Gaia's Face. New Mokolé emerging form a "ripple" in the stream (like a human generation) and often identify with each other.

Memory is all-important. A clutch defines itself by the memories it holds and passes down, generation after generation. Each ripple knows them again for the first time. Communion with the past is more than a religious belief for the Dragon Breed. It is the air that they breathe.

How to Keep Dragons

"Before, I was like a man. I'm nothing now, all broken up. So I'll remain in the water, and everyone will be afraid of me." He sang himself into a crocodile.

— "Becoming a Crocodile", Koori folktale, Daly River, Australia

This book is for anyone who loves dinosaurs, tropical rain forests, history and time. Its themes are evolution, memory, and the return of the lost. It contains information on how to flesh out Mokolé characters for your World of Darkness chronicle, as well as all-new information about roleplaying in the reign of the Kings. You'll need to have **Werewolf: The Apocalypse Second Edition**, obviously, but other World of Darkness books might help as well.

The book is laid out as follows:

- **Sunrise: Dragons in our Midst** — a summary of this book, including a lexicon.
- **Morning: Was** — A short summary of the past of the Mokolé, as Jeffo and Morwangu remember it.
- **Noonday: Us** — The four streams, as well as notes on Mokolé society.
- **Afternoon: Dragon Making** — Rules for character creation, including Archid-form characteristics and new Merits and Flaws.
- **Evening: Dragon's Eye** — Gifts and rites for the Mokolé, including many new ones.
- **Sunset: Dragon Lore** — Ideas useful for Mokolé-specific chronicles, such as clutch design, Mnesis questing and the like.
- **Night: Roleplaying** — An appendix of useful tidbits, including templates, famous Mokolé, details on the Mokolé's reptile Kin, dragon-specific antagonists and roleplaying notes for chronicles set in the Was.

Mokolé Lexicon

Age of Sleep: The time between the WonderWork and the beginning of mankind.

Ambalasokei: The neotropical biome; South America.

Archid: The intermediary ("Crinos") form of the Mokolé, resembling a dragon/dinosaur beast.

Bandaiyan: The Land of Fire; Australia.

Bata'a: African mages, often Kin to Mokolé.

Bête: "The Beasts." Shapeshifters other than Mokolé. Not an insult.

Big: Gigantic sauropods.

Blood-devil: A vampire.

Buaya: A Zhong Lung (or generally other Mokolé) obsessed with sex; a "scammer." Not a compliment.

Callsinger: A duckbilled dinosaur.

Champsa: The Nile crocodile varna of Entoban, first varna of Mokolé since the Age of Sleep.

Clutch: A group, especially a family group, of Mokolé.

Damned: Vampires.

Designer: The shaper of life, called the Weaver by Garou.

Devisor: The creative power, later called "Wyld" by the Garou.

Dinosaur Kings: The Archiosauria, including dinosaurs, pterosaurs, and crocodilians. Rulers of the earth for over 150 million years.

Dissolver: The Unmaker, called Cahlash by Bastet and Wyrm by Garou. Time after time, the Dissolver has cleared the Mother's face of life so that the Devisor could make anew.

Drachid: The "lost" form of the Mokolé, the shape of the Kings. No Mokolé hatched since the WonderWork has been able to assume this reptilian toolmaker form.

Dragon Kings: Legendary progenitors, found in the Umbra.

Dream Hunter: A monster inhabiting the depths of Mnesis, a dream of terror come alive.

Egg-smasher: A deadly insult, or description of the Garou.

Entoban: The ark-continent, birthplace of humanity; Africa.

Eshu: African fae, rarely Mokolé Kinfolk.

Farm Boy: Mokolé raised on an 'alligator farm' by human Kin.

Gendasi: The Nearctic Biome; North America.

Gharial: The gavial varna of India.

Gumagan: Saltwater crocodile and monitor lizard Mokolé of Oceania, including Australia and New Guinea. The Gumagan are a stream of Umbral travelers, Mnesis questers and visionaries.

Halpatee: The American alligator varna of the Mokolé-mbembe.

Homid: Human shape of Mokolé and Bête. Lowercase, a Mokolé born of human parents.

Innocents: The deformed and stillborn children of mating between two Mokolé: they become ghosts and haunt any Mokolé who enters the Umbra.

Inwitting: A unique storytelling art, combining Mnesis and a special Gift, which sends listeners into a shared memory-dream.

Jati: Human "caste" of India.

Karna: The saltwater crocodile varna.

Last Times: The First Times (paradoxically enough); the age between the awakening of the shapeshifters and the Wars of Rage.

Lineage: A family of Mokolé and Kin who pass Mnesis from generation to generation. A lineage can sometimes provide enough Mokolé for a clutch.

Ma'afa: The slave trade from Africa to Asia and the Americas, 1448-1865.

Makara: The Mokolé of India, the stream most beloved of humans. Can also refer to the varna of mugger crocodiles.

Mancala: The Mokolé game based on egg-laying. Now played by humans.

Matre: Mystic power gained through parentage.

Mnesis: Ancestral memory of the Mokolé.

Mokolé: The Dragon Breed; shapeshifters whose animal form is a lizard or crocodilian. Does not include the Nagah (serpents) or tortoises and turtles. The Mokolé breed is divided into four streams: the Mokolé-mbembe, Gumagan, Makara and Zhong Lung.

Mokolé-Mbembe: Ancestral Dinosaur King of the Congo Jungle.

Mokolé-mbembe: By extension, Mokolé-Mbembe's children, the Mokolé of Africa and the New World; a stream of warriors.

Monster of the Deep Shadows: The Dissolver, seen as opposed to the Sun.

Mother Cow: Gaia.

Olodumare: The Sun, or Face of God. Giver of heat, light and life to the Mokolé.

Ora: The Komodo monitor varna of Indonesia.

Perfect Clutch: A clutch with a member of each solar auspice. Rare.

Piasa: The American crocodile varna of the Mokolé-mbembe.

Proudest Monkey: Human.

Rats: Any mammals. Used by elders.

River Pact: The ancient accord between the Silent Striders and Mokolé-Mbembe of Egypt, enforcing truce between them. The treaty is assured by the totem Crocodile.

Ruler-Of-The-Tides: Mokolé name for Luna.

Salty: A saltwater crocodile; also "saltie."

Sharptooth: A carnosaur.

Stream: A great interwoven group of Mnesis lineages native to a specific area. There are four streams of Mokolé: the Mokolé-mbembe, Gumagan, Makara, and Zhong Lung. Each has its own strengths, and each is different. They are not "tribes" as such, but relatives who have grown apart.

Suchid: Reptile form of the Mokolé. Also (when lowercase), a Mokolé hatched of reptile parents.

Sun: The Face of God, Lord of All and Giver of Life. Also Olodumare, Surya, etc.

Sun bridge: Passage from one place to another "through the heart of the Sun," invoked through a rite.

Syrta: The caiman varna of the Mokolé-mbembe.

Tenrec: Ancient ratlike mammal, a "living fossil" surviving on the isle of Madagascar.

Two-legs: Human.

Unktehi: The (quite rare) Gila monster varna of the Southwestern United States.

Varna: The species of reptile into which any given Mokolé can transform. Each stream contains two or more varna: Mokolé of the same varna will have common interests and concerns, as well as the same Suchid form.

Wallow: Home of suchid Mokolé and other crocodilians or reptiles; a home for Mokolé and their Kin.

Wanderer: An office given to some Mokolé; indicates those who travel from wallow to wallow bearing tales.

Wani: The Dragon Princes of the East; mighty spirits who give their shapes to the Makara and Zhong Lung.

Was: The past, particularly the long-ago past.

Within, the (also "Great Within"): The inner world of ancestral memory, accessible through Mnesis.

WonderWork of the Wyrm: The Cretaceous-Tertiary Boundary event of 65 million years ago. The Dissolver-caused extinction of plants, sea creatures, and animals including the Dinosaur Kings.

Zhong Guo ("chung kuo"): The Middle Kingdom: China, Taiwan, Japan, Korea, Vietnam, Mongolia, Tibet, part of Siberia and so on.

Zhong Lung ("chung lung"): The Middle Dragons, Mokolé of Eastern Asia. They are great scholars and are renowned among the hengeyokai, the shapeshifters of the East.

Who knows for certain? Who shall here declare it?
Whence it was born, whence came creation?
The gods are later than this world's formation.
Who then can know the origin of the world?
None knows whence creation arose;
And whether he has or has not made it;
He who surveys from the lofty skies,
Only he knows — or perhaps he knows not.
— The Rig-Veda

Peter and Morwangu sat in the scanty shade of an acacia.

"How'd the world begin? Hell if I know! We weren't there!" Morwangu snorted and went on grinding pituri. The acrid smell of the root filled the air.

"What do you mean? Mokolé remember everything, I thought."

"No, only The Memory. Only what an ancestor saw, heard, knew. We aren't as old as the bloody world. Kings saw fossils in the rocks, older then than the Kings are now. Creation? It's as much a legend to us as to you!"

"Fossils? Huh?" Peter's head swam. Galliards sang of a First Time when Gaia had made all the Changers, all the beasts, a Garden of Eden. First the other changers, then the Garou, Her Warriors. The Mokolé fit into the song somewhere. And school taught that evolution had taken millions of years, but...

"Do Mokolé, do they, I mean, believe in evolution? I mean... I, uh, I guess I don't know what I mean. I mean, dinosaurs were real, I know they were, I was..."

"You have The Memory. Judge for yourself."

Peter began to think. The doors of Mnesis opened. He remembered dinosaurs, remembered being a dinosaur: not swamps of sluggish lizards but forests of pine and cycad, wingfinger herds wheeling in formation against a pure blue sky and treefern thickets where flocks of duckbills grazed. A landscape without flowers or mammals, filled with life that was broken remnants in Peter's time. Not the First Times of Cassandra's stories, but something so much more, a whole different world. Had he always known this? It was within his own soul.

Red struck his eyes.

"It's real. I mean, it's amazing, Morwangu! I remember — I remember everything, all that — Morwangu?" His skin was red as the sun that set. He'd sat entranced for hours, seeing what Was. The Mokolé elder was gone. *What can I learn? There were Mokolé before there were Garou. Okay, no surprise. What about the First Times? Well, they had to be, or there wouldn't be any Garou. And Gaia, She's as real as my snout. But he never said She wasn't.*

So who's right?

We both are.

Peter got up and looked in his rucksack for some sunburn lotion. This was going to be weird.

The most tantalizing hint had come from Morwangu. He said that there were those who came before the Kings — "else," he'd asked, "what did they remember? It seems to me that the Kings — well, that's another story." Peter wished he'd elaborated.

"Son, let us go." Morwangu beckoned Peter toward the combi that Jeffo had finally managed to start.

"Look, where are we going now?" Where was there a place more desolate and nasty than this?

"North." North from Arnhem Land was the ocean.

"Where north?" Peter picked up his bag. If they left, he was lost in this desert anyway.

"To where Wolaru is."

"Wolaru? What do you mean?"

"Wolaru must awaken. We will go to her now. You have come, and restored her to us."

"Look, if you mean the Wolaru I knew of, she lived, what, a hundred and some years ago. I mean, she has to be dead now." He hoped. There were worse things than dying in the world, and he'd met a few.

"She will awaken. She must. Her Memory is with us once more."

Peter shrugged and followed the old man to the combi.

Before Memory

It is ironic that the Mokolé, the eldest of the Changing Breeds, have no clear idea about how the world came to be. In general, they will tell an inquirer that they don't know, or tell the creation story that they know best. The Mokolé-mbembe prefer to believe that Gaia made them, as She made all things on her face. The Gumagan tell of ancestors who made the land of Australia and everything in it, in the Dreamtime. The Zhong Lung talk of Age after Age, as do the others of their land, while the Makara argue violently as to whether the world was created or not! Midnight Suns spin endless contradictory tales of gods, Gaia, and ancestors, but in the end no Mokolé claims to have the truth about what came before the Kings.

How the Mokolé Came to Be

Peter followed Jeffo and Morwangu up the hill. *Raijua? Why couldn't the Ancient be buried on, say, Bali?* Sun burned his neck where the bush hat didn't shield it.

We are going to wake up an ancient Mokolé. Or an ancient something. And when we do, Gaia help us. I am a Garou, for crying out loud! She'll kill me on sight! This is stupid. How could anyone, anything, be alive after hundreds of years underground? Vampires were another story — they were dead to start with. This thing, whatever it was, must be a fossil that they worship.

The Indonesian trip had been fun so far. They'd flown to Sumba, the big island nearby, and taken in the sights. There had been some local wingding with a massively overweight woman sitting under an awning: the native queen. Then they'd taken the boat over to this tiny place.

"Used to be all over trees — damn them for cuttin' em down." Morwangu's words were strange until Peter realized: The Memory. There weren't even stumps in the ground, and erosion furrowed it deeply. How long had the trees stood? How long had it been since they stood only in Memory?

They came to the summit, where there was brush and dry grass. There was a stone at the center of the place: white quartz with rainbow veins snaking through it. Peter approached, touched it.

Wolaru was there.

He knew her instantly, from the dreams pituri had brought: a regal woman with ebony skin and lively black eyes, scarred with the patterns that meant she was kin. He remembered her, and remembered being her.

"She's buried here, been so these hundreds of years. You were the one who found the Memories, Peter. You should be here." Jeffo was excited. Morwangu was solemn. "I have lived many rains and never thought to see this. No Mokolé alive has seen her—"

"Unless you count me a Mokolé," said the Garou. They squatted down and began the rite.

"Wolaru, wake; Wolaru, let your heart beat; Wolaru, let your blood flow, Wolaru, wake and see the Sun; Wolaru, speak to us your kinsmen, Wolaru, come to the daylight, Wolaru, Wolaru, show us your face..." They chanted on and on while Peter tried to join in, chanted till the sky grew red with sunset. Peter saw the play of copper sun on Jeffo's face, saw it disappear.

"Sun sees you," a voice said. Peter and Jeffo jumped. Standing a few feet from them was a tall and handsome black woman cloaked in kangaroo skin, with the setting sun eclipsed behind her figure. Had she slept centuries? Most people didn't act that collected after a half-hour nap.

"Sun sees you, Radiant Light, Crowning the Clutch of Scales-Of-Many-Colors. I am Jeffo, Shining in the Clutch of... the clutch of.."

"I am Morwangu, Concealing the Clutch," said the older man. He made gestures Peter had seen in the vision: reverence for Sun's Anointed. The woman smiled. Her teeth were white.

"And who is the invader?" For all that her speech condemned Peter, her manners were no less pleasant. "He is Bunyip? He cannot be. He looks like that other, the invader who became a dingo. But he knows our tongue; he can speak for himself."

"I am Peter Ward. I am a Glass Walker of the Garou, Gaia's warriors. These, my brothers, have brought me here because I sought the Mnesis of your clutch in the gullet of the Dissolver, and found it. I am the only Garou in all of time to have the Memory. I have your Memory. Sun sees you, Radiant Light." She seemed intrigued.

"Sun sees you. Is there wood, and a firestick? Let us speak more."

Idylls of the Kings

It was a night like this
Forty million years ago
I lit a cigarette
Picked up a monkey skull to go
— Don Was

Radiant Light spoke as the fire blazed.

"Call them the Lizard Kings, the Dinosaur Kings, the Reptile Kings, the Dragon Kings, the heesh, yilané, quintaglio or whileelin. The fact remains that there was a civilization on the Earth in the Mesozoic. How do I know? I remember it.

"That was the world as it should be. No mammals, no pollen to make us sneeze, no dogmen, just us and our Kin forever and ever. I remember walking the streets of el-Kaataar to the house of Wave-Without-A-Shore, seeing the hatchlings playing at spin-the-top as I wondered how old the game was even then. I remember Mother's tyrannosaurs driving her hornface herds east before a storm front on the Laurasian savanna, their talons scything sheets of water as they forded the Tkash, the westbirds scattering and diving for cover. I remember life after life, the continents themselves shifting so slowly that we simply rebuilt Alpeséak as a seaport when Tethys came in. Your people are proud of five thousand years of writing, of seventy thousand of talking. You are rats on your hind legs. The Kings cared for Mother Gaia for a hundred and fifty million years, so long that pine trees still grow tall to escape a Big's jaws, so long that you rats still tie memory to smell, still blame the Kings for being kicked out of the garden. Else what was the snake before Yahweh took his legs? The Time of the Kings, that was the garden. The Kings took many forms, many places and many times. But their reign endured."

"Wait a minute. You mean there were people — Mokolé — in the age of the dinosaurs? How — I mean, what did they turn into? Into people?"

"What are people? Are we people?"

"Humans, I mean."

"Not humans. No. The Kings were smooth-skinned, two-legged. Meat eaters mostly. Born with Memory even if they were Kinfolk, not Mokolé. But they had hands, eyes, minds all good as yours. Then Mokolé had three shapes, like now. Our Devisor shape was reptile and our Dissolver shape was great and mighty. But our Designer-shape was born from an egg. It was the Drachid shape, the shape of the Kings."

"But the fossil record—"

She shook her head. "Means nothing. Let me get to that part of the story."

Peter bowed his head, and then raised it again. "Were there other shapeshifters in the Mesozoic?"

"Oh, yes. All kin to us, you know. There were people who turned into sharks, people who turned into bristlecreepers—"

"What's a bristlecreeper?"

"Oh, they're little creatures that have hair and carry their eggs inside them till they hatch — mammals, I guess. But there were bird-people and so on. I think there might even have been a tribe of ammonite folk in the deep sea who fought the sharks."

Peter remembered Seeks' tale of the creation myth of the Rokea, of Qyrl, C'et and Kun, and the undersea nations that lived and died unknown to land-dwellers, and wondered. "There are still bird-people and rat-people today."

"Praise Gaia." She nibbled on the strip of dried wallaby meat.

"But things are changing, Wolaru. The Mother is dying—"

"Again? You woke me to see another WonderWork?" Awe covered her face. "I am honored. To see the world die and live again! "

"Wait a minute." Peter was amazed. "You want to see the Apocalypse? It's going to be the end of the world!"

"The world's ended many times before. Before the Kings there was a great dying, a great WonderWork. The Kings fell. You will fall. Each time the Devisor makes things anew."

"Wolaru — I have your memories, but I don't understand them.... You mean — this isn't the first Apocalypse?"

The Age of Sleep

Wolaru had gone to the bow to watch for the first sign of Australia she'd had in a hundred fifty years. Morwangu spoke as the ferryboat sailed across the Timor Gap:

"The Time of the Kings ended with the WonderWork of the Dissolver. We don't know just what happened. Why? Because no one who saw it lived to pass on the memory. It is the first of the Three Paths that no Mokolé can walk. Something terrible tore into the Mother, and then all the Kings died, along with their dinosaur kin, the ammonites and almost everything else."

"Why? I mean, was there a reason?" Day washed the ship's deck. Peter listened, worried that the customs officials would see right through the spurious papers that they had bought.

"I don't know why. The Dissolver has always been destroyin' so that the Devisor can make. But why every living thing would die? I don't know. Maybe th' Kings built things that poisoned the Mother and killed off other species, deserved th' punishment of Gaia. Maybe a nuclear war, or maybe droppin' stars on each other. Maybe the Dissolver went mad. Maybe they started using the kind of magic that humans now use, the kind that makes the Weaver write things out of existence — that'd make sense. Whatever it did, it took them out completely. You'll never even see so much as bones. You'll just remember.

"But enough Kin survived along with true Mokolé who slept in the mud that The People could be born again. These had the Memory, but didn't Change much, and never into the Drachid form. It was too full of bad memories. We sat dreamin'; it was better than doin' then, with all we'd lost. Our long punishment, the Sleep, had begun."

"We had two shapes then, Archid and Suchid. Usually wore the Suchid save for hunting, battle and rituals. Th' Memory was sharp and painful, with the glory of the Kings and their fall. We did argue, though."

"When have we not?" Jeffo sat by Peter and mimicked his fascination.

Morwangu scowled. "We argued about the rats. They were takin' over the world, y'know. The Quiet Pools said that the Mokolé should concentrate on the past. They were mindful of their duty as the Memory of Gaia and determined to keep Mnesis through the ages. The Way of the Water's Going wanted to shepherd the mammals, the new rulers of the land, makin' a toolmaker species who could help The Mother. To this end, they killed the weak and slow, instead of choosing according to how they tasted. In the end, the Designer brought sentience to humans anyway. To this day, there are Mokolé who regret not minding their own business."

"The Mokolé guided the evolution of the human race? Is that what you're saying? That can't be true!"

"That's exactly what we did. Been regrettin' it ever since. It was a mistake. We won't repeat it."

"What? When would you "repeat" it? When would there not be any people? You mean — the — the Apocalypse! The Apocalypse?!?"

Jeffo spoke, a mischievous expression on his face. It was a moment before Peter realized that he was quoting:

"For the end of the world was long ago
and we dwell today as children of a second birth
like a strange people left on Earth
after a judgment day."

"You mean..." He struggled to control rage and fear. "But we are fighting, dying to stop the Apocalypse. To save Gaia. You don't even care?"

"No. It is much more than that." The elder looked at him seriously. "The WonderWork came and went and we still were. We did lose by it, though. But before the Kings was a Dying greater still, one that left Her Face almost empty. Who reigned before the Kings? We don't know." He took a deep breath.

"If you fight, maybe it can stop. Maybe the End won't come. Maybe it will. Maybe fighting makes it worse. The more you destroy, the more is gone. Don't stop fighting. But we will go on."

Morwangu looked up at the blue, blue sky and fell silent. Peter wondered what patience it had taken to shape humans from rats. What mammal could match it? Mammals scurrying from burrow to hunt to mate to die while the Kings basked lazily in the sun, hairy little things sniffing in the dark to find food or a mate, gorging and gorging to stoke their ravenous metabolisms—

He started. For a moment — how had it happened? He had seen wolf and man through the eyes of a reptile.

He was becoming Mokolé. The certainty filled his mind. In a world of darkness, here were Sun's Chosen. He had seen himself from far away. How many Garou, how many anything, had ever been given that gift? Peter felt grateful.

Grateful and sunburned. Australia was visible ahead.

The Last Times (the First Times)

She was born in the eye of a hurricane
Laughter all around the bed
At night the Sun was looking down
Into a hole beneath the sky
The songs of angels filled her head

— Chris Leitch, "Julula"

The four sat in the shade of a rock outcrop tufted with mulga. Wind spirits drew on the desert sand. Morwangu and Jeffo wore the lizard-shape, to stand the heat. Their ancestor coiled by the cliff, wind waving her crest. Resting her head across the coils of her body, she spoke.

"We had chased and driven you, saved the smart ones, eaten the dumb ones. We had watched and waited while forest and ice walked back and forth on the land. We never spoke. You needed your own words. We never used tools before you. You needed to learn by yourselves or make the same mistakes we did.

"That's the worst thing about those damned bloodsuckers. They fiddle with your lives and herd you like cattle. But they never think that you might do better than them. How could they know what's best for you any better than you can? We never made that mistake. But when we saw you dipping water from a stream in gourds, we knew the Way had worked. There was another toolmaker species. Someone had to bridge the gap then, restore what we had lost in the WonderWork.

"Two Thumbs was the first. She was a Shining. She stole your shape with a Gift, learned how adaptable and how clever you rats could be, and used her sense of humor to find a mate, Lightning Crashes, among the human band who camped by her wallow. She bore seven children, who became the first Mokolé with three forms since the Kings failed. Two Thumbs always joked that if anyone had warned her how much it hurt to hatch a human egg then the Age of Sleep would never have ended. Her eldest, Mokolé-Mbembe, was born when day became night. He was the greatest of all, the Mighty One, the King. They say he lives still in the heart of Entoban."

"Where?"

"Africa," Jeffo interjected.

"No one remembers the First Changer or what Breed he was from. This is the second of the Three Paths that we can't walk down. We were stirred by the ancient memory of the Kings, so we joined with the new toolmakers in Entoban. Your own Shrouded Suns know that. We remember a time when there were no Garou, but you can't remember a time when there were no Mokolé.

"Gaia washed Her face with ice to clean off the corruption of the Dissolver, washed it four times. We spread with humans. We liked warm weather the best. Two other Breeds divided from our own. There were some Mokolé who remained with Sun but gave up Mnesis in return for the powers of the Umbra. They became the Corax, messengers of Gaia. Likewise, the Mokolé who had no limbs made a special contract with Gaia. In return for losing Mnesis, they would gain the power to judge and slay Her lawbreakers. They kept our sun auspices and our reptile coolness. They're the closest to us in blood, if not in mind and heart. Sometimes, one of them will have flashes of Mnesis. If we could awaken the Memory that lies sleeping in them a great fissure in Gaia's mind would close and She would move closer to being One.

"The Bears were the First to waken. Why? It was Gaia's will. They taught humans to walk on two legs and store food for the winter. This was when they and their two-leg cousins learned to paint and draw on cave walls, when they learned to sing and dance. We never knew till later — they were too far north. But like us, they culled humans who broke Gaia's Law. Later we taught the bears to Sleep like Dragon."

"Then we learned of other shapeshifters, the Bête."

"What is that?"

"I think it means 'beasts.'"

"Oh."

Many Tribes or None?

The Nuwisha and Kitsune, because of their shapes, seem to the Mokolé to be Garou themselves, and Mokolé distinguish them chiefly by the fact that they did not help the Garou in the Wars of Rage. The Mokolé do not know that there are many Garou tribes who dislike each other. Unless a Mokolé has Garou Lore (a rare Knowledge among the Dragon Breed), she may assume that the atrocities of the Get, Fianna or possibly even the Black Spirals are sanctioned by all Garou elders. The fact that all Garou belong to "the same varna" makes the idea of having many tribes seem strange to Mokolé.

"The Shrouded Suns explained that Gaia, mother of all, had made them and that each had their purpose. The Bastet were the Mother's eyes. The Corax and the Camazotz were Her messengers; the Grondr, the boar-skins, cleaned and groomed Her. The Ananasi wove and unwove the Great Web, and the Ratkin and Apis nursed and protected Man. The many Bête were one, parts of the Mother's body, and Gaia was whole. It hurts me to remember this time. Many adepts who do so have fallen from despair. Last came the Garou, who were the Warriors of Gaia, and their cousins the Nuwisha."

"What was that time like?"

The serpent shook her huge, plumed head.

"You may not believe it, but in the Last Times we were all friends. I remember it myself, and even I don't believe it. The wolf-skins sat wide-eyed at Midnight Suns' tales of the mighty Kings, hunted with the Rising Suns, and exchanged Gifts and rites with the Shrouded Suns. Some of you joined our wallows, especially females of breeding age, as the Dragon Breed's skills could ensure more and healthier offspring. Many pups saw the Moon's light in the arms of a dragon-nanny. Mnesis, the true labor of Sun's children, meant that none of the shapeshifters invented writing. Mokolé sat to watch your tales and rites so that they could not be lost, and we witnessed contracts and treaties. Usually the contract made that a condition.

"Many Gifts entered into Mnesis then. We have some you've forgotten. We gave you everything. Even the Memory, when you had a reason. You swam into the Memory with us, deep into time, and saw the dawn age of Gaia."

"We did? Wow, we have changed."

"We have not.

"Then the Dissolver became trapped in the Designer's web, and went mad. You know the story. That was bad. But what followed was worse."

The Wars of Rage and the War of Shame

Raphus cucullatus had become rare unto death. But this one flesh-and-blood individual still lived... She no longer ran, she waddled. Lately she was going blind. Her digestive system was balky. In the dark of an early morning in 1667, say, during a rainstorm, she took cover beneath a cold stone ledge at the base of one of the Black River cliffs. She drew her head down against her body, fluffed her feathers for warmth, squinted in patient misery. She waited. She didn't know it, nor did anyone else, but she was the only dodo on earth. When the storm passed, she never opened her eyes. This is extinction.

— David Quammen, *The Song of the Dodo.*

Wolaru spoke, the academic bent of her lecture trying to hide grief and failing:

"The tale is told elsewhere of how the Wars of Rage began. It is told many times, all different. The Garou blame the Gurahl, the Bastet blame the Garou, and the Nagah blame themselves, assuming that any Nagah can be found to tell the tale. And we are the Nagah. The Wars began in the forests of northern Eurasia. The Mokolé, far removed in their tropical homelands, never saw the coils of plot and counterplot that led to the slaughter. They knew of the War only when Garou clutches began to destroy wallows. At first, we thought that you had fallen to the Dissolver. The truth was far worse. This is the Third Path we cannot walk. If we were responsible, we have paid and paid and paid, so dearly that the Mother herself may not live.

"We fought for centuries, then for millennia. One by one you could not face us, but war packs were able to kill even the Setting Suns if they caught one alone. Because you had abandoned the culling of humans, you coaxed human 'heroes' to fight us too, to 'slay the dragon.' Why did we take humans? They killed all the proper prey! There was no food!

"You could not out-think us either. Each of us recalled thousands of hunts, millennia of battles." Her snout twisted with disdain. "You turned to trickery. 'Peace' offers brought us to the killing grounds, and disguised Kinfolk entered wallows as 'travelers' to spy on the Dragon Breed. When they simply could not lure the Mokolé from their jungle strongholds, you set the forest aflame, killing every living thing within. Your Concealing extracted poisons from plants and spewed them into drinking water or the waters of a wallow; they bribed spirits to sabotage the magic of the Shrouded Suns. Your most savage trick was to step sideways and attack from the Umbra, which was harder for The People to enter. As the War raged on, you forgot how it had begun, and forgot that you had ever been friends with the giant reptiles. There was only war between Wolf and Dragon. So terrible was the conflict that you began to call the Dissolver 'The Wyrm' to insult us. Jeffo tells me that everyone says that now.

"The People retreated further and further. We ate less than you. So we could survive in smaller areas of wild land. Clutches lost track of each other, and many died out altogether. Some entered the Sleep of the Dragon to wait for better times. With us almost gone, you tried to protect the Mother alone. No wonder She is dying."

Peter remembered Nyi and Trees Dream. How could anyone want to destroy creatures who named every plant in a rainforest and every star in the sky, who remembered the days of the dinosaurs?

"There is a tale they tell in Entoban. It says that the slaughter went on until clutches could hardly bury their dead. Finally Dives Backward, Shining for the Congo Clutch, led the ultimate retreat. Calling all the Mokolé he could find, he went into a Mnesis trance and plotted the location of every City of the Kings. From this, he deduced that a part of Gondwanaland lay to the west; if it had held Mokolé before the Time of the Great Freeze, it could do so now. Dives Backward led seventy Mokolé across the ocean, swimming in their Archid forms. Clinging to their backs were a hundred Kin and three Bastet, who flourished in the new land as well. Their descendants are still there.

"The Wars of Rage severed connections between the Mokolé of Entoban, Gendasi and Ambalasokei and their kin in Zhong Guo and Bandaiyan. Travel was too difficult, and use of the Umbra more so, with Garou ready to attack any Mokolé they saw. The Mokolé of Zhong Guo, isolated for millennia, redreamed themselves into the dragon shapes of the Middle Kingdom, and became the eldest of the hengeyokai, the Bête of the East."

"The East was no haven. It was also wracked by war and sorrow. The blood-devils of the East tricked the hengeyokai into attacking each other. The result was the War of Shame, in which the outnumbered and outclawed Garou of the East, the Hakken, were no more to blame than their peers. But after many years, a truce ended the War. It was too late to save the Okuma, the Children of Bear. But the Beast Courts of the Emerald Mother came to be home to many Changing Breeds, who worked and fought together to save Gaia. Although the Zhong Lung, the Mokolé of the East, are on speaking terms with all the other hengeyokai, they have a special fondness for the Same-Bito, the shark-warriors of the Pacific. Long ago they became guards for the Zhong Lung in return for their tutelage. It is very common for the two Breeds to be clutchmates, or even to breed together so that their children are Kinfolk to each other.

"In Ambalasokei—"

"Huh?"

"It's—" she conferred quickly with Jeffo— "South America, and the land to the north, Gendasi, the People met wolves also. But these had no hostility toward them. They were the Croatan, who built great mounds of earth and worshipped our sister Turtle. They were Croatan's brothers, fierce Wendigo and sage Uktena. They lived in peace for many, many rains. But you know that tale, as I can see."

Oannes

Radiant Light spoke, the sun cutting her shadow into earth like a hole:

"The Impergium was broken, some say, by the Children of Gaia and their hyena-shaman, Lore-Speaker Grahn. Other claim that bloodsuckers first herded mankind into the cities of Jericho and Catal Huyuk to control their 'herds' of human prey. However, we remember a hero. His name was Oannes. I did not know him. But Beautiful Is The Being of Sun, Concealing the Clutch of Crocodilopolis, remembers reading a book in the Library of Alexandria." Radiant Light spoke in a rising-falling language that Peter didn't know, maybe Greek. Then she caught herself at his bewilderment, began to translate.

"'In the first year there appeared from that part of the Erythrean Sea which bordered upon Babylon, an animal destitute of reason, by name Oannes, whose whole body was that of a fish, that under the fish's head he had another head, with feet also below, similar to those of a man... His voice, too, and language, was articulate, and a representation of him is preserved even to this day. This being was accustomed to pass the day among men... and he gave them an insight into letters and sciences, and arts of every kind... At this time there also appeared other animals like Oannes.'

"That was one of the Dragon Breed. No doubt. Who else on the Mother's Face knew how to read and write, how to plant crops, how to build a city? But our minds could guide your hands. The memory of the Kings finally had a use. The clutch must have been overjoyed. Our punishment was finally over.

"But the blood-devils took the city from us. The night was theirs, and by day, humans they'd enslaved fought against us. There are all kinds of stories about a big mighty hero fighting a Mokolé. Marduk, Yahweh, St. George, call him what you will. But the cadavers lie when they say they invented civilization. They have never invented anything, only stolen what others made. They are dead and should lie in their graves forever."

"Is that why you people hate... them... so much?"

"We are the Children of Sun, who is the Face of God. If they aren't damned, why can't they look Him in the face? Every other thing in the world can do that!"

"I guess you're right." The Garou were night creatures too, Peter thought. Was that why the Mokolé hated them so much? He didn't want to ask.

The Unchanging

The Mokolé remember not only the past of the Changing Breeds that still walk Gaia's face, but that of the lost Breeds, those slaughtered by the Garou in the Wars of Rage. While Midnight Suns tell of the were-skunks, werewhales and weresloths, these breeds were only jokes. However, the Mnesis adepts can name several Breeds who exist now only in Memory. These creatures, the "Unchanging" or the "Lost Ones," are ritually mourned by clutches who carry Mnesis from the Wars of Rage. Note that because of the ceremonial exchange of mates as well as shared Kin, there are Mnesis lineages who hold the memory of the Lost Ones. These memories are fragmented, imperfect, and difficult to understand because non-Mokolé minds experienced them. They also carry the threat of Harano — the loss of the Unchanging is even more horrifying to anyone who remembers being one, and many adepts who have sought the lost Gifts of the Unchanging have found madness. The Merit "Mnesis of the Lost Ones" allows a character to roleplay this.

The Grondr were the "boar-skins" half-remembered in Old European mythology. Dwelling in forests and swamps, they were the cleaners and groomers of Gaia, using their Gifts and rites to remove filth, parasites and taint from Her body. They rooted in Her forests and mudflats to remove impurities. The Grondr had five forms, like the Gurahl: a human, a near-human with great tusks, a "battle-boar" seven or eight feet tall with sharp, slashing hoof-hands, a near-boar shape with inch-thick armor hide, and a wild pig shape. They had three breeds: homid, suid and metis. Their metis were warriors and questers, whose inability to breed meant that they had nothing to lose if they died. Grondr sounders (the equivalent of clutches) had Kings and Queens who won their titles by sparring jousts.

When the Gurahl were attacked by the Garou, the Grondr rose to help them and slew many packs of Garou. However, once the Gurahl departed in sleep or death, the Grondr fell to Garou claws, Brazentusk Mightyhoof being their last King. The Mokolé who went to aid the Gurahl remember the battles, and some, out of grief, entered the Sleep of the Dragon directly thereafter. Humans of the First City soon after seized the last Kin of the Grondr, and enslaved them. The beast Kin were also broken and made into domestic pigs. Many say that the bloodsuckers who ruled the humans were behind this evil deed. The last true Grondr Kin sought the aid of the Dissolver and devolved into dark beasts called Skull Pigs. Feeding on death and suffering, these eaters of the dead still exist.

The Apis, the "moon-bulls," were the matchmakers and sages of Gaia. They grazed, meditating on the Sun and Moon, and sought the time and place to bring Man and beast together to fulfill Gaia's plans. Despite Garou legend, they were never kin to domestic cattle; they were aurochs through and through. Their forms were human, aurochs, and a powerful minotaurlike battle form. Though herbivores in their aurochs form, they had sharp teeth in their battle form, and ate humans who were foolish enough to hunt them. Their Gifts worked slowly, as the Earth and sky turned, but their insights were deep. The Mokolé remember their wise sayings to this day. They were frequently consulted on brood kenning and marriage matters. The Apis fell when the Garou war packs entered the Near East. They are revered to this day by the Mokolé-mbembe, who say that their sacrifice stopped the Garou from ravaging Africa and exterminating the Mokolé and Bastet completely. The last memory of them was preserved by the Children of Gaia, who tell of Kin birthing an Apis in Crete long ago.

As the Corax were to the day, the Camazotz were to the night; as the Corax were to the north, the Camazotz were to the south. The werebats were Gaia's second group of messengers, who covered the lands the Corax couldn't reach. Theirs were gifts of hearing and darkness and night. However, they were routed by Garou in the War of Rage, and the Black Spiral Dancers later hunted down the survivors wherever they could reach them. By the second millennium CE, the only Camazotz to survive were those of Central America, and they too fell when the European Garou arrived with the conquistadors. To this day, their extinction is one of the few things that makes Shadow Lords feel remorse.

It is important to remember that the Mokolé were cut off from the Gurahl (whose far northern habitat meant that few or no Mokolé cared to look for them) and that the Nagah also vanished in the Wars. The Mokolé count both Breeds as casualties. In fact, a few Nagah survived and disguised themselves as Mokolé, and the Gurahl merely went to sleep as the Mokolé had taught them long, long ago. To date, none of the newly awakened Gurahl has contacted a Mokolé clutch, and so the Mokolé number the bears and serpents among the fallen, even if they cannot remember the death of either.

Khem

How manifold are thy works, o sole God, like whom there is no other!

— Akhnaten, Hymn to the Aten

Morwangu spoke:

"The Wars of Rage and the struggle with the Dissolver eventually led you to abandon the Impergium. But we were at war with you. We didn't hear about the new idea and would not have cared for it if we had. In the tropics, we continued to cull humans who stepped over the line. However, one Mnesis lineage of the Mokolé-mbembe stream changed its ways.

"The battles with the Dissolver and the ravages of the first human farmers dried up the Sahara plain and made it a desert. The one river that still flowed was the Nile, and here two-legs began to build a civilization. As the work of Oannes had gone so well, the Mokolé decided not to slaughter humans any more than we had to. Khem came from that. The Greeks called it 'Aiguptos.'

"We coexisted with humans in this land, and our wallow was in the oasis city of 'Crocodilopolis,' where two-legs worshipped us. They were called the Hem-ka-Sobk; they're still around. A Crowning would serve as the god enfleshed. When they had lived a long time, the two-legs wrapped them in bandages and they slept the Sleep of the Dragon in their tombs. The others of the Mokolé clutch were fed, worshipped and mummified when they died also. The Mokolé were allies of the Bubasti and the Silent Striders; they still won't hurt us. The Breeds shared Gifts, Rites and Totems, including Crocodile, Sobek, who is beloved of the Striders to this day.

"We preached Sun to the Khemetic people and they made him into many gods. Eventually, a Mokolé Kinsman of royal blood, Amenhotep IV, ascended the throne. His friend Mentu-Hotep had a passionate conviction that Sun alone should be worshipped. Their beliefs transformed the land of Khem and cost Akhenaten his kingship and his life. There are some who revere him even now. But I know that Mokolé-mbembe shake their heads when I ask about him.

"After his time, Crocodilopolis declined, and the blood-devil Followers of Set gained more and more power over the two-legs. Eventually, in the first century AD, all the Mokolé-mbembe left Khem for the Sudd and the tropics of Entoban. Their descendants remain to this day. The Mnesis of Khem has been carried to many lands.

"Many rains, and no one has sought to waken the sleeping elders who lie beneath Crocodilopolis in their mummy cases. But we say they're still there and they have a lot of Memory. Wakin' them up, that would be a great deed."

American Mokolé and the Slave Trade

Jeffo spoke as the sky wheeled overhead, stars of the Southern Hemisphere making half-familiar shapes. A fire of mallee wood cheered up the night. Peter held a mug of tea and listened:

"Just when we thought the worst was over, the humans' numbers culled by the Black Death, the Wars came to us again. Bad times for Mokolé and Kin. You call the year 1448, when the Portuguese humans landed in Mother Entoban to buy slaves with guns and liquor, and you call the next four hundred years the 'slave trade.' We call it the Ma'afa, the 'unspeakable.' We did the best we could to protect our Kin. They say that eleven million went to the New World, but the number whose lives were destroyed was much higher. We didn't know what was happening until too late. The lines of Matre were cut and Mnesis borne by Kin vanished forever.

"The Shrouded Suns wrapped themselves in bloody bull-hides and asked the dead for knowledge. The Kin who had died of hanging, beatings for 'discipline,' smothering or had jumped overboard told them that the Kingdom of the Dead would suck those white men down. But the Crowning tried to help the living too. Some Mokolé went voluntarily onto the ships to aid Kin who had been sold. Many ships disappeared, presumed lost, as the dragon-folk saved those aboard them. Your books record one hundred fifty "slave revolts." Cinque aboard the Amistad managed to return thirty Kin to Entoban. There were many more that whites never knew about. The Decorated Sun, Fenda Lawrence, known to her own people as Seeks-the-Forgotten, came in 1743 to Georgia as a free black immigrant to search for lost hatchlings born in the nightmare world of the plantations."

"But slavery is over! And it was white men who abolished it." Peter felt momentarily grateful for being a Canadian. Cassie's great-grandmother had helped twenty-nine ex-slaves to Ontario before the Civil War.

"Yeah, but it was one of us started the War! Striking named Liberation, she was. She shot the cannon into Charleston Harbor, first shot of the War." He looked more serious. "But you know damn well that whites still profit from black folks' misery. Nobody got their eyes open doesn't know that."

"I think you're right. But it's not black and white we're talking about. It's green and scaly."

They talked longer. Peter heard tales of Zhong Lung who had fought to keep their Kin from journeying to near-slavery in the Old West, of the Kinfolk cowboy who had found "dragon bones" in the rocks of Colorado and the

elders who had made them speak. They talked of the death scream of the last Camazotz and the repentance of the Shadow Lords who'd killed him, and of the Mokolé who followed what seemed to be a Garou ghost to a riverboat filled with vampires. His head swam with the millennia of time that were life and breath to the Mokolé, that ocean of memory that his own folk had crawled from. What could he learn? Just what it meant to be a Mokolé. If that could bring enemies together, maybe it would be enough.

• • •

Far away, a great, hulking thing padded over red sand. An awful blend of dingo and demon, he sniffed for scent and caught one he didn't recognize. His head snapped around and he began casting back and forth for trail. As Luna sank, he found a three-clawed footprint greater than any bird's.

"Wyrmspawn," growled Mamu the Red Talon. His tail lifted with pleasure.

Now, what was that Weaver-thing's true name? He needed a favor.

I heard a clatter of loose stones along the bank, and looked up to see a monster approaching. It was a giant lace-monitor, the lord of the mountain, Perenty himself. He must have been seven feet long. His skin was pale ochre, with darker brown markings. He licked the air with his lilac tongue. I froze. He clawed his way forward: there was no telling if he'd seen me. The claws passed within two inches of my boot. Then he turned full circle and, with a sudden burst of speed, shot off the way he'd come.

— Bruce Chatwin, *The Songlines*

The Four Streams

The Mokolé do not have tribes, as do several of their younger siblings among the Changing Breeds. Their Mnesis has preserved a degree of unity among the isolated clutches that has led some outsiders to assume that the Mokolé are so rigidly traditional as to be unable to change. This isn't completely true: environment and time have shaped the Mokolé on Gaia's face into four branches, called "streams" by the Wanderers.

The four streams aren't enemies, but they do have different interests; they aren't allies, but have much in common. Each is a collection of Mnesis lineages organized in a geographic area with its local Gifts and rites; each has a different approach to the problems that the Mokolé face.

The streams are all shaped by the nature of their chosen lands and the reptile Kin found there. In this, they're more like Bastet tribes, split by feline and human Kin, than they are like Garou tribes, divided by territory and philosophy. Even so, the word "tribe" just isn't appropriate. However different a high-caste Bombay Makara and a Louisiana Mokolé-mbembe might be, they consider themselves of one family — even if each looks on the other as one of those "crazy second cousins."

The Mokolé are fairly widespread, although there are far more of them in the Southern Hemisphere than in the Northern. There are no Mokolé in Antarctica, although it's said that once there were. With Mnesis 4 or 5, a true adept can see the southern continent as the green and pleasant land it was before the coming of the ice. Mokolé regard Antarctica as a nightmare and the Garou who go there as deserving of frozen death.

Gumagan
Dreamers of the Fire Land

Morwangu spoke, taking the Suchid form, his long beard wagging.

"When the Kings died, old Gondwanaland shattered with a broken heart. As its fragments voyaged apart, the Mokolé on the separate continents began to diverge. Their Suchid forms became new varna and their lineages of Mnesis began to grow apart.

"The fragment of Gondwanaland nearest the South Pole drifted slowly closer to the Pole and grew colder. As the Ice began to cover it, its Mokolé took themselves and their suchid Kin across the sea to their nearest neighbor. This land made its way into warmth, its back in the tropics. It became a home for Fire-spirits, and even now they ravage the bush. You called it Van Diemen's Land and Australia, but it calls itself Bandaiyan. We are its people, the Gumagan, the Voices of the First Day."

Jeffo spoke:

"Dreams walkin' around, chump. That's all we are. Shakes y' up, if y' think about it. Dreams was where we came from. Long, long time ago. The Ancestors walked first to Ulungan, here, where the world began. Then walked the ways of the law, south, east, west, all over Bandaiyan's body. Where they walked, y' can still see, if y' can see with the eyes of truth. Perenty Man, Wallaby Man, Goanna Man, Bandicoot Man, all of 'em walking, walking. Then Bandaiyan is green, full of trees and grass. Gulbirra Man huntin' in the forest, Ninya Man in the mountains. Two men went from Ulungan to the south sea, Jungga and Gulgabi, White Goanna an' Black Goanna. Everything that is has a spirit, y'see. And everythin' that has a spirit, has a dream.

"All of 'em dreamin' real."

Morwangu spoke:

"When did we awaken from the Sleep? We don't bother with calendars. I know that the whitefella gal what dug up old bones, said there were bones from 'a hundred thousand years ago.' She thought they were a 'lost race' from before Kooris. But we were here when the first two-legs came, and the first Bunyip. Long time, however you count it.

"We could use Sun Bridges to reach wallows outside the homeland, but didn't want to most of the time. The desert was the heart of the land, the perenty's home. The desert and the sea were the two poles that held us. Salties were our warriors, perenty our wise ones.

"We welcomed the Bunyip, children of Dog-Faced Possum. We knew nothing of your people. You never came to Bandaiyan to attack us. Our two Breeds used different habitats, but made common cause against the Dissolver. The last news that came from the world outside was when some man-dogs were sent to Bandaiyan as a punishment. They called themselves the Bloody Claws. All born dingo, hated their human side. They set about trying to tell us to kill humans, to protect the Mother. We didn't need to hear that. Then they wouldn't talk to us at all. Sometime after that they were hunting Dissolver-things and the Bane-Chief at Greatrocks ambushed them and killed many. They hated us then and the Bunyip too. But the land was ours, and they could do nothing as long as we held the desert and the Dream.

"We remember the day the world ended. You call the year 1788. When the First Fleet dropped anchor in Botany Bay, dogmen came on your canoes and six Sunlost bloodsuckers with them. You invaded Bandaiyan; do you wonder why the Bunyip would not talk to you? Garou 'explorers' hunted and killed Gumagan. You still do. When whitefella reached Ulungan and called it 'Arnhem Land,' the blood-devils accompanied them, moving from station to station to drink from the whites and blacks there. Eventually the undead discovered the Rainbow Stone, sign of the Rainbow Serpent and source of power for the Gumagan. They attacked the clutch of Scales of Many Colors and chased them to Raijua: we died there, but killed them all. Then Wolaru slept, until we awakened her.

"White men came, took our land, shot and poisoned our Kin. Wallows became prison camps for the weird animals whitefellas eat: sheep, cows. We kept retreating. Last of all we moved our most sacred wallow to the isles of the Torres Strait. A mighty one named Guards-the-Path protected us. He dies as we do, and lives again. He is not Gumagan but has great, great magic. The Clutch of the Scarred Gums, they are. They're the ones who managed to save the last few Bunyip Kin — too late to save the tribe, though. They all live together on an island in the Straits. Whitefellas call it a School for Aborigines. We call it our last stand."

The Gumagan are the Mokolé of Bandaiyan, called Australia by whites. They also occupy Tsalats (New Guinea) and assorted islands. Known as the stream of fire, they are the Mokolé most commonly found away from water, and indeed some spend their whole lives in deep deserts. Once found all over the continent, they are today only a remnant of their previous numbers. Their prowess at Umbral voyaging and Mnesis questing is undiminished, however. Gadimargara, first of the Gumagan, came in the Last Times. Choosing perenty lizards and saltwater crocodiles as his mates, he trekked the Dreamtime and created the songlines, roadways paved with Mnesis. As aboriginal culture developed over forty thousand years, the Gumagan cooperated with their cousins, the Bunyip, to create the most complex array of beliefs known to humanity. The twin seas of water and sand were opposed poles in their world and equal as sources of wisdom. The Dreamtime remains central to their lives even on the brink of the Apocalypse. In order to further their understanding of it and preserve its lore, they work with elders and wise men (and women) of Aboriginal cultures.

The Gumagan never knew of the Wars of Rage until Europeans came, bringing vampires with them. The perfect clutch of Scales of Many Colors, dedicated to the Rainbow Serpent, was the most prominent of the Gumagan clutches. Then the undead attacked it, and the Mokolé survivors fled to Raijua in Indonesia, where they were slain by the vampire elder who arrived in the First Fleet. However, the bloodsuckers were themselves killed when Wolaru-Radiant Light, Crowning the Clutch of Scales of Many Colors, invoked the power of Dream Semblance and burned

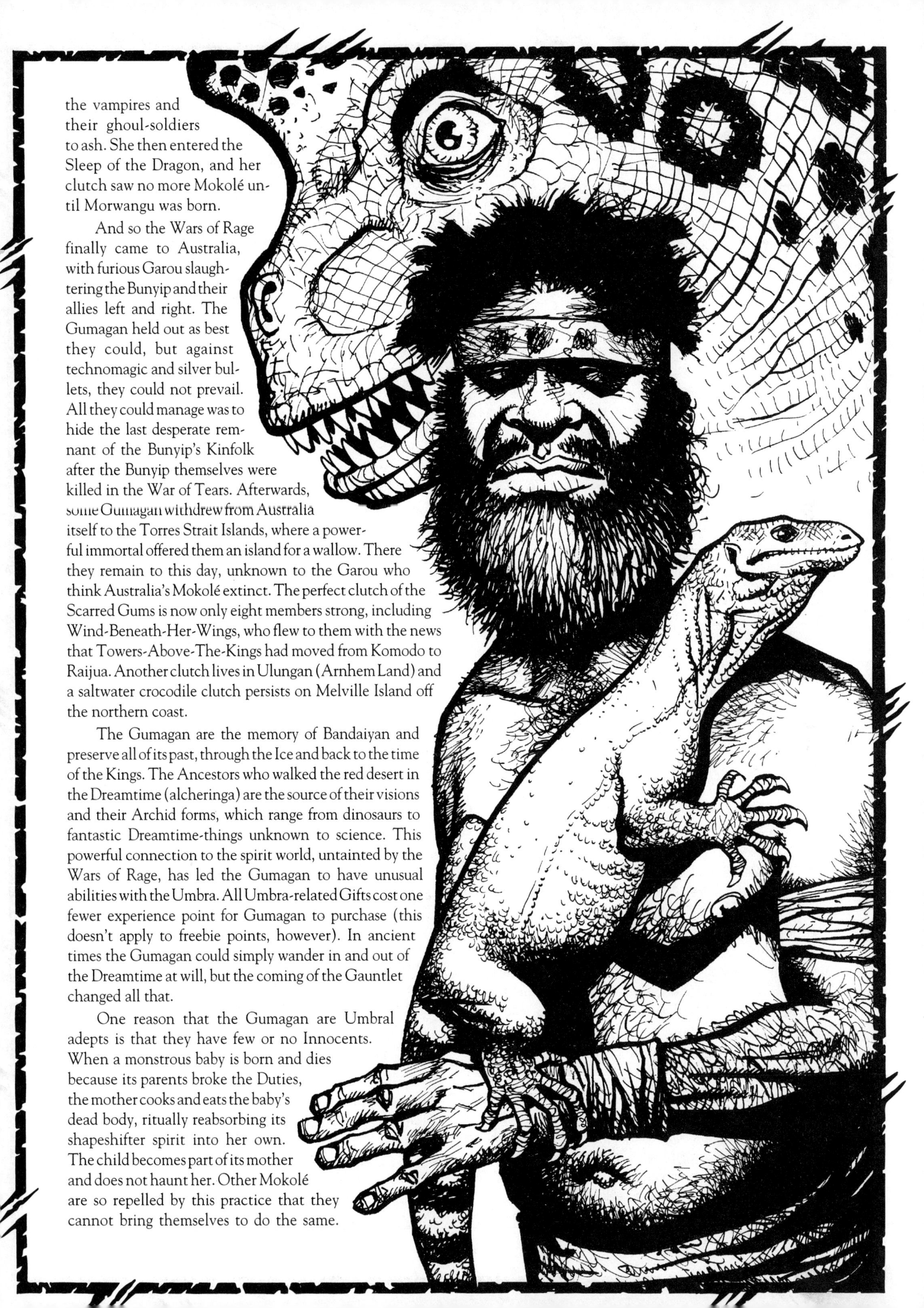

the vampires and their ghoul-soldiers to ash. She then entered the Sleep of the Dragon, and her clutch saw no more Mokolé until Morwangu was born.

And so the Wars of Rage finally came to Australia, with furious Garou slaughtering the Bunyip and their allies left and right. The Gumagan held out as best they could, but against technomagic and silver bullets, they could not prevail. All they could manage was to hide the last desperate remnant of the Bunyip's Kinfolk after the Bunyip themselves were killed in the War of Tears. Afterwards, some Gumagan withdrew from Australia itself to the Torres Strait Islands, where a powerful immortal offered them an island for a wallow. There they remain to this day, unknown to the Garou who think Australia's Mokolé extinct. The perfect clutch of the Scarred Gums is now only eight members strong, including Wind-Beneath-Her-Wings, who flew to them with the news that Towers-Above-The-Kings had moved from Komodo to Raijua. Another clutch lives in Ulungan (Arnhem Land) and a saltwater crocodile clutch persists on Melville Island off the northern coast.

The Gumagan are the memory of Bandaiyan and preserve all of its past, through the Ice and back to the time of the Kings. The Ancestors who walked the red desert in the Dreamtime (alcheringa) are the source of their visions and their Archid forms, which range from dinosaurs to fantastic Dreamtime-things unknown to science. This powerful connection to the spirit world, untainted by the Wars of Rage, has led the Gumagan to have unusual abilities with the Umbra. All Umbra-related Gifts cost one fewer experience point for Gumagan to purchase (this doesn't apply to freebie points, however). In ancient times the Gumagan could simply wander in and out of the Dreamtime at will, but the coming of the Gauntlet changed all that.

One reason that the Gumagan are Umbral adepts is that they have few or no Innocents. When a monstrous baby is born and dies because its parents broke the Duties, the mother cooks and eats the baby's dead body, ritually reabsorbing its shapeshifter spirit into her own. The child becomes part of its mother and does not haunt her. Other Mokolé are so repelled by this practice that they cannot bring themselves to do the same.

Another reason for their skill is that the Bunyip were Umbral travelers and passed along much lore to the Gumagan.

Two varna are known in Bandaiyan: saltwater crocodiles and perenties, which are huge lizards related to the Komodo dragon. No other varna survive at the present time. New Guinea and other islands can boast many salties, but the perenty is restricted to Bandaiyan's own body. The Homid shapes of Gumagan are aboriginal peoples of the lands where they are born. No Gumagan are known to have been born elsewhere (although it is seemingly possible).

The Gumagan hold that the role of Sun is as one among many spirits. The Mother, Gaia, called Waramurungundi by their Kin, is where all beings came from, but Meeka (the Moon) is as important at night as Gnowee (Sun) is in the day. Oddly, Gumagan agree with their Aboriginal neighbors that the Sun is female and the Moon male. They are the only Mokolé to believe this and revere Sun as a Great Mother. Like the Mokolé-mbembe, they recognize seven solar auspices, one for each "moment of the sun." They also revere the Dreamtime ancestors who made the world and became it. A stone may look like a stone to a whitefella, but to those who know, it is the body of the ancestor. They teach that at the origin of the world there was only alcheringa (Dreamtime) but that at one point the waking world became separate from Dreamtime. Thereafter, only those with special abilities could reach the otherworld. Of these, some (bone men) could work what magic they dreamed. Others, Bunyip and Gumagan, could shapeshift and also trek the Dreamtime. The coming of whitefella and Garou has meant extinction for the Bunyip, but the Gumagan aren't gone yet. The Dissolver has forced them and their Kin nearly to extinction. It's time to fight.

Breeds and Territories

Homid, or "koori" Gumagan are born to human parents from a native nation of Oceania: Australian Aborigine, Papuan, Melanesian and the like. A homid's Suchid form is invariably that of a saltwater crocodile or perenty. Suchid, or "gadimargara" Gumagan hatch from saltie or monitor eggs; a suchid's Homid form resembles the humans who live near her nesting ground.

Gumagan are known to live in the deserts of Bandaiyan, in Ulungan (Arnhem Land), Tsalats (New Guinea), and the Torres Strait Islands. They are also found in isolated island mobs elsewhere, such as the Yirrakapauwei Mob on Melville Island. In southern Australia there were no Gumagan left after the Wars of Rage came in 1788. As to whether there are Gumagan elsewhere in the world, who knows?

The Gumagan's entry to the adult world is their Rite of Passage, celebrated with elaborate ceremony among the aboriginal peoples and Gumagan mobs themselves. These rites involve dancing, chanting, long seclusion for the visions of Mnesis, impersonation of ancestors to trigger Mnesis, and scarification or circumcision. The teacher plants, such as tobacco or pituri, may open the way to the great vision.

Forms

• **Homid:** Gumagan in Homid are typically Australian Aborigines or islander natives. A few Gumagan have had mothers and fathers who were Kin to the Zhong Lung (such as the Japanese who came to New Guinea or the Bajini who came to Bandaiyan).

• **Archid:** The Gumagan draw on the vast dreaming of Bandaiyan for their Archid form, and therefore appear as gigantic Megalania lizards, the lost dinosaur Kings of Bandaiyan, and the Dreamtime beasts that once roamed the burning sands. They are colored and marked with the thorns, ridges and sandy tones of their native earth.

• **Suchid:** The Suchid form is a perenty monitor or saltwater crocodile.

Auspices

The Gumagan recognize seven solar auspices based on the movement of Sun through the day and night. They view the seven auspices as pieces of a whole, and acknowledge this in their daily lives. Their functioning is embedded into the mobs of human and reptile natives of Bandaiyan. Their auspice roles are similar to those of the Mokolé-mbembe, except for the Eclipsed Suns; Gumagan Crowning are directors of life and ritual, often taboo persons because of their immense sanctity. They forego the idea of government, and are far from secular rulers.

All Gumagan begin play with Willpower 3, regardless of sun auspice. They may purchase Backgrounds according to breed, as with other Mokolé. Kinfolk, Wallow and Allies are common Backgrounds, but Resources are not normally available to them. Technological skills are also usually unavailable. Gumagan cannot take non-Australian totems (such as Anaconda or Snapjaw) unless the chronicle demands otherwise. Each character begins play with two Gifts. As mentioned before, Umbral Gifts cost one experience point less for Gumagan to purchase. The Gumagan's Mnesis has the following thresholds:

Mnesis	Timespan
•	You can remember the time since whitefella came.
••	You can remember aboriginal life for many lifetimes.
•••	The Ancestors.
••••	Before the Bunyip.
•••••	Time of the Kings.

Stereotypes

• **Makara:** They all want to be humans. Don't they remember our duty?

• **Mokolé-mbembe:** Colors are the deeds and sufferings of light. They have suffered much. Let us hope that they can remember something more cheerful.

• **Zhong Lung:** Snooty dragons. There is more honor in following your own dreams than the words of a hundred sages.

Makara
The Water Monsters of India

Skandadasa dreamed. He saw Mitra rising over the harvest-horizon. He remembered his grandfather, a Shudra laborer in the village. He felt the spirit of the Trimurti Dissolver-Uncorrupted, Shiva, beckon to his gavial breed. Agni, the Face of Dragon amongst Men, the receiver of Oblations, the Fire, awoke within him. "Jya, mother-earth," he cried out in his sleep. "It is too much. I cannot bear it." The rivers of time flooded the fragile banks of his mind with the silt of thousands of years. The Wani, the Dragon-Kings, roared to him from the ancient past. "Agni, it is too much; I cannot bear it."

Skandadasa felt the breath of the Dragon upon his face and it burned like the sun. "You must fulfill your dharma, child. I have burned away the demon-dreams and you have escaped the Destroyer of Time. You will reach the Wani and accept their gifts."

He awoke in the river, on a tiny islet. The gifts of the Wani still graced his body: fins, a spined tail, webbed feet. The others awaited him on the shore, and Skandadasa scurried out of the water to meet them, relieved that he had survived the Sushupthi and become Smaranabhu, Memory-Born. The mud felt good against the new skin of his toes. He remembered a thousand childhoods playing in the river mud, as a boy, as a girl and as a gavial. However, the moment that his boyish form returned to him, he felt sick and vomited upon the rocks. Fish and bones splattered everywhere, but amongst the bile he saw something gleaming. He picked it up before he even thought of the pollution of the unclean to his person.

"You have taken upon yourself the stain; look at what you have," the Bhatta Ma said to him. Her aged voice did not sound so disapproving as he had expected. Skandadasa opened his hand after swirling it in the Ganga's waters. There lay a golden swastika. "What does it mean to you?"

"It is the sacred sign. But is also the heritage of a legacy of terror in another land. It is the jewelry of the dead. I do not know what it means, Bhatta Ma."

"You are of the Zarad and a Shudra. It is a sign of your duty. The

west and the mystic and the artisan. You must return the symbol to its glory."

"How will I do that? I am but one."

"No, Swallows-the-Sign, you are many. You must teach the ancient truth before the sign was tarnished by the Western wind of corruption."

Skandadasa knew he had no choice. The Namakarana had been done and he had a new name. It was a name to remind him of his dharma, his duty.

Mokolé in the Indian subcontinent derive from the unique blend of religious culture amongst humans and populations of crocodilians. Known as Makara, two of the mighty Water Monsters are even mentioned in the Bhagavad-Gita. The Stream of the Makara also refer to themselves as the Stream of the People. They are the stream associated with wind, their homeland swept each year by monsoons that bring death and destruction but also water the land to make it fertile. More than any other Mokolé, the Makara see themselves as preservers of Gaia's living thinkers, not just memories of the long-dead.

The Makara of India regard Sun as their source of enlightenment. Also of great importance is Dragon, the Father of the Wani, or Dragon Kings. Hindu Mokolé in particular usually interact with spirits through the sacrifice of fire, and revere Dragon as Agni, the God of Fire, the Conveyor of Oblations, the Speaker of the Wani. Of course, their images of Agni are more reminiscent of the Wani than of humans. They also acknowledge Chandra the moon. Above all, the Makara place Rta, Jya (or Gaia) and the Trimurti.

Beneath Jya the Makara place the Trimurti, composed of the Creator, Preserver and Destroyer. An interesting difference between most Makara and many of the other Changing Breeds is that they believe in Rta, or the cosmic order. Rta, the all, came before Jya and will be after her. Some human-born Makara prefer to think of Rta as a supreme spirit and call it Brahman. Many suchids simply shrug and note that the Makara are not meant to know that, for it is beyond Jya.

The Makara divide themselves up in three distinct ways: breed, varna and auspice. First, all Makara are either born to a human or a crocodilian. As they believe that their souls are reincarnated many times, and that they have been both reptiles and humans in many past lives, the Makara do not consider either form to be superior and freely intermingle. Breeding between two Makara is forbidden in the manner of all Mokolé, however, as it inevitably results in a child who dies in the dreams of the First Change and becomes one of the Innocents. The Makara are no more lenient about this rule than are any other Mokolé. Secondly, there is the breed of reptile (varna, or "colors") the Makara's suchid form takes. Three varna are native to India: the saltwater crocodiles, the mugger crocodiles and the gavials. Finally, the Makara divide themselves into auspices according to the season of the year.

Breeds and Territories

Homid Makara are almost always Indian-born, and as such belong to one of the castes, or *jati*. Their suchid forms take the appearance of their dominant ancestors' reptile genus. Most are born to low castes; it is extremely rare for a high-caste child to be discovered to be a Changer, as most of the ancient high-caste Kinfolk were slain in the War of Rage.

Suchid Makara are hatched from the eggs of a saltwater crocodile, mugger crocodile or gavial. The suchid's Homid form takes an appearance based upon their ancestors' Homid features.

The native crocodile of India is endangered, however, and each year fewer and fewer Makara are hatched. Sun's-Hand, Crowning the Clutch of Kanpur, is concerned about this, and has sent at least one Wanderer out to ask advice from other clutches. Sun's-Hand is so worried that when Lakshmi Devadasi of the Nagah openly approached him for aid recently he refused; she eventually sought out Towers-Above-The-Kings in an epic pilgrimage.

Forms

• **Homid:** The Homid form of the Makara is almost exclusively ethnic Indian; very few Makara have ever been born anywhere else. They are found in all levels of Indian society, but most often among the merchant, peasant and

The Caste System

It is important to note that all homid Makara are born to one of the Indian jati, the social castes that divide all of the nation's people into various classes. There are over 3,000 distinct castes, but they fall into four general castes derived from the Rig-Veda and the class outside, the Untouchables.

Most homid Makara are assumed to be of the Shudra caste, for it is the most common. Shudra Makara receive no special penalties or benefits other than being a commoner. Of course, great wealth can alleviate the discomfort of this caste. Shudra are supposed to serve the Vaishya, Kshatriya and Brahmin castes.

Some Makara are of the Dalit, or Untouchables caste. Also known as Harijan, these are members of the lowest caste in India and suffer great prejudice. Others are born into the Vaishya, which is the caste of respected farmers or merchants.

The highest castes are the Kshatriya, the traditional caste of warriors, and the Brahmin, the priest caste. The Brahmin is highest of all; although it is no guarantee of wealth or good fortune, even beggar Brahmin are treated like Brahmin.

Of course, this is just the briefest look at a caste system that's only part of a very old and very rich civilization. In many ways, it doesn't do Indian society justice. We encourage interested readers to learn more.

priest castes. Makara acknowledge that each caste has its place, although they are likely to ignore human caste when choosing a mate; the Makara are themselves not entirely of human castes, and are not tied by human rules.

• **Archid:** The Archid form of the Makara takes shape from the dreams of the Wani, the ancient Dragon Princes. Some are gigantic water-beasts, archaic crocodiles, serpents, or even fishlike sea-dwellers. Others are many-headed things resembling the serpent nats, or even Eastern dragons.

• **Suchid:** In Suchid form the Makara is one of India's native crocodilians: a gavial, mugger crocodile or saltwater crocodile.

Auspices — the Seasons of the Stream

Like the Zhong Lung, the Makara divide their auspices according to the sun, but in regard to the season rather than time of day. The role of the Makara within Mokolé society is determined by this seasonal auspice, though all Makara are expected to try to aid Jya's other children in order to carry out their duties as the stream of diplomats.

The **Hemanta**, or winter auspice, are the tricksters and rogues. They are expected to be crafty, but are often attributed with frivolous behavior. The Hemanta have a beginning Willpower of 2 and the same sun dice as the Shining.

The **Zarad**, or autumn auspice, are thought of as mystics and spiritualists. Those of backgrounds that preclude priestly duties often become bhagats ("godly ones"), who try to blend their daily life with the rituals of religion. The Zarad have a beginning Willpower of 3 and share the sun dice benefits of the Concealing.

The **Grisma**, or summer auspice, are the judges and police of the Makara. They are expected to seek truth and justice. This can be a rigorous duty in a society born of strong beliefs in duty according to caste and karma. The Gharials most fierce in their service to the Trimurti of the Dissolver are usually of the Grisma auspice. The Grisma have a beginning Willpower of 4 share the sun dice of the Gathering.

The **Vasanta** are the spring auspice and are the warriors of the Mokolé of India. They are also travelers and are the most ready to hear of new things. The Vasanta have a beginning Willpower of 5 and the same sun dice as the Striking.

Stereotypes

• **Gumagan:** Savages, but masters of arts long lost to us.

• **Mokolé-mbembe:** So scarred from endless war that they hardly know peace when they see it. Their karma must be deeply tainted, but all of us are bound to the Wheel.

• **Zhong Lung:** Prideful creatures! They give themselves too much credit for their status — we didn't start the Wars.

Mokolé-mbembe
Right Talon of Sun

Morwangu opened his mouth. But memory spoke through him.

How long did we sleep? When did we awaken? I don't know your numbers and names. But when the Kings walked Gaia's face, you were rats. Look at you now. The stars have moved, the continents have moved. Was it Mokolé-Mbembe who first opened human eyes to see Lord Sun? I don't know.

We awakened in Entoban, the world's heart. Sun, streams, sand. These were all we knew. But Mnesis opened within us and we remembered all. The Last Times began.

The Last Eggs lay in the warm sand of the Congo. The Sun took seven stations, seven moments. "Look!" He said to His children, "I am Lord above all. Follow me and do what I do." Eggs hatched as He rose up red in the sky and the Rising Suns rose up like Him, hungry for new things.

Lord Sun sat atop the sky in majesty and saw all the world. No thing that was could cast a shadow. No evil could hide. Then the Judges were born. The Noonday Suns looked to the sky for His wisdom and learned to see all bathed in light, to find all evil and destroy it.

The evening came and Lord Sun went down drawing the drapes of his sleeping mat about him in crimson and gold and purple. The evening wind began to blow. The Setting Suns hatched then and huddled against the night. "Darkness comes," they said, "but let us prepare." And they worked to ward the clutch from all harm.

Darkness covered the world. There was no Sun when the Shining hatched. "Sometimes, light is darkness," they said. "Make your own light however you can." They made light of the darkness. They still do.

But eggs lay still in the sand. Sun shone the next day in clouds. The Shrouded Suns hatched then, and knew, though his face was covered, where he was. This was where their knowledge of hidden things began.

The Sun showed his face, but a ring surrounded him. And lights shone beside him. There were three Suns! Then the Gathering hatched. They were not confused. "Lord Sun tells us to bring all together. There is much to do." There was one egg left. For a long time, it did not hatch. Then Sun seemed to blacken. His face vanished and a crown of fire shone in the sky. The Gathering had assembled the Mokolé and they all saw the Last Eggs open, as the stars shone at Midday. "It is a Rising Sun," said the Striking. "No, this is the greatest of Mokolé, and there are no shadows now. It must be an Unshading," said the Noonday Suns.

"The Sun is dying, so it is a Warding who has come," said the Setting Suns.

"No, it is night and day both. It is a Midnight Sun, who sees the stars instead of the Sun when he is born." The Shining danced and capered.

"The Sun is covered and this new child is one of us," said the Concealing.

"No, no, this is much greater than that. The Sun, moon and stars all shine at once. This new child is the greatest of us all," said the Gathering.

And the Crowning, the greatest of Mokolé, was born.

Clutch after clutch took human shape, and human Kin went century after century to new places, waking Dragon from his eternal dream.

The Mokolé-mbembe are the first stream and currently the most numerous as well. Named for the progenitor of their kind, the Mokolé-mbembe are the furthest-flowing stream and the bloodiest. They claim they shepherded the human species to sentience over sixty million years by eating the stupid — the truth of this is unknown. Born of Africa, the Mokolé-mbembe have traveled to the Americas as well. They are "the Mokolé" to the Garou, and to the few others who know of the Dragon Breed. Theirs is the stream of earth, and their origin is from Mokolé-Mbembe himself.

The first of their kind was Mokolé-Mbembe, the Crowning son of Two-Thumbs. He and his siblings were the first true Mokolé born after the Age of Sleep. He founded the Congo Clutch on Lake Tele deep in the rainforest of Africa, and his seven Mokolé children hatched in the warm mud to form a perfect clutch. Tales have it that through life-extending Gifts and his sleeping the Sleep of the Dragon, Mokolé-Mbembe has prolonged his life to the present, living most of it in the Umbra. He warded the jungle home of the Mokolé with deadly Fever-spirits to save his people. He saw the First City, then Egypt, Sumer and Rome rise and fall, and has sired endless hatchlings on his Kinfolk mates. When the Wyrmcomers at last colonized the Congo basin, Mokolé-Mbembe knew that the wards of fever that he had built long before would not stand against the Weaver-things that the white men had made. He and his clutch removed Lake Tele into the Umbra, where he reigns still. However, his descendants sagely nod, the Gauntlet is so weak in the swamp that human searchers have seen the great king more than once.

The Mokolé-mbembe are renowned among other saurians for their rage and their prowess in battle. Of the four streams, they suffered more than any other in the Wars of Rage. First they saw the Grondr, Apis and Khara die, then they themselves were driven nearly to extinction. A few clutches swam to the Americas, and eventually so many Mokolé had fled, died or gone to sleep that the Garou gave up the War. Khem, where both breeds were strong, saw the River Pact sworn between the Striders, Mokolé-mbembe and the totem Crocodile. To this day, Crocodile demands that his children leave Mokolé alone, if they do not befriend them.

Breeds and Territories

The Mokolé-mbembe are the most racially diverse of the streams; they are most commonly Africans, Native Americans, and biracial or triracial people in their human forms. The Mokolé of Africa and the Americas alike have always flowed in the same stream. As Mnesis tells of the days when the ocean was a mere rivulet, this is appropriate.

In their Suchid forms, they are caimans, American alligators, crocodiles, Nile crocodiles or even Gila monsters. Varna vary, but a shared heritage of slaughter and strife bloodies the stream. The Archid forms of the Mokolé-mbembe are great amalgamated dinosaurs, dragons, and prehistoric reptiles, almost too varied to name. Even so, they are often the most primeval in Archid, borrowing only very rarely from their homelands' dreams of dragons.

- **Entoban**

Entoban, the African ark-continent, home of humanity, is also the home of the most ancient stream of Mokolé. Called the warriors of the Dragon Breed, they have been attacked endlessly in the Wars of Rage; their extreme hatred of the Garou is a mere reflection of the Garou's own mistreatment of them.

The great rivers that flowed across the Sahara dried when Gaia shed her mantle of ice, save for one — the Nile. Its moisture enabled the rise of one of the first human civilizations. Naturally, the Mokolé saw it all. The Mokolé of Khem were and are Nile crocodiles, the Champsa varna. They were allies of the Bubasti in their long struggle with the Followers of Set, and remain cordial with the few Egyptian werecats that remain. When the bloodsuckers finally triumphed, the Mokolé mostly left Khem and headed upriver. A clutch of Mokolé-mbembe remains in the Sudd, the immense tropical swamp of Sudan. To this day, they fight against undead worshippers of the Darkness, who are said to have a monstrous temple beneath the nearby sands.

But further into Entoban there are living legends. Mokolé-Mbembe, last of the Dinosaur Kings, is said still to dwell in the Umbral swamps of the Congo River. The Congo clutch remains to this day. Currently it is nineteen Mokolé strong, and seven hundred Kin live in a swamp nearby. Swims-In-Mbembe's-Wake crowns this clutch. With the recent political trouble, the Mokolé have been moved to act; they recently devoured 33 fomor mercenaries in a dictator's entourage. They are searching at present for the Spear of Mokolé-Mbembe, the greatest weapon known to the children of Sun.

The great temple at Ibadan, in Nigeria, houses the temple clutch of Sees-The-Sky, headed for many years by the albino Mokolé White-Like-Sun, who has since passed into Gaia's Memory. The human Kinfolk priests and the local cult keep four Mokolé safe and sound. This clutch remembers the bloody history and prehistory of West Africa and the reigns of the Kings. Lagos, also in Nigeria, is home to a lagoon clutch of sacred crocodiles who were once given human meat in return for controlling the flow of the Niger river. Sabou, in Burkina Faso, houses another temple clutch, guarded well by human Kinfolk. There are also temple crocodiles in Angola, Tanzania, and Uganda.

The clutch Where-The-River-Bends, on the lower Gambia, is in dire straits. It currently has only three full Mokolé, all fairly old, and no more have been born in decades. The reason for this is unknown.

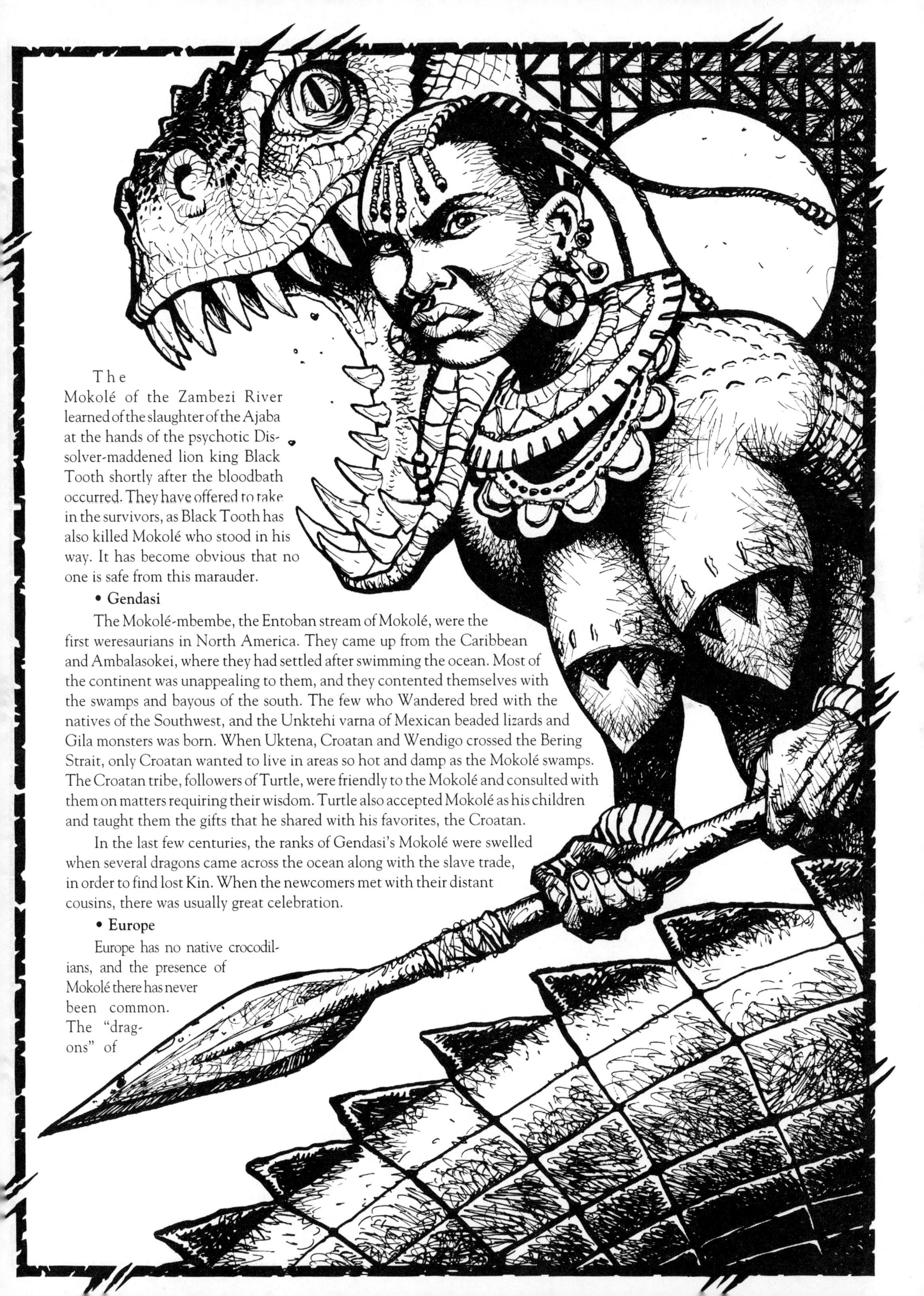

The Mokolé of the Zambezi River learned of the slaughter of the Ajaba at the hands of the psychotic Dissolver-maddened lion king Black Tooth shortly after the bloodbath occurred. They have offered to take in the survivors, as Black Tooth has also killed Mokolé who stood in his way. It has become obvious that no one is safe from this marauder.

• Gendasi

The Mokolé-mbembe, the Entoban stream of Mokolé, were the first weresaurians in North America. They came up from the Caribbean and Ambalasokei, where they had settled after swimming the ocean. Most of the continent was unappealing to them, and they contented themselves with the swamps and bayous of the south. The few who Wandered bred with the natives of the Southwest, and the Unktehi varna of Mexican beaded lizards and Gila monsters was born. When Uktena, Croatan and Wendigo crossed the Bering Strait, only Croatan wanted to live in areas so hot and damp as the Mokolé swamps. The Croatan tribe, followers of Turtle, were friendly to the Mokolé and consulted with them on matters requiring their wisdom. Turtle also accepted Mokolé as his children and taught them the gifts that he shared with his favorites, the Croatan.

In the last few centuries, the ranks of Gendasi's Mokolé were swelled when several dragons came across the ocean along with the slave trade, in order to find lost Kin. When the newcomers met with their distant cousins, there was usually great celebration.

• Europe

Europe has no native crocodilians, and the presence of Mokolé there has never been common. The "dragons" of

Greco-Roman and Germanic stories might be Mokolé who had turned; Mokolé-mbembe say that any Mokolé who lived so far from Sun would go crazy. Western dragons make for poor player characters — of course, a game of **Werewolf: The Dark Ages** might prove interesting if there was a chance to play "the other side."

A few Mokolé-mbembe wander through Europe at present, but no wallows have existed there since the Ice Age. Those who come often remember the days when Europe was tropical, part of ancient Laurasia.

• **Ambalasokei**

The caymans arrived at the party dressed in their best.

— "How Iwariwa the Cayman Learned To Share," Yanomamo folktale

Ambalasokei, called South America by the whites, was the New World of the Mokolé-mbembe. The rainforest had abundant prey and an ideal climate. The African Kin who came on the slave ships faced first the horrors of the Middle Passage, then the burden of bondage. But many escaped into the jungle, often with native help. Their African-style villages were human wallows run by true Mokolé and offering sanctuary to any refugee.

The destruction of the Amazon rainforest has awakened the Mokolé to the dying of Gaia. Elders such as Nyi the Feathered Thunder and her clutchmate Horned Thunder have awakened to find that the jungle is disappearing. Pentex poisoned the wallow of Hooark-Oark and the Mokolé abandoned it; Feathered Thunder, a Midnight Sun, has gone so far as to cooperate with the Garou Ghost Raptor pack in order to protect her nest. This wallow, Gr'rrash-takknyrr, is the largest remaining in Ambalosokei, and is a famous nesting ground; it has been in continuous use for over five hundred thousand years. It is the home of six Mokolé, including Feathered Thunder and a Rising Sun named Song-of-Younger-Days who has distinguished himself in the Amazon War. His kinsman, Strikes-like-Lightning, annihilated a Pentex First Team with the help of the Balam Smoking Mirror Wind. The memories of Trees Dream, the clutch's Setting Sun, contained the key to curing the deadly "snow plague" that threatened the Garou nation. The Garou who carried the plague, Peter Ward, became the first Garou to receive the gift of the Memory.

Stereotypes

• **Gumagan:** Lost in time, lost in space, or just plain lost? The Sandwalkers need to wake up and smell the coffee, if any are left at all.

• **Makara:** They like humans too much. How can they cull them properly? It could be nice to have two-legs at your beck and call like that, though.

• **Zhong Lung:** What we'd be if it weren't for the wars. I'd like to see if their fancy courts and philosophy schools could survive Garou attacks. They *are* very wise, though.

The Zhong Lung

Servants of Heaven

Wolaru spoke.

I remember the strangers. Bajini came a little while ago. Not by your measure, by ours. Four hundred years? Five hundred? Long enough for their houses to fall, their books to rot. Long enough for white men to say "We discovered Australia."

Bandaiyan hadn't seen strangers since the Ice. The Bajini were small, gold-skinned, with straight black hair. They came to fish. "No fish back home?" we wondered. They took sea slugs, dried them till their boats were full, then back on the greatstorm they sailed. Our women went to them because that means peace. They gave the clean food, the white, clean food, rice. That was good eating — but too much work to grow it. They brought us more. Among them were shapeshifters like us. And we learned from them that the Wars were over, that the Wolves had forgotten us. No one knew that Bandaiyan was even there, lost in the south sea. These were the Middle Dragons of Zhong Guo, the kingdom white men called "China." Mokolé? Yes, but from a different world. They remembered Dragon, not the Kings, and they worshipped Sun through the year, not the day. Still, they knew the Speech, and we learned a lot from each other. Zhong Guo has bled white in my own time. I might be a blackfella but I'm not blind and deaf, Peter. The great dragons live in my memory. Sun grant that they still fly in the waking world.

The hengeyokai, the shapeshifters of the East, recognize three kinds of dragons. The High Dragons are the great Dragon-spirits of the Mother, highest-ranking lords of the spirit world. The Low Dragons are the alligators, monitors and crocodiles of the land, the dragons made purely of flesh. And the Middle Dragons, the Zhong Lung, are the Mokolé of the East. Eldest among the hengeyokai, they serve the Beast Courts of the Emerald Mother as sages, scholars, and mighty warriors. They are the strain of Mokolé associated with water, and control the rivers and streams of legendary Zhong Guo.

Where and when Mokolé first came to the Middle Kingdom is unknown, although the Zhong Lung say that the Dragon Kings are their progenitors. According to their tales, the Wani, the Dragon Kings of the Eastern world, gave five of their eggs to the Queen Mother of the West. She bore the eggs into the Middle Kingdom where they became the first Zhong Lung. Of course, there's little evidence of this, and the truth remains unclear. The other hengeyokai are no help on this matter, as they all regard the Zhong Lung as eldest among shapechangers.

The Hwanlung xi, the Kinfolk "dragon-rearing families" of old China, survive to this day in the Yangtze river valley. They have served the Zhong Lung as Kinfolk since the Xia Dynasty. Their vigilance is necessary, as the egg of a Zhong Lung can remain viable and incubate for centuries, sleeping the Sleep of the Dragon before its birth.

The Wani are the Dragon Princes of Zhong Guo, ruling the clouds and the rising and falling of water, presiding over royal houses of mankind, and puzzling humans for their "nine resemblances." When they choose to appear in their formal visage, they embody human dreams by having stag's horns, a camel's head, demon's eyes, a snake's neck, a clam's belly, scales like a carp, eagle claws, soles like a tiger and ears like a cow. The memory of the Emerald Mother holds all who have lived on her face, and so one and the same shapeshifter can easily draw on many branches of the tree of life.

The Zhong Lung's Mnesis is not any deeper than that of the Mokolé-mbembe, but they make a different use of it. What is certain is that the distinct spiritual texture of Zhong Guo has worked profound changes. Like all Mokolé, the Zhong Lung are the Memory of the Mother. Like their kin the Makara, they revere the years of Sun, not His days. Wherever the Dragon Princes may be in the present Fifth Age, the Zhong Lung remember them, and not the dinosaurs unearthed by Sunset People. Their Archid forms are more like dragons than those of any other Mokolé; only they have such features as gills, manes (too mammalian for the other streams), and fiery pearls. The Wars of Rage did not reach Zhong Guo, and so the Zhong Lung do not hate and fear the Hakken as the Mokolé-mbembe do the Garou. They are foes of Kuei-jin and other Yomi-things, and their physical prowess is helpful when combating such creatures. In sentai (clutches of more than one breed of hengeyokai) Zhong Lung often serve as Pillars (guardians much like Wardings) and Fists (warriors and generals).

They are often noble and wise before the First Change. Their ability to look deep within other's souls (and their own) is legendary. Alas, there are not many Zhong Lung left. Wars, the destruction of reptile species, and their own slow breeding have taken their toll. But long life is common for them. Some sleep the Sleep of the Dragon, while others dose themselves with elixirs to perfect the balance of yin and yang, prolonging their lives. By shedding old skin and even old bones, dragons can live for centuries. They are revered by their Kin and used to be fed and worshipped in return for bringing rain.

The awe of other hengeyokai is apparent when they deal with the Zhong Lung; the ancient legacy of the Kings shows through. When a Zhong Lung in Archid is present, any other Eastern Changer must make a Willpower roll at difficulty 6. If they fail, they suffer a +1 penalty to shapeshifting difficulties.

The beliefs of the Zhong Lung are those which they have imparted to their cousins among the hengeyokai. They revere Earth, called the Emerald Mother, and Sun in his yearly cycle. They hold that next to these are the Wani, the dragon ancestors. The fact that hengeyokai often negotiate with Kuei-jin rather than simply attacking comes from their attitude toward the Triat. Like the Makara, the Zhong Lung believe in the Balance, a supreme principle governing the entire universe. The Balance of yin and yang, light and dark, of the Devisor, Designer and Dissolver, is more important than the inherent goodness or badness of one of the Three. Like the Makara, the Zhong Lung pay careful attention to the Dissolver's true role, and don't simply condemn all of its servants. However, war is a part of maintaining the Balance and their Tung Chun don't shirk their duty.

All Zhong Lung begin play with Willpower 4. They may purchase backgrounds according to their breeds, as with other Mokolé. Like them, they cannot take Past Life. They often have Pure Breed, which represents direct descent from the First Eggs. Their Mnesis is roughly equivalent to that of the other streams, but expressed differently:

Mnesis	Timespan
•	Events of the Fifth Age: "human history"
••	The end of the Fourth Age: The Wars of Shame
•••	The entire Fourth Age: Before the War of Shame
••••	The Third Age: Legends of the great wars
•••••	The Second Age: The Wan Xian and the first shapeshifters

A few Zhong Lung have shared Mnesis with the other streams, but the memories of the Sunset dragons are strange to them.

Breeds and Territories

Homid Zhong Lung are born to humans from one of the East Asian nations: China, Japan, Korea, Tibet, Vietnam, Kampuchea, Laos, Thailand, Myanmar, Malaysia, Indonesia, and so on. Each homid's Suchid form will be the shape of the varna most common in the land where his ancestors are buried. Suchid, or draco Zhong Lung, are hatched of alligator, saltwater crocodile or Komodo monitor eggs. Other varna are not native to East Asia and would not incarnate Zhong Lung souls. A suchid's Homid form will resemble the people native to her varna's habitat.

At present, the Zhong Lung avoid cities when they can. In China itself, they inhabit communes along the Yangtze river, which are populated entirely by Kinfolk and dragons. They thus escape attention. Many solitary elders retreat to the mountains to contemplate. The purges and slaughters of the twentieth century have not left the Middle Dragons unscathed: Hei Lungren, Spring in the clutch of Seven Pearls, shudders when she tells of Kuei-jin gorging on the spoil heap of Mao's death camps, bloated almost mindless with Yin chi from the dead. Her scars from fighting them mark her even today. Two clutches of Zhong Lung lost Kinfolk during the Cultural Revolution when gangs of Red Guards attacked while the dragons were absent.

The island clutch of Fang Zhang, in the Pacific, has taken in several refugees from China's troubles. Less and less often do the dragon-lanterns beckon Zhong Lung and Kin to gather in sacred sites. China's environment is in deep trouble; the Chinese alligator is nearly extinct. Therefore fewer and fewer suchids are born, and the Shrouded Suns have taken long journeys elsewhere to seek reptile mates for their hatchlings.

Indonesia's troubled politics have meant ill for the ancient clutch of Towers-Above-the Kings (on Komodo Island). The royal family of this island was unseated and forced to retreat to the nearby island of Raijua when the tools of the Designer attacked Komodo. The Komodo dragon

is endangered, but adroit maneuvers by Kinfolk have placed it under protection and scattered Kinfolk breeding pairs to America.

Among humans, there are very few Japanese or Koreans who carry the Old Blood. The lack of reptiles in these lands has led the clutches to "lose the dragon." Some Japanese and Korean Zhong Lung send abroad for mates, although this is socially taboo. Southeast Asia's sorrow has led many of the Middle Dragons to flee or enter the long sleep, but a few clutches remain. At Samutpraken Crocodile Farm in Thailand, six Zhong Lung guard clutches of eggs in the jungle. In Indonesia the dragons are still strong, as they are in the Sea Realms beneath the Pacific. The aborigines of the Philippines and the Andamans are Kin to the Zhong Lung, and clutches exist on both island chains.

Half of Gaia's Face is under the waters of the Dragon Kingdom of Umi, and this is one of the last strongholds of the race. Here Zhong Lung bide their time, waiting alongside their Same-Bito comrades and many other supernatural denizens of the Middle Kingdom. Zhong Lung swim as far as Fiji and mate with the saltwater crocodiles who made the crossing long ago.

Forms

The Zhong Lung have three forms, as do all Mokolé since the Age of Sleep. They take their Archid form from the great vision which comes to them at their First Change, although their dreams drift toward the sinuous grace of the Wani rather than the hissing, thundering great beasts that their Sunset cousins recall.

- **Homid:** A human of the East Asian world. The Zhong Lung, as the eldest of the hengeyokai, breed with common folk and aboriginal tribes rather than nobles or cityfolk.
- **Archid:** Archid forms differ from clutch to clutch and from dragon to dragon, but Zhong Lung tend to resemble the dragons of their homeland rather than reptiles or dinosaurs. Chinese Mokolé, for instance, are most distinctive. Bull dragons are called k'iulung in Putonghua ("Mandarin"). They are splendidly whiskered, often bearing the "heaven-shattering thunder-erupting demon-repelling fire pearl" under their chins in Archid form. They often have a horn, which undulates and is curved and thin. Their sisters, called chi'lung, are gifted instead with narrow, clever snouts and crests of colored feathers, which rise and fall according to their mood. They often have thin scales and a strong tail. Zhong Lung are more flexible and agile than other Mokolé when in Archid, due to their more serpentine bodies; their Archid-form Dexterity is equal to that of their Homid form.
- **Suchid:** In this form the Zhong Lung is a reptile of the appropriate varna: the rare Chinese alligator, Komodo monitors, or the saltwater crocodiles. Mating in Suchid form is common even for homids, as it is believed to be interestingly erotic.

Auspices

The Dragons recognize four auspices, depending on the season when a Zhong Lung is born.

The **Tung Chun** are the warriors and lovers, born in spring. Their color is blue and green, and the east wind blows on them. They resemble the Rising and Setting Suns in demeanor. They begin with a Rage of 4 and receive the same sun dice as the Rising Suns.

The **Nam Hsia**, born in summer, are the judges and lawgivers. They are favored by the South wind and its warmth. They are most like the Noonday Suns or even the Eclipsed Suns. Their color is the emperor's yellow, the color of summer, and they begin with a Rage of 3. Nam Hsia have the same sun dice benefits as the Decorated Suns.

The **Sai Chau**, whose color is deathly white, are born in autumn. They are the seers and scholars among their scholarly people. The are the Shrouded Suns of their people, and somewhat like the Decorated Suns as well. They are also the keepers of the wallows of the east, called "dragon nests," and often reside in them all the time. The West Wind from the Queen Mother blows on them, and their beginning Rage is 2. Sai Chau receive the same sun dice as the Shrouded Suns.

The **Pei Tung**, whose beginning Rage is 1, are the jokers and tricksters. Born in winter, they are warmed by the North wind, and like the Midnight Suns, are contrary and love paradox. Their color is black, the "black of the daylight," as they say. They share the same sun dice benefits as the Midnight Suns.

Stereotypes

• **Gumagan:** We have watched their decline for centuries: are there any left? Had the Middle Kingdom yet ruled the seas this would never have happened.

• **Makara:** Enmeshed in human coils, the Water Monsters forget what came first. I only hope that they don't lose sight of the Emerald Mother's purpose for them.

• **Mokolé-mbembe:** Brutal warriors savaged by the barbarians' way of life. Harmony between Heaven and Earth is the way, and soldiers are less than peasants, for they only destroy.

Gathers

The gathers of the Dragon Breed are quite different from the moots of the Garou. Since the decimation of the Mokolé in the Wars of Rage, and their subsequent difficulty in regaining their numbers, gathers are also less frequent: though the Mokolé are gregarious, they are few in number. However, Mokolé all over the world learn of gathers through Mnesis, and more or less know what to do in one. They hold gathers before wars, at the summer and winter solstices, when a Crowning takes office and for some other occasions. The tenor of such an event is slow and solemn, with a great deal of bowing and courtly speeches. Mokolé usually announce their full names, including sun auspice, when they begin to speak ("*I am Cinnamon In His Light, Gathering the clutch of Towers-Above-The-Kings*"). While a gather ideally includes all seven sun auspices, sometimes requiring that several clutches meet, necessity demands that a Mokolé act in substitute of any sun auspice which is not represented. In particular, when no Eclipsed Suns are present, an elder takes the role of supervising the gather instead. The Decorated Sun has no explicit role, unless he is called on to report. Instead, he coordinates the gather, making sure that the clutch is not disturbed and providing anything needed.

The gather opens at sunrise, and begins with the time of the Rising Suns. The eldest Rising Sun acts as sergeant-at-arms to open it, and the morning is spent discussing war plans if any, hunting territories, new hatchlings, newly Changed Mokolé, and anything new. It is the part of the gather devoted to the future.

The sun approaching zenith is the time for the Noonday Suns to take over. They sit in judgment over any cases which require their authority, such as violations of the Duties, legal disputes, or matters involving Kinfolk. The eldest Noonday Sun is chief judge but must reach consensus with the others present. Any impasses are appealed to the Crowning, but this rarely happens. This is the part of the gather devoted to current events and the present.

As the sun sinks and the legal affairs are disposed of, the part of the gather devoted to the Was begins. The Setting Suns approach and begin to recall the past glories of the clutch, of the Mokolé, and of the Kings. Renown is distributed and Rank is settled. Mokolé are recognized for heroic deeds and given new Ranks if necessary. The Mokolé prepare for evening and the time of the Midnight Sun with songs and the telling of tales. As the evening shadows lengthen, inwitting and Mnesis often remind the Mokolé of the past. The Shrouded perform rituals to restore Gnosis, summon the spirits, and so on. The time at which they do this is dependent on Sun. If he covers his face with clouds, the gather begins the Shrouding phase of activity. If the whole day passes without clouds, then a canopy is brought to cover the Shrouding in the afternoon and they perform the rites then. The Mokolé see gathers at which the whole day is cloudy as times for endless performance of ritual, and the cloud cover a sign that much needs to be done.

The darkening sky marks the time of the Midnight Suns. The No-Suns make the whole night into a time of no rules. Usually food and drink are present in abundance, and Mokolé can celebrate. By ancient tradition, no reprisal can be taken for actions performed at this time. The Crowning can be insulted, the Duties mocked, and the whole structure of Mokolé society turned on its scaly head. The deranged and rococo pranks of the Shining are often bizarre beyond belief.

The celebration must end with the sky's reddening once more. When the gather ends, Mokolé return to the business of the clutch and their lives as humans or reptiles.

Kin: The "Eighth Sun"

I met you in a cave
You were paintin' buffalo
I said I'd be your slave
Follow wherever you go
— Don Was

Mokolé human Kin are usually traditional peoples of the tropics, Old World and New. As Westernization erodes their traditional way of life, they have moved closer to the Designer. However, many have sought to combine the best of old and new.

Kin who parent a true Mokolé are accorded great honor, as well as the titles "Siring" (for fathers) and "Carrying" or "Bearing" (for mothers), along with their clutch name. Fathers can make more true Mokolé, but the work of bearing them is with the female, and so the two receive equal honor. Kinfolk characters do receive Matre dice for parenting true Mokolé, although they do not have full awareness of their Matre; they call on it instinctively rather than consciously. Mokolé court and arrange matches carefully using Brood Kenning, so that happiness and many children will result: romantic love matches are unusual. Kin also aid in Mokolé clutch business, often organized by the Decorated Suns. In a gather, they speak when there is a matter that concerns them. Human Kin jokingly call themselves the "Eighth Sun."

Mokolé Kin seldom manifest Gnosis, and like all shapeshifter Kin, they can never have Rage. A very small number of Kin do manifest first-level Gifts, and a similar few Awaken as mages, usually Orphans or members of the tropical crafts such as the Bata'a or the Kopa Loei. Mage or Gifted Kin are often admitted to full membership in a clutch and called by a Sun Auspice, as true Mokolé are. As the number of true Mokolé drops, using Kin to fill up a clutch has become more and more accepted.

Kin do not undergo the Rite of Passage and do not have true Mnesis. The memories are latent within them, though, and Kin with Gnosis may have the occasional dreams or visions of ancestral memories at the Storyteller's discretion. Kinfolk are also responsible for the Mokolé alligator farms of the American South. Unlike other, more conventional gator farms, these aren't sources of food or skins. They are wallows of refuge for homid and suchid alike. Kin alligators are matched to produce true Mokolé, while non-Kin are raised for "wilderness reclamation" or to stock zoos. Human visitors are encouraged to see the alligator show for a fee — it rarely includes true Mokolé performing elaborate tricks. Notably, the American alligator has increased in number from a few hundred to over one million through human and Mokolé intervention. Of course, the Midnight Suns say that these are actually "human farms" where gators lounge at their ease while scurrying two-legs feed them. At some, true Mokolé are present as guides, but none has managed a complete clutch. Traditional Mokolé elders fret and fume that such places are no better than prisons and that no good will come of them. They may be right: at least one "farmboy" has fallen to the Dissolver and risen to a place of power among the Dissolver's human support network.

Stereotypes

It has been related that dogs drink at the River Nile running along, that they may not be seized by the crocodiles.
— Phaedrus, *Fables*

"What do we — I mean, you —I mean… Uh, what do Mokolé think of the other kinds of creatures? Do all of them hate each other?"

Jeffo pondered — accessing the Memory, Peter wondered? "Not like y'might think. Mostly it's just that the wolves don't like us. But take, f'r instance, the...

Ananasi

"They're some freaky people, no foolin'. The Mokolé-mbembe who came as a Wanderer to Scales-of-Many-Colors told us about them. Spiders who drink blood. They do the dirty work of Maker, Unmaker, Shaper, you name it. I never met one, that I know of, and don't know that I'd want to.

Bastet

"The Catskins, now, they'll deal with anybody. Just about. Moon-children, like me. You wolf-types useta' fight 'em. But they like the hotlands, like us, so we help them, and they us. 'Specially in the Amazon—"

"Yes, I met two when I was down there with the Ghost Raptors. Cat who walks by himself, kind of. But they took everything in — nothing got past them."

"The Eyes of the Mother, innit? They used to pass it all on to us, till all that got buggered up good'n'proper. But today—" Was Jeffo the only Mokolé who knew that word? How many Mokolé knew what a century was, let alone which one they were in? "—they help us when they can, we help them. Not much talking, though. We should do more of that."

"I guess we all should. You said Mokolé were related to the..."

Corax

"Sun's own eggs. But they gave up The Memory, 'cept a few little tricks like that eye-plucking rubbish. Got t'be Her postmen instead. Don't think I'd fancy that."

"The Ravens — Jeffo, you might know. Did they really used to be white?"

"In the Memory, I saw a white one, a long time ago. Long, long time ago. But it doesn't prove that all ravens are black, just because y' never saw a white one, now does it? The Ravens are friendly enough, but not many of 'em left, and most live where it's too damn cold. The Mother's parts are severed — it's part o' why She's dyin'..."

Gurahl

"...and no one to help her. Things were different then. There used to be bear-men. Women too. They were the first changers since the Age of Sleep. They could heal anything, even dead people. They say that — I don't remember it. But they could heal the Mother too. We taught them a lot — how to sleep like Dragon, how to use herbs, all that."

"What happened?"

"Wolves killed 'em all. If there's any left, they're way up north out of sight. Hope there's a few. Mother damn well could use 'em."

Nagah

"The moot I was at, where I talked about the Dragon Breed-there was another Garou present, Gere Hunts-the-Hunters. He talked about some things that sounded like Mokolé — snake people. They were all dead, though. I mean, are they?"

"The last we heard, not many left. They were Mokolé — Makara, really, in India. They made a deal with the Mother. They would give up the Memory if She let them enforce Her laws. Not something that makes y' real popular, follow me? The clutch of Towers-Above-The-Kings met one. Maybe she was the last. We remember the Camazotz dying, the Grondr and the Apis, but don't remember the Nagah dying. Maybe there's a few left, but they're not talking."

"There are other shapeshifters too. What about the..."

Ratkin

"Small mouthfuls. Look, all mammals used to be that small. The rat-folk at least stayed that way. I've never met one, but they don't seem to like us much. I don't know that they like anybody. If they are the keepers of man, they're not doing a good job. We get along better with the..."

Rokea

"Friend to the Undertow, y'know? They cull stupid humans; so do we."

"Damnation! The were-sharks! I knew a warrior once who met one. What are they really like?"

"I know them only from The Memory, but we do talk from time to time. They live long, hundreds of years, or thousands, so sometimes one knows us from before. We remember him. There are clutches that knew the same shark for centuries. What are they like? Cold, fast, silent. Deep. They love the Ocean, that much we can tell. We swap information: where reefs open, where the hunting is good, safe waters for breeding. Who knows what else is under there? Could be anything."

"Anything? There are a lot of other weird creatures in the world, I know. Ever meet a vampire?"

Kindred

"Stalkers of the night! Easy enough to step on them. You think you hate those things? Imagine how we feel. The blood-devils are destroyed when they see Sun's face. I hear that there are a lot of different kinds of them. Those who serve Set are the worst. They took Egypt away from us and destroyed it. From Kin I hear that the blood-devils fight each other. Maybe they'll kill each other. That would be good."

Mages

"There are different kinds of witches and spook-men too. The Bata'a are friends to our Mokolé-mbembe cousins in Africa and America. The mob knows another kind called Dreamspeakers. They have some honor; many are Kin. In Khem there were some cunning men called Hem-ka Sobk a long time ago. They worshipped Sobek, Crocodile spirit of the Nile, and were good to us. Of the rest we know little. Don't they destroy Garou wallows? Then they're not all bad. Oh... sorry, Peter."

"It's okay. I know Garou have done a lot of bad stuff to you."

"No. You aren't the only ones at fault. We both fought in the Wars of Rage. We both have to fight to make peace. Not just fighting our own people when they want to keep up old grudges, but fighting ourselves, when our rage tries to control us. Fighting to become more than we are. It isn't easy."

For the first time Peter saw how difficult and scary this must have been for Jeffo's mob. Garou were slaughterers, squatters, killers of Bunyip and Gumagan. How many wallows would have invited a Garou to visit them? To become one of them? How many Garou had been offered the chance to see themselves as others saw them? That alone was priceless. He was grateful. He had to try.

Mummies

"But in Egypt the Memory tells us about another kind of immortal, women and men whose bodies died, but who kept coming back. Guards-the-Path is like that. He dies, but lives again."

"What, like 'The Mummy's Curse'?"

"Yeah. Mummies and such. Made 'em by magic, so they'd never die. We know it worked. The Memory sees 'em. They like us because everyone else has forgot the world they lived in. So every so often they'll seek us out for a chat. One came to see us about fifty years ago, Morwangu told me, name of Psammtik, something like that. The old chap was just full of gossip about Hatshepsut's sex life. Kept Morwangu jawing all night, he did. Wonderful conversation."

"What are they like, then? Like vampires?"

"No, not at all — well, most of 'em. Got some odd Gifts and rites, but they don't eat people, drink blood, all that rot. Rather weird, so we heard. When I see them in the Memory, they're right sad. Can't die, and their world is gone. Fight each other, I'd think. It's all they have left."

"'Most of 'em... and the others?"

"Well, there's some as is worse. Time ate 'em, they fell to the Dissolver. They're name-eaters, memory-eaters. Or they were. If any are still around, I don't know. Nasty old rotters. Run if you meet one."

Wraiths

"What about real ghosts? Have you met any?"

"Real as your hand, mate. Buggers what die bad don't stay in the ground, that's all."

"But Garou who die, they don't become ghosts. I mean, do they?"

"Whole mob o' wolf ghosts, Pete! The Bunyip, don't y'know? Whitefella killed 'em and they didn't stay dead. Makes the Shadow scary as hell! They don't bother us, 'coz we got along fine before you came. But I saw a whitefella wolfie torn to pieces, and the pieces, they just kept screamin.'"

"Don't Mokolé have a harder time entering the Shadow, though?"

"Yeah. 'Coz of our own ghosts. When a Mokolé covers another Mokolé, the brat always dies, and dies bad, real bad. They don't leave us alone, either." Jeffo shuddered, shivering in the blazing sun. "Maybe the other ghosts, the regular ones, take care of ours. I hope so."

Changelings

"There's other odds an' sods out there too. Some callin' 'emselves eshu. Blackfellas from Africa. Good enough blokes. Like to visit Gathers for the party. They have lots of good stories, all full of knights, princes and castles. Maybe it's all true, somewhere. I wouldn't know."

The Duties

For when you have done this, you will see a youthful god, beautiful in appearance, with fiery hair, and in a white tunic and a scarlet cloak, and wearing a fiery crown. At once greet him with the fire-greeting.

—The Mithras Liturgy

The Sun has given his Children a series of moral and personal imperatives by which to live their lives. Called the Duties, these are the Mokolé precursor to the Garou Litany.

Each Duty is connected to one solar auspice, although all Mokolé are bound by them. Violations of the Duties merit reprimands, loss of status, and other punishments. Serious offenders are eaten. The Unshading enforce the laws, although even Midnight Suns will chastise an undutiful Mokolé. Mokolé who have reached their First Change alone (lost hatchlings) are sometimes seduced by the Dissolver. These Mokolé, if they Fall to the Dissolver, lose solar Gifts and Mnesis. Sometimes they return to the Rite of Passage and manifest monstrous, non-reptilian body parts. They are readily recognizable; they shun the Sun and seek darkness, often after descending into drug use to recapture the dreaming. Usually other Mokolé hunt down and kill these monsters before it is too late.

The Rising Sun says **Cull the Fallen**. The creatures of the Dissolver, Mokolé who have fallen or broken the Duties, and Gaia-wrecking humans are fair game. The corollary of this Duty is the obligation to avoid unlawful prey. Likewise, Mokolé do not hunt Garou or other shapeshifters wantonly.

Reality: Mokolé can't keep killing humans, or so many reptile Kin will be killed in return that more Mokolé can't be born. Garou, thinking that the Mokolé themselves are Dissolver-spawn, have slain so many of the Dragon Breed that missions against the Dissolver are rare. The Mokolé have enough problems of their own.

The Noonday Sun says **Let No Shade Accuse You**. At all costs, avoid breeding with other Mokolé. When judging, judge fairly. When making war, remember the death that it brings. Accept a surrender when you can. There are not enough Mokolé left to waste. Moderation is the way to bring justice to Mokolé society.

Reality: Mokolé seldom breed with other Mokolé, and regret it when they do because of the Innocents, who harry any Mokolé in the Umbra. Mating rites ensure that Mokolé have suitable Kin partners. Mokolé often deal leniently with violations of the Duties, as so few Mokolé remain that the harsher punishments would only weaken Sun's children further. Duels are almost unknown anymore save in Mnesis.

The Setting Sun says **Guard the Wallow**. Children, Kin, and old or sick Mokolé as well as the sacred sites and objects of the Dragon Breed need protection. The laws of sanctuary mandate refuge for the needy. Likewise, respect another wallow's territory and Memory, including the wallows of Nagah and Corax. As for the wolves, stay away. Setting Suns never ask how many foes there are. Only where they are.

Long ago, rivalry between Mokolé and between clutches ended in violence. Nowadays, the rarity of Mokolé means that the lives of the Dragon Breed are too precious. To kill a clutchmate is the ultimate horror. Warding Mokolé have recently asked whether, as Gaia dies, non-Mokolé shapeshifters could also be clutchmates.

Reality: The Setting Suns are still ready to die on a heap of the slain to save the clutch. Merely fighting isn't enough, though. Mokolé now have to manage things like acquiring legal title to land and protected status for their reptile Kin. Strangers are more and more commonly accepted as it becomes painfully obvious that the Mokolé need help just to survive. Killing a clutchmate is still punished by death. Unlike the Garou, the Mokolé enforce tending a relative's sickness, rather than forbidding it. The hurt and sick can be tended more easily in the wallow than on the trail with a wolfpack.

The Shrouded Sun says **The Veil Must Not Be Lifted**. The Veil ensures the Mokolé's survival, and their existence must be kept secret. Likewise, the lore of Mnesis is for those who can use it, and is to be kept for its rightful owners.

Reality: The Delirium helps out a lot here. As the Mokolé drop in number, even the other shapeshifters begin to believe that they are extinct. In most chronicles, a non-Mokolé character will need Mokolé Lore even to know that the Dragon Breed exist at all.

The Midnight Sun says **Test the Clutch**. The tricksters see what other Mokolé don't. They prepare their clutchmates for the unexpected by being it themselves. Many tales mention the elaborate practical jokes and teaching pranks of the No-Suns. There are tales, dances and shapeshifting plays that convey the wisdom of the Midnight Suns in a way that everyone can understand and enjoy.

Reality: The Shining perform their function gladly, to the chagrin of their clutchmates.

The Decorated Sun says **All Are Of Gaia**. Know that Kinfolk, humans, reptiles, and other Awakened are here for a reason. You have a place, and so do they. Respect the Crowning, listen to the Concealing, follow the Gathering. Leaders may be questioned, but authority does not come from winning a fight. Honor the Eighth Sun, who enable the Mokolé to survive. Make sure that all resources, including food, are distributed fairly and in proportion. Heal the sick, help the wounded, allow the dying spirit to pass on into Gaia's Memory.

Reality: The Mokolé do not understand why many Garou treat their Kinfolk so brutally. Mokolé are much more concerned with having children than the Garou, but their attitude is that mating is there to be enjoyed. The Zhong Lung are the most dedicated to the "play of clouds and rain," and have made endless "pillow books" and "springtime pictures" about the art of love. Both same-sex and opposite-sex love have their places in Mokolé society, although opposite-sex Mokolé couples must not exist.

The decimation of the Mokolé in the Wars of Rage means that the old hierarchies are gone. Few clutches have a Crowning, and many Mokolé are without a clutch at all — they are born to 'clutches' of Kinfolk who wait lifetimes for a true Mokolé to come.

Food and money were distributed more equally in the old days when human Kin were tribal. Nowadays, as social inequality worsens in the tropical nations where they live, observance of this Duty is fading. Mnesis helps a great deal in making this Duty real, however. Mokolé know the pain of childbirth, the bite of hunger, and the lash of slavery. Almost all Mokolé have Mnesis from members of the opposite sex, from humans and reptiles. This makes them unusually understanding (as residents of the World of Darkness go).

The Eclipsed Sun says **Remember**. Sun made you Mokolé for a reason. You are part of the Memory of Gaia. Don't forget this.

Reality: Many Mokolé are too busy fighting for their lives to worry about Gaia's great plan. However, their mere existence and the perpetuation of the Dragon Breed are enough to assure that Gaia has a Memory.

Mokolé Names

Suchid Mokolé have deed names, similar to those of the Garou. Names can be simple or complicated and can be earthy or very religious. Examples include Moss, the guardian of the Dismal Swamp, Stands Against The Tide, a warrior from Indonesia, and Winter Cannot Conquer Him, leader of the Mokolé clutch in Detroit. Names can also refer to ancestors or describe the Mokolé ("Cinnamon-In-His-Light").

Homids have a name appropriate for the land of their birth, and usually end up taking a Mokolé name at their First Change. Often they keep their human name for all but the most formal functions, as human names sound silly in the Dragon's Tongue. For gathers and courts, a Mokolé introduces herself by name, clutch and sun auspice.

The Mandates of Earth

The Mokolé of the East, the Makara and Zhong Lung, adhere to the Mandates of the Emerald Mother, the hengeyokai law. These rules are somewhat different from the Duties, but are based on the same principles.

Shirk Not The Tasks Which Have Been Given You

The Dragon Breed are the Mother's Memory and may not forget "all that's past." Their special powers are their compensation, and they should not desert the Way to live as an ordinary human or reptile. This rule does allow for different kinds of service, however — as long as they're taken in addition to rather than instead of the Memory.

Guard The Wheel, That It May Turn In Fullness

The hengeyokai, half human and half beast, are by their very nature keepers of the Balance. They must aid and abet the progression of the Mother through the ages of time, even if forward motion brings them and their Kin more death and sorrow. Some dragons have studied Marxism and found its belief in a future "workers' paradise" to resemble the prophecy of the Twelfth Age, when Heaven and Earth will again be in harmony. However, neither utopia is anywhere in sight.

Honor Your Territory In All Things

This Mandate means guarding territory, and requires respect for the land and its creatures, including Kin. The Makara and Zhong Lung both cherish human and reptile Kin and work closely with them. With Kinfolk help, they also work to keep up the flows of earth-energy.

Let Mercy Guide You In Our August Mother's Court

Eastern Mokolé must abstain from killing allies or potential allies, especially other hengeyokai. However, other Awakened are not protected by this Mandate.

Honor Your Ancestors And Your Elders

The Zhong Lung and Makara are the most reverent of all the hengeyokai toward those who have gone before. Mnesis is the reason. In fact, blind obedience to this rule has made for inflexibility in their culture. Another result of this duty is the reverence for descendants. There must be someone to live after you when you die; therefore, these Mokolé surround breeding with great ritual and reverence.

Honor The Pacts With The Spirit World

This ordains that Mokolé must regularly perform rites and rituals. As the bloodlines die off, the lineages of Mnesis stretch and break, and the Wall hardens, the Zarad and the Sai Chau are less able to do this. As a result, serious trouble has come on the Breed.

War Not Upon Human Nor Beast

This forbids excessive hunting as well as fighting to exterminate any nation or tribe. As the Mokolé are more philosophers than fighters, this has never been difficult to obey.

Let No One Or Nothing Violate The Sacred Places

This simply means that wallows and dragon nests are worth the lives of the Vasanta and Tung Chun who guard them. However, any Mokolé would fight as valiantly as the Warriors when defending a sacred site.

And so I was led from a word to a word,
From a thought to another thought.
— The Hævamæl

Jeffo spoke. "I always knew I was Gumagan. Mum talked about it to me, like anything else about us, like about the Dreamtime. I was about five when I knew she didn't talk about it to anyone else but Morwangu. She didn't talk to the welfare lady or the preacher."

"Yeah, I was like that. My mother, Cassandra, was a Fury, and she raised me at the caern and I knew lots of Garou. But we couldn't talk about it to anyone else. But a lot of Garou are lost till they change. Their parents aren't knowing Kinfolk."

"Mokolé can't be like that. We have the Memory. Now, y' can be Mokolé but not know another. Some go their whole lives like that. No clutch, sometimes just Kinfolk. Sometimes Kinfolk keep the wallow long, hoping for a Mokolé to be born. That's what happened to Wolaru's mob, our mob. Morwangu was born when only one granny was left who'd known Standing Stone and Wolaru."

"Wow. They remember that long, and keep everything the same?"

"Even Kin are good at remembering. They don't have The Memory, that's all. You never get it till you get the djunggawon, the man-making."

"What's that?"

"When I first became my dragon-self."

"Was that your First Change? Or whatever you call it?"

"Not the Change that's the big deal — it's dreaming it. I was, oh, I guess, thirteen or fourteen. Gone walkabout down to Jabirru with me mates and felt a shakin'. Morwangu wasn't anywhere near, so I told 'em to go on, an' laid down with some water."

Jeffo's eyes were bright, focused on the Was. "Next thing, I was crawling across a mudflat, cold as a squatter's heart. Had to find food, but I could barely move. Then Lord Sun showed His face on the land. I turned my side to him, and the crest on my back drank His light. Soon I was moving, fastest thing on the block. I took a greatfrog who was barely awake — it tasted really good."

"I woke warm in the desert, staring up at thousands of stars. There was a power in me that I had never felt before. I could reach back with my mind, through life upon life, time upon time. I was greater than myself. I was Mokolé. Morwangu found me at moonset, and then he started teaching me the old ways. It's been a long road."

Children of the Sun — Aspects

Sun laid nine eggs
rock, cloud, water, sand, great, rings, wind, blue, snow
Water laid nine eggs
scum, worms, weeds, fish, frogs, us, Kings, wombs, man
Who laid Sun?

— Mokolé riddle

The Mokolé revere Sun as the giver of life and source of heat for their bodies. As such, the sun determines the identity of a Mokolé. The Mokolé-mbembe and Gumagan recognize seven solar auspices; each aspect provides a special advantage ("sun dice") to those born under it. Just as in Garou society, repeatedly acting outside one's auspice is considered inappropriate and disrespectful.

The Rising Sun — "Striking"

These are Mokolé born between the reddening of the eastern sky and noon. Striking Mokolé are the soldiers, hunters, explorers, seekers and doers of the new in Mokolé society. Often they are the only Mokolé who interest themselves in the present. They joke that the sky reddens with the blood of their foes. Throughout their lives they gain an extra die to their initiative dice pools.

Beginning Willpower: 3

Steretoypes:

• **Unshading:** Our teachers of the law. They are strict: maybe too strict.

• **Warding:** Hold the fort. I'll be back before long. I hope.

• **Concealing:** How does that work? What do you mean, no one knows? Can I learn? Hey, did you see this? No, really, try it...

• **Shining:** They have some crazy ideas. Some of them are so crazy that they actually work.

• **Gathering:** Busybodies! I wish they'd listen to good ideas when we have them. They can get you help when you need it, though.

• **Crowning:** Listen to me! I am trying to help us! I don't care how you did it in the Ice Age! The past is over — this is a new time.

Quote: *Oh, do not fear, little one. There shall be companions for our deaths.*

— Teeth-Of-The-Kings, Striking for the clutch of Scales of Many Colors

The Noonday Sun — "Unshading"

These Mokolé come into the world while the sun is high in the sky. The shadowless are the police, judges, and enforcers of the Duties. They apply the laws of Sun, and enforce the will of the Crowned. These Mokolé may subtract one die from the dice pool of any foe related to the dark (including vampires, fomori, Black Spirals, Spectres, Nephandi mages and Banes). They may do this once per scene, and may only affect one dice pool at a time. Of all the auspices, this one has lost the fewest members to the Dissolver.

Beginning Willpower: 5

Stereotypes:

• **Striking:** Impetuous. They are forever rushing headlong into their silly "new" ideas. Mnesis shows that there is nothing new and the Duties tell us how to live. That is what is right.

• **Warding:** How a warrior should act: sturdy defenders of the clutch and wallow.

• **Concealing:** Their mysteries have an appropriate place. They can be useful at the proper time.

• **Shining:** Annoying tricksters! I do not care for their foolish pranks.

• **Gathering:** Excellent for seeing that the right course of action is carried out. They leave me much time to study the Law and advise the Eclipsed Sun.

• **Crowning:** Givers of orders, they are in turn given orders by Sun.

Quote: *You think that the darkness will hide your actions, but I have eyes of Sun and can see you wherever you cower.*

— Giant Footsteps, Unshading the clutch of Great Bayou Mother

The Setting Sun — "Warding"

These Mokolé are born while the Sun descends, before the sky darkens. Warding are the guards, nurses, healers and caretakers of children. Warding add an extra die to their dice pools when they defend others, retreat or follow specific orders. They say that the Sun reddens the sky with the blood that they shed to defend their people.

Beginning Willpower: 3

Stereotypes:

• **Striking:** They are great in battle. That is good.

• **Unshading:** The No-Nights tell us what to do. Sometimes the Sun blinds them to what *is*, though.

• **Concealing:** How can you follow something that no one can see? Practical matters are more important.

• **Shining:** They say many silly things. That's good, because I need to laugh.

• **Gathering:** They talk too much. But sometimes some good comes of it.

• **Crowning:** Sun's chosen. Glad it's not me.

Quote: *Lord Sun dies in blood, and so shall I. But you shall die first.*

— Stands-Against-The-Tide, Warding the clutch of Towers-Above-The-Kings.

The Shrouded Sun — "Concealing"

Concealing Mokolé are born while the Sun is clouded. The Concealing gain an extra die on Stealth rolls or when they camouflage anything. The Concealing are the mystics, teachers of spirit lore, and knowers of secrets in Mokolé society. They are most skilled at magic or Gifts and are subtle hunters. Many have the Merit: Spirit Magnet or are mediums, allowing friendly spirits to possess them for the benefits. They are known to associate with human shamans more freely than does any other Mokolé.

Beginning Willpower: 4

Stereotypes:

• **Striking:** The Rising Suns are rash and hotheaded. There is more to Sun than His heat.

• **Unshading:** They judge and condemn too freely. Sun is no tyrant.

• **Warding:** These stalwarts know too much suffering and loss. Sun sinks, but He does so that He may rise.

• **Shining:** They see the great mystery: sometimes light is darkness.

• **Gathering:** How often do sundogs shine?

• **Crowning:** There is more than one way for Darkness to cover Sun's face.

Quote: *You who look into darkness, know that there are also mysteries in light.*

— Coils Within Coils, Mokolé Wanderer

The Midnight Sun — "Shining"

The Mokolé born while the sky is dark are called Shining. Lovers of contradiction, paradox and riddle, they see humor in a solar auspice without any sun. They can draw on an extra die when they are faced with hopeless odds. They are guides of the dead, tricksters, and mythmakers, as well as the jokers, artists and poets of the Dragon Breed.

Mokolé born at night divide themselves into three groups. The Night-Suns are born under Luna, and joke about moon auspices, or seek Gifts of the moon, saying that she is the Sun of the Night. Of course, they do have difficulties finding moon creatures to teach them Gifts. The Many-Suns are born under the stars, and say, "Every star is a sun." Therefore they claim to be thousands of times more blessed than Mokolé born in daylight. They say that there are as many paths to truth as suns, and often get into trouble for their crazy ideas. The No-Suns are born under the lightless sky, and are the most mysterious of all: they say, "Sometimes light is darkness." They draw wisdom from the empty spaces between the stars. The Unshading fear that they may fall to the Dissolver because of this.

Beginning Willpower: 4

Stereotypes:

• **Striking:** Hey, ya hear this one? Two Mokolé walk into a wallow, see...

• **Unshading:** There is more than one Sun.

• **Warding:** The Darkness will come, whatever you do. So praise it also.

• **Concealing:** Clouds hide the Sun from you, but Gaia hides Him from us.

• **Gathering:** Here, hold this.... (sputtering noise followed by explosion)

• **Crowning:** Give us no orders and we must obey; command us and we have to undermine your authority. Nothing personal.

Quote: *Maggots from meat, weevils from rye*
Dragons from stars in an empty sky...

— Morkeleb the Black, Shining the clutch of Million-Season Jaws

The Decorated Sun — "Gathering"

A special blessing follows the Mokolé who are born while the Sun is accompanied by "sundogs," the rings, rays or flares of light surrounding His Face. The Gathering are the matchmakers, organizers, and coordinators of the Mokolé. The Crowning may reign, but the Gathering get things done, as Mokolé say. They are workers, listmakers and busybodies. They receive an extra die to dice pools when they act in a collective effort to benefit the Mokolé.

Beginning Willpower: 5

Stereotypes:

• **Striking:** Excellent warriors and wanderers. Even so, they talk too much about impractical concerns.

• **Unshading:** Useful in keeping the clutch in line.

• **Warding:** Our guardians and foster parents. The assurance of our future.

• **Concealing:** If they would explain their "mysteries" more clearly then they would be more useful.

• **Shining:** AAAAAUUUUUUUGGHHHHHH!!!!!!!

• **Crowning:** The ordained rulers. The less they actually do, the smoother things usually run.

Quote: *Even a dragon cannot do everything alone.*

— Cinnamon-In-His-Light, Gathering the clutch of Towers-Above-The-Kings.

Solar Eclipse — "Crowning"

Those born when Sun is eclipsed are the ruler-priests of Mokolé society. Mokolé mothers sometimes try to use the Rite of the Nesting Mound to bring their eggs to term while an eclipse is in progress. The Crowning are rare creatures; all other Mokolé defer to them. However, they usually look to the Concealing for advice and the Gathering for know-how. Tyrants among the Mokolé end up without followers.

There are four types of eclipses and therefore four types of Crowning Mokolé. A total eclipse is the birthday of the Jewel-Crowned, who are priest-kings. They lead the worship of Sun and proclaim His prophecies. They get one extra die to apply anywhere the sun shines.

The Crescent-Crowned are born in a partial eclipse. These are warrior kings who lead Mokolé and Kin into battle. They are born slightly more often than their jeweled siblings, but their occupation means that few of them live to old age. They get one extra die to apply when making war.

The Ring-Crowned are born in annular eclipses, and are the Unity Kings: they forge alliances between different clutches, inspire their people to great-hearted deeds, and amass treasures and wealth. They have an automatic extra die when making connections between other creatures or when working with their wealth (even suchids).

The Moon-Crowned are born in lunar eclipses and are the backwards rascal kings of Mokolé society; they should well be Shining, but law places them among the Crowning's ranks. Their "reigns" are eruptions of loony policies, wild parties, and deadly practical jokes; they are the kind of crazy hero whose ideas end up saving the day. In the present dire straits of the Mokolé, their weird stratagems might be necessary.

Beginning Willpower: 5

Stereotypes:

• **Striking:** Cleanse our territory to the last Dissolver-spawn and *then* tell me about what the next clutch is doing.

• **Unshading:** Find the kinslayers and bring them to me for judgment.

• **Warding:** Keep an eye on the wallow. That's all I ask.

• **Concealing:** You can do what? Are you sure it's safe?

• **Shining:** (irritated ruffling of royal crest feathers)

• **Gathering:** Organize the Mnesis holdings, the food warehouse, and the hatchlings' nursery and then report to me.

Quote: *Sun be with you, and with us all.*

— Malesi, Crowning the clutch of Towers-Above-The-Kings

Breeds

Peter lay in the sun, reflecting that even with SPF 45, this was going to give him the tan from hell. There was something to be said for spending most of your time active during the day.

"So, Jubati told me a long time ago that you guys can't enter the Umbra like we can. What's the deal?"

"Oh, many of us can. All we have to do is remember you doing it, you know. But there's a reason to stay right here."

Jeffo shuddered, which was strange to watch in a reptile. "The Shadow is full of fear for us. Sun warned us long ago not to make children with other Mokolé, or we we'd regret it. But in the Wars of Rage, there was a Midnight Sun called Night's Fire. The wolves caught her, tortured her for days with brands of silver to get the location of her clutch." Peter kept silent, horrified at the cruelty Garou were capable of, and even more horrified that Jeffo hadn't heard this tale: He had lived it. "Cut her to the bone, then clotted the wounds with fire. She was called She Burns after that. She told them, and her whole clutch died, her children with them."

The dinosaur took a deep breath, his sides heaving. "Then they let her go, and she went mad to become a mother again. She mated with another Mokolé. Their child died when she first Changed. She Burns died too, by her own claws, but when Light Between The Leaves, Concealing the Clutch of Hooark-Oark, passed into the Shadow after that, She Burns' daughter attacked him and he barely lived to see Sun's light. No-Face, he named her. She was the first of The Innocents."

"Innocents? What are those?"

"The lost children. Born from Mokolé and Mokolé. Sun sends them no dreaming, and they die, to haunt us forever. They are hellish to see and deadly foes. Pray that you never remember them." He shot away into the brilliant outback. Peter turned over in the sun and wondered if he would ever understand the Dragon Breed. Why would dinosaurs be afraid of babies? These were some scary babies. Maybe the Garou had it easy.

Breed Characteristics

As mentioned before, Mokolé have only two breeds; their metis die before they are born. Homids, the human-born, are at a distinct disadvantage in Mokolé society because their awareness of their reptile side is mostly learned rather than instinctual. Suchids make fun of them for their ineptitude at hunting and swimming. Homid Mokolé begin the game with 2 Gnosis.

Suchid Mokolé, those hatched from a reptile's egg, are as limited as lupus Garou when it comes to purchasing Abilities. They cannot purchase Drive, Etiquette, Firearms, Computer, Law, Linguistics, Medicine, Politics or Science with initial points, only with freebie points or experience. Furthermore, they may not buy Resources, Allies, or Contacts at character creation, save with freebie points (although they're free to make friends and accumulate wealth during the course of play). Their only Kinfolk are reptiles. In the First Times, most Mokolé were suchid, but as reptile species become endangered, homids have become as numerous as suchids. Suchids begin play with 4 Gnosis.

New Abilities

Skills

Brood Kenning

Brood Kenning is the ability to match mates so as to maximize the chance of a desired offspring, a happy union, or some similar goal. If trying to maximize the chances of a Mokolé babe, the matchmaker observes her charges carefully, anywhere from a day to a month or more, and finally makes a Brood Kenning roll (usually paired with Intelligence, Perception or Wits at the Storyteller's discretion). The difficulty is typically 9, but can be reduced with extra observation. The number of successes is added to the chance for a Mokolé offspring; a particularly insightful and ridiculously lucky matchmaker could thus increase the odds of breeding true up to 20%.

This skill can only be used once for any given couple, at least when enhancing the odds of breeding true. It can also be used to make matches that will wind up happy, or to recognize the signs of hidden trysting (such as if two Mokolé are secretly mating and might produce an Innocent). Brood kenners are compensated and esteemed, whether they are Mokolé or Kin. It is a common choice for Gathering.

- • You can arrange blind dates that aren't total disasters.
- •• Your clutchmates sneak off to you for romantic advice.
- ••• You patch up stormy, confused teenage relationships on a regular basis.
- •••• If you'd been present in Verona, Romeo and Juliet would have lived happily ever after.
- ••••• Even the fiercest Crowning bows his head to you and calls you "auntie."

Knowledges

Maieusis

Originated by Greek and Egyptian philosophers, the rare skill of Maieusis enables a practitioner to bring out memories lost in the recesses of another's soul. Called "the midwife's art," it involves questions, ritual dialogue and the pronunciation of syllables whose meaning is obscure. The player must specify how many levels of Mnesis he wishes to evoke in the subject, or how many memories he wishes the subject to recall, and the two participants must speak the same language (usually the Dragon's Tongue). The subject must have the Mnesis to do this, or the potential to remember the subjects involved. The practitioner must spend a number of hours equal to the level of Mnesis desired to call out the memory, then make a Manipulation + Maieusis roll. The difficulty is 6 for ordinary memories, 7 for Mnesis, and 8 for difficult or obscure subjects. For each success, one memory is recalled.

Maieusis is a daring art. Memories long forgotten can emerge, and a soul be made anew. The Unshading sometimes send lawbreakers to receive the midwife's art rather than die, hoping that their memories will contain enough righteousness to return them to good. It is said that the Fallen have been overcome with grief when subjected to Maieusis, realizing the horrors that they have become, and have died voluntarily in their remorse.

- • You can remind your partner of that night in Rio.
- •• You can bring new insight to people.
- ••• You are known as a lover of wisdom.
- •••• You are revered as a teacher/counselor.
- ••••• Watch out for the hemlock...

Mnesis Emulation

This strange knowledge may be learned only by Mokolé. It enables a Mokolé to "learn" almost any skill or knowledge that could have been known to an ancestor.

The Mokolé must meditate on the ability desired and enter a Mnesis trance. The trance is usually not long — perhaps one night. Finally, she makes a Mnesis + Mnesis Emulation roll, difficulty 7. For every two successes, the seeker gains a dot in the given Ability for one day (rounding up); she may spend dots to increase the duration, however. For instance, five successes could give her a skill of 3 for one day or a skill of 1 for three days. Mnesis Emulation cannot grant any supernatural abilities (such as Gifts, rites or powers of other Awakened creatures). For example, a Mokolé may use Mnesis Emulation to learn the language of the Bastet, but would not be able to turn into a cat even if she had a Bastet ancestor.

- • You can call up a hint of memory.
- •• You can usually see the right place and time.
- ••• You have something to say to everyone.
- •••• You are at home everywhere.
- ••••• You can imitate anyone who has ever lived.

Saurimancy

The giant reptiles of the world, because of their profoundly different thought processes, have always fascinated humans. The slither of alligators and the chirping of lizards have for ages been thought to hold mystic insights. This skill, the art of saurian divination, allows Kin and Mokolé to divine the future or the will of Sun from saurian omens. It is most common among Kin in India. The diviner must listen to lizards chirping at dusk, meditate on the tracks of crocodiles, or use a similar method. For each day that she spends in such study, she may make a Perception + Saurimancy rating roll, difficulty 7. For each success, she may gain one "insight" of the Storyteller's choice. The omen may be vague or quite clear, as the Storyteller thinks appropriate.

- • You heard a lizard once.
- •• You knew when Father had died.
- ••• You know tomorrow's weather.
- •••• You are a famous fortuneteller.
- ••••• The alligators tell all.

Backgrounds

Mokolé characters gain the same five points in Backgrounds as do all other **Werewolf** characters. They may not purchase Past Life or mammal totems at character creation. In addition, many Mokolé have at least a dot in Mnesis, the Background of their racial memory.

Mnesis

One of the most important traits of the Mokolé as a race, Mnesis is the Memory — the racial memory that stretches back to the birth of the Dragon Breed. This Background determines how far back a Mokolé may remember on a Mnesis quest.

- • A century or so
- •• A millennium or so
- ••• The Impergium and the beginning of human civilization
- •••• Up until the Last Times
- ••••• The time of the Dinosaur Kings

Mnesis can actually vary from stream to stream; the differences are listed in the previous chapter. When remembering, a Mokolé can remember only what an ancestor of his might have seen or done, and gather a vague impression of what that ancestor might have felt about the events witnessed. Further details on Mnesis questing are given in the Sunset chapter.

Wallow

You have ties to a Mokolé wallow, one with some history and other Mokolé residents. If you are a homid, this may be a village, rural homestead, or isolated island such as Komodo. If you are a suchid, it may be an ancient temple, jungle swamp, zoo or gator farm. Any Allies, Contacts or Kinfolk you may have likely live at the wallow.

The wallow is a place where you can meditate to regain Gnosis in Sun's light, hold gathers and perform rites. You may live there all the time; of course, if you don't have Resources, your home might not be very luxurious.

- • A poor wallow. One Mokolé lives there or perhaps only Kin.
- •• No palace. A few Mokolé and Kin live there.
- ••• The wallow has lots of land (maybe a national park) or places to live.
- •••• A nice place: a village, isolated creek, or lake.
- ••••• A temple, alligator farm or large village.

Dragon's Blessings

The Mokolé share many of the benefits and disadvantages common to all the Changing Breeds, as well as some characteristics uniquely their own. They are a powerful bunch, to be sure, but the gifts of Dragon and Sun combined give them even more flexibility, even as they hinder the Mokolé in other ways.

Regeneration

Mokolé regenerate as do Garou, healing back a health level every turn unless the damage is aggravated; to do this in combat or during other heavy exertion requires a Stamina roll, difficulty 8. Like Garou, they can return from below Incapacitated with a Rage roll; like Garou, they also run the risk of gaining battle scars. They cannot be harmed by any disease that isn't supernatural.

The Umbra

Mokolé, like several other Changing Breeds, cannot step sideways without assistance. They must learn a particular Gift to be able to enter the Umbra on their own. When they do travel the Umbra, they most often use outside assistance (such as pathways or rites) to visit the High Umbra rather than the Middle Umbra. For more information, see the Sunset chapter.

Rage and Gnosis

The Mokolé have as much Rage as any Garou, and use it in much the same manner — they may frenzy, gain extra actions, change forms instantly, recover from stunning, or make Rage rolls to remain active when critically wounded. They regain it in similar fashion, when angered or humiliated, or between stories as usual. Furthermore, Mokolé regain Rage the first time that they see Sun during the day, such as at sunrise. The amount recovered depends on how bright Sun is.

Light Conditions	Rage Regained
Sun is completely obscured by mountains, buildings, etc.; the Mokolé is indoors.	None
Sun's disc is hidden by clouds or is seen through windows.	1
Sun's disc is visible through clouds or fog.	2
Sun is low or dim.	3
Sun is bright.	4
Sun is blazing directly overhead.	5

Any Mokolé seeing her sun auspice gets back all Rage.

Midnight Suns get back Rage from seeing their "sign," not the Sun. They may not recover their full Rage if the moon is clouded, or the stars are dim. No-Suns cannot see the empty sky and Many-Suns cannot see the stars if smog or city lights block their view.

Zhong Lung and Makara regain all their Rage each day of the season of their auspice when they first see the sun, but recover Rage piecemeal if it's "not their season."

Mokolé may not regain Gnosis when cut off from the sun, save when sleeping the Sleep of the Dragon. The less Sun is visible, the more time Mokolé must spend meditating in his Light. Naturally, Mokolé are usually uncomfortable in cities, unless they are in the tropics. They regain Gnosis in the typical fashion of meditation (which they must do while basking in sunlight) or by bargaining with spirits, and may regain Gnosis between stories as usual.

The Dragon's Tongue

All Mokolé inherit knowledge of the language of Dragon even if they have no other Mnesis, unless they have the Flaw: Speechless. The Dragon's Tongue was the common language of the Earth in the time of the Kings, and all the Awakened of that era spoke it. Most could read and write its elaborate script as well. Many old-fashioned Mokolé refer to it as "the Speech" and will refuse to admit that "rat's chitter" is capable of fluent expression.

Mnesis brings knowledge of the Speech when a new Mokolé dreams her shape. If the newly Changed one has never heard the Dragon's Tongue, she will understand it but be hesitant to speak until she has heard more. Expression is idiomatic in the Dragon's Tongue, and figures of speech are common. "She has dug her nest" means that someone has made up her mind, while "to lash my tail" means to move towards a goal. The Speech can be written phonetically but is more often written using the original claw-print script. In classic tales, hand and body motions accompany the speech. The Dragon's Tongue is also the language of Mokolé in Archid, and even Suchid form allows some halting, primitive converse in the Speech. Shrouded Sun adepts tell their students that the original form of the language was as a dance. The hand and body movements are called the Language of Claws and must be learned separately. Someone who knows this language can speak volumes without making a sound.

It's an arduous task to learn the Dragon's Tongue, and only Mokolé Kin are likely to have the time and opportunity to do so. A rare few Corax, Nagah, and Bastet allies have managed to squeeze out some remedial knowledge of the language, but almost none are fluent. The language is not strictly a secret, but it is difficult to understand. Add in the fact that Mokolé themselves don't learn it, but know it through Mnesis, and the boosts in experience point costs for learning the language (three times that of gaining another dot in Linguistics the usual way), even if a Mokolé agrees to teach it.

Mokolé and Gold

So Cortes said, "Send me some of it, because I and my companions suffer from a disease of the heart which can be cured only with gold."

— Francisco Lopez de Gomara, *Istoria de la Conquista de Mexico*

Peter asked, "Silver hurts the Garou because we are the Moon's children..." feeling a twinge of fear as he let out the secret that wasn't a secret, the truth that Cassie had warned all the cubs not to advertise. But every cheap horror movie tore the Veil— "...but what about the Mokolé? You can't be Moon's children too, are you?"

Jeffo took another pull on the cane spirit and offered Peter the flask. Peter declined; the stuff was too strong and foul for his taste. "Well, I'm a Midnight Sun. I was born in the darkness, so I'm a Moon-child too. So is Feathered Thunder. It's why we talk to you — we're all crazy and do everything backwards. But you asked about silver. Silver burns us like it does you; the Rage opens us to it, I suppose. But gold does too."

"Gold? You mean someone with, like, gold bullets or a golden klaive?"

"Yes. The People are Sun's children — even me. So we can be hurt or killed by gold. But the joke's on the hunters. A Shadow Lord conquistador once spent, musta been two million on ammo and didn't kill one Mokolé — his fortune never recovered!"

Both gold and silver cause one level of aggravated damage to Mokolé per turn of physical contact (save in Homid form, or in Suchid if of suchid breed). Gold affects the Mokolé and their kin the Corax because these two Breeds are children of the Sun. However, the Mokolé born at night have maintained a tie between the Dragon Breed and Luna; and at any rate, the Mokolé are filled with Rage, called Luna's gift. Therefore Mokolé are also vulnerable to silver. Garou can hunt Mokolé with gold weapons while themselves unhurt by the gold.

Of course, this isn't exactly an open secret. Most non-Mokolé and non-Corax have no idea of this vulnerability whatsoever. What's more, gold doesn't have to be 24k to harm the Dragon Breed, but gold-plated items don't do any good. What strikes the Mokolé must be gold, and gold plate, leaf, foil or "wash" doesn't do any more than make them itch a little. Gold-plated weapons will lose their gold coating after striking the scaly hide of a Mokolé, and do no damage. Electrum is so impure that it is ineffective, just as it is useless against silver-allergic creatures. Mokolé can be hurt by punching them with a gold ring or by punching with gold chains wrapped round one's fist, but something so small could not possibly cause more than one health level of damage no matter what. Gold weapons cannot be bought anywhere and must be made by the hunter. Gold costs up to $800-1000 an ounce, and a sword weighs at least 3 pounds ($48,000.00). In addition, the weapon will dull instantly (half damage after each battle unless it is pounded back into shape by a goldsmith) because gold is so soft. Note that any goldsmith will be curious about why anyone owns a golden battle-ax and will ask a lot of questions. If the hunters "silence" such a person, the police will be suspicious, because gold dealers often receive stolen property.

Bullets weigh 9-10 grams each and there are 35g in an ounce. Gold bullets will therefore cost hundreds of dollars each, assuming that someone can be found to make them (Goldsmith skill). Once fired they are gone. A drum of 43 rounds would therefore cost at least $8800.00 for the gold alone. Not even the immense wealth of the Catholic Church would suffice to hunt Mokolé for long. Mokolé are not hurt by gold or silver when in their breed form and no Mokolé in Homid form is hurt by either, although a weapon will do normal damage. For each gold or silver item carried, 1 point of the Gnosis pool is lost. For every five gold or silver items carried by members of a clutch, each clutch member loses one point of his Gnosis pool. Note that normal items of jewelry (such as a ring) cost only one Gnosis for all the jewelry worn. Unless the item is also a weapon or tool, it does not count separately. If a Mokolé carries both gold and silver, she suffers the Gnosis penalty only for one or the other, not both.

The Three Forms

Like their Corax relatives, Mokolé have only three forms; really, it's all they need. The difficulty to shift into each form is 6, making shapeshifting rather easy; to go from Homid to Suchid requires a mere two successes at an average difficulty.

• **Homid:** The Homid form is effectively indistinguishable from an ordinary human. The actual ethnicity depends on the Mokolé's stream (see the Noonday chapter), but they are almost always from warmer lands.

• **Archid:** The intermediary form of the Mokolé is a shape taken from the dreaming, which comes at their Rite of Passage. In this mystical experience, the Mokolé relives the lives of her ancestors and her Archid form creates itself from their body shapes. The Archid form usually resembles a dinosaur or dragon, although there are pterosaur and sea-serpent Mokolé. Of course, a Mokolé may have body parts that in nature didn't occur on the same animal, such as armor on a carnosaur — their forms are dreamed, not strictly remembered. The Archid form causes the Delirium just as does the Crinos form of the Garou, save in other Awakened beings and Kinfolk. The Mokolé do not cause a lessened Delirium — it is enforced in full.

When creating a Mokolé character, the player purchases various Archid-form characteristics to represent the Dragon's war form. This is done by taking the character's final Gnosis score, and "spending" points to purchase characteristics; for instance, a Makara with a final Gnosis of three could take three Archid-form characteristics. Some of these characteristics, such as Huge Size or Multiple Heads, may be purchased more than once; the aforementioned Makara might choose to sink all three Gnosis points into Huge Size, resulting in an Archid form which isn't particularly armored or armed, but is certainly immense.

In all cases, the Storyteller has final approval of the Archid form, and may veto forms that seem silly, overly bizarre, or illogical.

• **Suchid:** This is the reptilian breed form of the Mokolé, which is drawn from one of the several varna. Varna include alligators, crocodiles, and large lizards such as Komodo dragons. The Rage of these varna is different, because of their different body shapes: Mokolé say that the Rage of Gila monsters is what makes their poison so strong.

The Halpatee varna represents common American alligators and shares the same statistics as the Piasa (American crocodiles); running speed is halved in this form, and swimming speed equals the Homid form's land speed. The bite attack inflicts Strength + 3 damage.

The Ora are monitor lizards, anywhere from 4 to 12 feet long. Their running speed is equal to human running speed, and sprints at higher speeds are possible. They can swim at negligible speed, and bite for Strength +1 damage.

The Unktehi are Gila monsters; they have only half human running speed, and cannot swim. Their bite inflicts Strength -1 damage,

Form Statistics

Archid	Suchid (Halpatee/Piasa)	Suchid (Ora)	Suchid (Unktehi)	Suchid (Karna/Champsa)	Suchid (Gharial/Syrta)	Suchid (Makara)
Str: +4	Str: +2	Str: +0	Str: -1	Str: +3	Str: +1	Str: +2
Dex: -1	Dex: -1	Dex: +0	Dex: +0	Dex: -2	Dex: +0	Dex: -1
Sta: +4	Sta: +3	Sta: +2	Sta: +1	Sta: +3	Sta: +2	Sta: +3
Man: -3	Man: -2	Man: -4	Man: -3	Man: -4	Man: -3	Man: -4
App: 0						
	Rage: 4	Rage: 5	Rage: 5	Rage 2	Rage 3	Rage 4

but is poisonous and very painful; those bitten must make Stamina rolls, difficulty 7 to resist the venom. If they fail, they drop to the Wounded health level, and remain there until the poison has run its course. Creatures smaller or larger than human-size could alternately be killed by the venom, take less damage or not be affected at all, at the Storyteller's discretion.

Both the Saltwater crocodile (Karna) and Nile crocodile (Champsa) share the same statistics. Running speed in this form is halved, and the Mokolé cannot run continuously for long, but swimming speed equals the Homid form's land speed. These crocs can reach 20' in length or more. Their bite attack inflicts Strength + 3 damage.

The gavial (Gharial), caiman (Syrta), and Chinese alligator varna also share the same statistics. The Makara (or mugger crocodiles) are larger, but all four varna halve their running speed in Suchid but swim as quickly as the Homid form's land speed. All three varna bite for Strength + 2 damage.

Archid Form Characteristics

Can I hit people with my tail?

—Bob the Dinosaur, *Dilbert*, by Scott Adams

Mokolé dream their Archid form out of the Mnesis of their ancestors. The Archid form is the size of a Crinos form werewolf unless the Mokolé dreams of Huge Size or belongs to the Unktehi varna. All Mokolé have an Archid-form bite and claw attack (both Strength + 2 damage, aggravated), unless they dream of the more vicious Long Teeth and Terrible Claws. In the case of Mokolé with beaks, flippers, or the like, bite or claw attacks may be impossible.

The Archid form that a Mokolé dreams when coming of age is hers for life: Gnosis bought through experience *cannot* be used to buy extra appendages after the character is created.

- **Air Sacs (Chuckwalla)** — The Mokolé can "swell up" with air until he is huge, frightening any creature who does not know what is going on. All opponents who do not have specific Mokolé knowledge react as if their Willpower were one point lower for purposes of the Delirium Chart. In addition, the Mokolé can wedge himself into tight places and swell up, making it impossible for others to pass. He is also unsinkable, even if he can't swim.
- **Armor (Ankylosaurus)** — Two extra soak dice (three extra for 2 Gnosis points).
- **Back Sail (Dimetrodon)** — One extra die to soak attacks from the rear; the character also gains the Merit: Temperature Control at no extra cost, as the sail can be used as a radiator fin or solar panel.
- **Binocular Vision (Troodon)** — All sight-related Perception tasks are at -2 difficulty.
- **Color Change (Chameleon)** — The difficulty to spot the hidden Mokolé rises by 1. This characteristic can be taken more than once, although the difficulty to spot the Archid-form Mokolé can never go over 9.

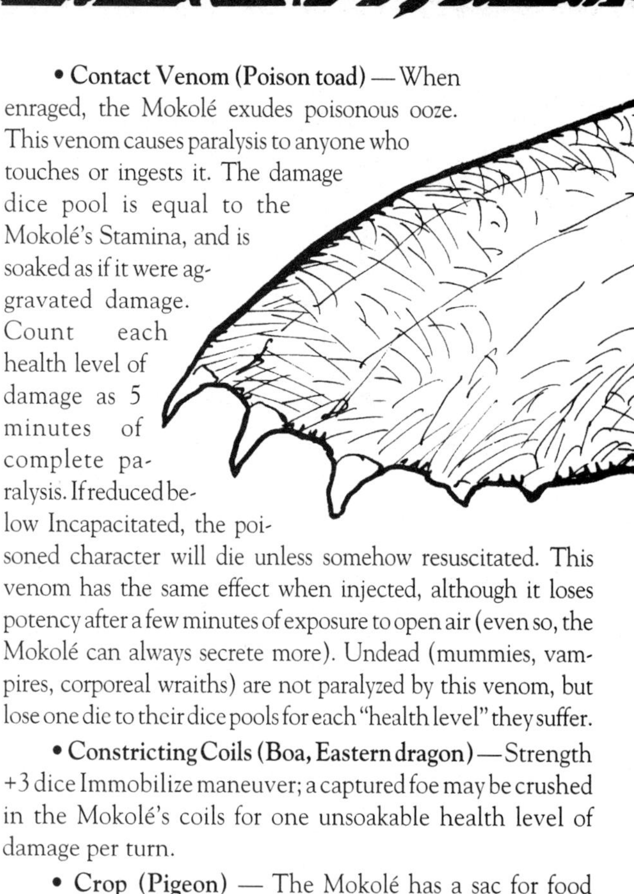

• **Contact Venom (Poison toad)** — When enraged, the Mokolé exudes poisonous ooze. This venom causes paralysis to anyone who touches or ingests it. The damage dice pool is equal to the Mokolé's Stamina, and is soaked as if it were aggravated damage. Count each health level of damage as 5 minutes of complete paralysis. If reduced below Incapacitated, the poisoned character will die unless somehow resuscitated. This venom has the same effect when injected, although it loses potency after a few minutes of exposure to open air (even so, the Mokolé can always secrete more). Undead (mummies, vampires, corporeal wraiths) are not paralyzed by this venom, but lose one die to their dice pools for each "health level" they suffer.

• **Constricting Coils (Boa, Eastern dragon)** — Strength +3 dice Immobilize maneuver; a captured foe may be crushed in the Mokolé's coils for one unsoakable health level of damage per turn.

• **Crop (Pigeon)** — The Mokolé has a sac for food storage and can feed the ill, aged, or hatchlings with "crop milk" regurgitated from the crop. As much food as the Mokolé cares to eat can be stored in the crop and brought back as crop milk.

• **Deep Lung (Mosasaurus)** — This allows the Mokolé to swim underwater for up to an hour, or hold her breath for up to five minutes in combat.

• **Disarticulating Jaw (Snake)** — The Mokolé's jaw can dislocate, allowing her to swallow anything that can fit into her stomach. She never has to chew. A creature swallowed alive has a number of turns equal to her Stamina before she begins to suffocate. She may, of course, try to escape, and if she is able to somehow slash open the Mokolé's gullet (3 or more health levels of aggravated damage), she can get loose This form of eating is unnerving to watch.

• **Dragon Masque (Dragon)** — The Mokolé has an awe-inspiring face in her Archid form, similar to Dragon Himself. The Mokolé gains an extra die when using Bellow, Dragonfear, or any terror-inducing Gift or rite, if the targets can see her face. Her opponents react to the Delirium chart as if they were at -1 Willpower. When seeking the favor of Dragon, the Wani or of any ancient reptile totem, the Mokolé gains a -1 to Social difficulties.

• **Duck Bill (Hadrosaurus)** — Two extra dice of Expression

• **Extra Limbs (Dragon)** — Must be purchased with Sacral Plexus. The Mokolé has one extra limb per Gnosis point spent. If she wants them to have claws, be useable as hands, etc., she must buy these as separate characteristics. This may be taken more than once, but Mokolé with too many legs are looked at strangely by their peers: even clutchmates may wonder about their devotion to Sun.

• **Eye Cones (Chameleon)** — The Mokolé's eyes are mounted on movable cones; the Mokolé has a 360° field of vision and can look in any direction without moving her head. It is very difficult to sneak up on her.

• **Feathers (Longisquama)** — Effective Appearance 3 in Archid

• **Fiery Pearl (dragon)** — Three extra dice on Intimidation rolls versus vampires, Kuei-jin, fomori, and other creatures of darkness. This pearl often appears in the Mokolé's forehead or beneath his chin.

• **Fins (Mosasaurus)** — Doubles swimming speed

• **Food Storage (Gila monster)** — The Mokolé can live for one season per point of Stamina without eating anything. The storage may be fat sacs beneath the tail, a hump (like a camel's), or an obese belly. The Mokolé must gorge in order to refill her fat storage.

• **Fur (Sordes)** — The Mokolé can withstand cold weather, including arctic regions.

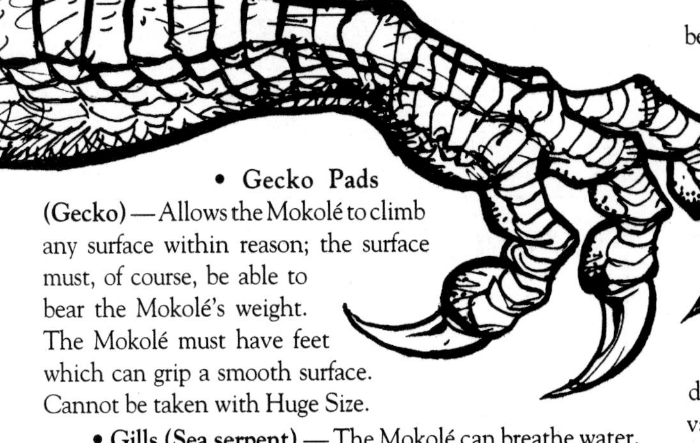

• **Gecko Pads (Gecko)** — Allows the Mokolé to climb any surface within reason; the surface must, of course, be able to bear the Mokolé's weight. The Mokolé must have feet which can grip a smooth surface. Cannot be taken with Huge Size.

• **Gills (Sea serpent)** — The Mokolé can breathe water.

• **Grasping Hands (Troodon)** — The Archid form has full Homid manual dexterity.

• **Hard Skull (Pachycephalosaurus)** — Three extra dice to soak damage to the head, and three extra dice of damage on head butt attacks (not cumulative with Horns).

• **Hollow Bones (Pteranodon)** — +3 to Dexterity for purposes of movement, and the Mokolé can soar effortlessly for hours if he has wings. However, his bones may break more easily (Storyteller's discretion as to rule effects).

• **Horn (Triceratops)** — Strength +3 head butt (aggravated)

• **Huge Size (Apatosaurus)** — One extra dot of Stamina, and two extra damage dice to Body Slam or Overbear maneuvers. The Mokolé is up to 20' longer per Gnosis point spent on Huge Size, and gains weight in proportion to added size. This can be taken more than once, and some Mokolé are up to 100' long in Archid form. This also grants one additional Health Level each time it is taken. It is not clear exactly how large a Mokolé can be, but extremely large Mokolé cannot use Stealth, sneak up on someone, hide, or walk on ordinary floors. Taking this characteristic more than four or five times, then, is asking for trouble.

• **Jacobson's Organ (Snake)** — May sense infrared radiation, using a Perception roll to "see" in the dark. The organ is located in the roof of the mouth.

• **Long Neck (Diplodocus)** — May grant bonuses to Perception dice pools, depending on the situation. Also allows the Mokolé to bite from a distance.

• **Long Teeth (Tyrannosaurus)** — Bite damage becomes Strength +3.

• **Long Tongue (Chameleon)** — The Mokolé has an tongue as long as her Archid body. It has a Strength of 1, although for each extra point of Gnosis spent on this trait, the tongue's Strength is increased by 1. The tongue is covered with sticky goo and can be used for feeding, picking things up, or for grabbing objects or people. It has the same Dexterity as the Mokolé's Archid form.

• **Multiple Heads (Naga)** — The Mokolé has an extra head in her Archid form for each point of Gnosis she spends. This head does not add to Mental Attributes. Any characteristics such as Long Teeth or Horn must be purchased anew for each head. This allows use of the Wishbone maneuver, and grants one extra die per head for the purpose of splitting dice pools for multiple bite attacks. In unusual circumstances, the different heads of the Mokolé may demonstrate slightly variant personalities — nobody knows why this is.

• **Neck Frill (Triceratops)** — Two extra soak dice against frontal attacks.

• **Nictating Membrane (Alligator)** — The Mokolé may see normally underwater.

• **Poison Sacs (Snake/Gila)** — May inject venom on bite attacks (2 health levels of aggravated damage in addition to bite damage). This may be purchased more than once (reflecting a more potent venom), adding a health level to the damage inflicted each time. It is claimed that Nagah are immune to this venom, and that some vampires actually benefit from it. The truth is unknown. The Mokolé may choose to specify that sacs are located elsewhere than his mouth, and may dip his claws into them instead of biting to inject the venom.

• **Prehensile Tail (Snake)** — The Mokolé may grasp objects or people with her tail. The tail has as much Strength and Dexterity as the Mokolé's other limbs. If bought with the Sacral Plexus characteristic, the character may add the sacral plexus dice to the tail's Attributes instead of other skills.

• **Regeneration (Salamander)** — The Mokolé may spend a point of permanent Gnosis to regrow a lost body part over a long period of time (at least several months, possibly longer). The process is extremely painful, so much so that living as a cripple is often preferable. The Storyteller will have the final say on whether a body part can regrow, how long it will take, and any special care required (such as healing baths, food, rest, etc.).

• **Royal Crest (Parasaurolopus)** — +2 dice to any Social rolls involving Mokolé and Nagah.

• **Sacral Plexus (Stegosaurus)** — The Mokolé may tap into a secondary brain located in the spinal cord. For each Gnosis point spent on the sacral plexus, the Mokolé can add one point to an Ability involving the lower body, such as Dodge, Brawl or Expression (dance). The sacral plexus can perform actions without involving the brain, and therefore the Mokolé can take extra actions without spending Rage if they involve the skills of the sacral plexus — however, these extra actions are limited to three dice total, plus an extra die for every time this characteristic is bought.

• **Snorkel (Brachiosaurus)** — The Mokolé may remain underwater or under earth and breathe comfortably with only her nostrils exposed. The snorkel is usually on top of the head. Difficulty to spot her is usually 10.

• **Spitter (Dilophosaurus)** — Must be purchased with Poison Sacs, but the Mokolé can spit his venom 1 yard for every point of Rage he has.

• **Tail Blades/Spikes (Dragon, Stegosaurus)** — Can attack with a tail lash for Strength +2 damage (aggravated).

• **Tail Club (Ankylosaurus)** — May attack with a tail lash for Strength +3 damage (not aggravated).

• **Terrible Claws (Deinocheirus)** — Claw damage becomes Strength +3.

• **Thorns (Thorny Devil)** — The Mokolé is covered with spines, dealing out two health levels of aggravated damage to anyone who strikes her bare-handed.

• **Throat Sac and Wattles (Chuckwalla)** — +1 Expression, and two extra dice when using the Gift: Bellow. This can also be a hollow crest with resonators inside.

• **Upright Walking (Goanna)** — Enables tool use in Archid form.

• **Webbed Feet (Hadrosaurus)** — These allow a Mokolé to swim at one-and-a-half speed and walk more easily on soft mud. They impose an additional -1 penalty to Dexterity when on dry land.

• **Wings (Pteranodon)** — The Mokolé can fly at 20 mph or so. Mokolé with Hollow Bones can soar for hours; others can fly for 1 hour per point of Stamina, then must rest for the night. Cannot be taken with more than one level of Huge Size or with Armor. Mokolé who are too large and heavy simply cannot fly (although they may have wings anyway). In addition, certain body shapes, such as a Velociraptor or Tyrannosaurus, cannot fly at all.

Mokolé Renown

Peter flipped open the cellphone and dialed the phone's own number, the un-number that alerted the technospirit. "Look, Webby, I know you're mad, okay. I mean, not only am I hanging out with Mokolé, but I'm in a place where there are no roaches! But I'll make it up to you. Look, I know nostalgia isn't what it used to be, but every time I think about the past, it brings back so many memories! Hey, these two Garou walk into a bar…"

The spirit listened in the Shadow, and when Peter was done, made plans of her own. She heard a lot, what with one thing and another, and maybe she could find someone who paid higher than Taddle Creek Sept…

Mokolé gain temporary Renown and convert it into permanent Renown the same manner that Garou do. They also use the system of Glory, Honor and Wisdom, acknowledging five ranks. Mokolé gain 1 point each of Glory, Honor and Wisdom for passing through their coming of age Mnesis trance. They do not get Renown for subsequent Mnesis use. The Mokolé-mbembe and Gumagan use the same Rank system.

Character Creation Chart

• **Step One: Character Concept**

Choose concept

Choose breed (homid or suchid)

Choose stream (Mokolé-mbembe, Makara, Gumagan or Zhong Lung) and varna (alligator, crocodile, monitor, Gila monster)

Choose solar auspice (if Mokolé-mbembe or Gumagan) or seasonal auspice (if Makara or Zhong Lung)

Select Nature and Demeanor (optional)

• **Step Two: Attributes**

Assign Attributes (7 Primary, 5 Secondary, 3 Tertiary)

• **Step Three: Abilities**

Prioritize the three categories: Talents, Skills, and Knowledges (13/9/5)

Choose Talents, Skills and Knowledges

• **Step Four: Select Advantages**

Choose Backgrounds (5 pts)

Choose one auspice Gift and one common Mokolé Gift.

• **Step Five: Finishing Touches**

Record Rage (by varna), Gnosis (by breed), Willpower (by auspice) and Rank (1)

Spend Freebie Points (15)

Pick Merits and Flaws (if desired)

At this point the Storyteller may wish to tell you the tale of your coming of age, usually including the great vision that opens the powers of Mnesis to you. At the end, record your Archid form characteristics.

Breed

• **Homid:** You were always thoughtful, even as a child. Now thoughts of endless ages before your own have come to you. The Change has awakened wisdom, power and Rage in you. Whether or not your parents told you of Dragon's Breed, you were amazed when the visions came.

Beginning Gnosis: 2

• **Suchid:** You were hatched as a giant reptile and lived as such until the Change came. You are suddenly one of the most powerful creatures in the world, but tool use and language are new to you. The changes can be overwhelming. Sleep in the sun? Maybe, when the Duties are fulfilled.

Restricted Abilities: Drive, Etiquette, Firearms, Computer, Law, Linguistics, Medicine, Politics, Science

Restricted Backgrounds: Resources, Allies, or Contacts

Beginning Gnosis: 4

Backgrounds

• **Allies:** Those you trust among humans, reptiles and Mokolé

• **Contacts:** Those you know and who prove useful to you.

• **Fetish:** A magical item containing a spirit, which has certain powers.

• **Kinfolk:** The humans and reptiles who share your secret and your ancient blood. Your family, though you might not know them all.

• **Mnesis:** The ancestral memory of Mother Gaia, known to Mokolé alone.

• **Resources:** Money and other good stuff that you have or can get.

• **Rites:** The number and level of rites which you may know.

• **Totem:** The patron spirit of your clutch.

• **Wallow:** A place of refuge for you and your clutch.

Freebie Points

Trait	Cost
Attributes	5 per dot
Abilities	2 per dot
Backgrounds	1 per dot
Gifts	7 per Gift (Level One only)
Rage	1 per dot
Gnosis	2 per dot
Willpower	1 per dot

Players of Mokolé characters may choose a Nature and Demeanor from the Archetypes listed in the **Werewolf Players Guide.** Typical Mokolé natures include Survivor, Traditionalist, Curmudgeon, Alpha (for clutch leaders) and so on. However, a Mokolé Bon Vivant, Reluctant Shapeshifter, Worker, or Dilettante is possible. Characters can regain Willpower either by acting according to their auspices or by following their Nature.

Renown for Gumagan and Mokolé-Mbembe

Striking and Warding

Rank	Title	Glory	Honor	Wisdom
1	Hatchling	1	1	1
2	Son/Daughter	4	2	2
3	Brother/Sister	6	3	3
4	Father/Mother	8	4	4
5	Grandfather/Grandmother	10	5	5

Unshading and Crowning

Rank	Title	Glory	Honor	Wisdom
1	Hatchling	1	1	1
2	Son/Daughter	2	4	2
3	Brother/Sister	3	6	3
4	Father/Mother	4	8	4
5	Grandfather/Grandmother	5	10	5

Concealing and Gathering

Rank	Title	Glory	Honor	Wisdom
1	Hatchling	1	1	1
2	Son/Daughter	2	2	4
3	Brother/Sister	3	3	6
4	Father/Mother	4	4	8
5	Grandfather/Grandmother	5	5	10

Shining

Rank	Title	Any Combination
1	Hatchling	3
2	Son/Daughter	9
3	Brother/Sister	14
4	Father/Mother	19
5	Grandfather/Grandmother	24

The Makara and Zhong Lung use a Renown system that corresponds closely to the Garou Renown system (**Werewolf**, pg. 195). Assume that the Garou auspices correspond to the Mokolé as follows:

Garou Auspice	Makara	Zhong Lung
Ragabash	Hemanta	Pei Tung
Theurge	Zarad	Sai Chau
Philodox	Grisma	Nam Hsia
Ahroun	Vasanta	Tung Chun

When awarding Renown, allow for a few differences from the Renown chart in the **Werewolf** rulebook. Some examples:

• 3 Wisdom for completing a Mnesis quest

• 1 Wisdom and 1 Glory for inwitting a good story

• 1 each for awakening a Sleeper

• 1 each for surviving a long sleep (more than a human lifetime) in Sleep of the Dragon

• 3 Wisdom and 3 Honor for retrieving lost Mnesis

• 1 Glory for wandering for a year

• 3 Wisdom for mating and producing a child of any sort

• 1 Glory for producing a Mokolé child

• 1 Honor for mating as is best for yourself, your clutch and the Mokolé, that is, choosing a proper mate. Monogamy is not mandatory.

• 1 Honor for each year of proper mating

• -1 Honor for mating unwisely

• -7 Honor for mating with another Mokolé

Special Combat Maneuvers

• **Tail Lash:** This involves swinging the tail and slapping an opponent. Suchid-form Mokolé may only use this maneuver on enemies directly behind them.

Usable by: Archid - Suchid

Difficulty: 7 **Damage:** Strength +1

Actions: 1

• **Head Butt:** This requires a charge forward, head lowered. This works like Body Slam maneuver (**Werewolf**, pg. 232) except that the Mokolé does not suffer damage if in Archid form, and the target isn't unbalanced unless knocked down.

Usable by: Homid - Archid

Difficulty: 8 **Damage:** Strength + extra successes

Actions: 1

• **Jaw Shear:** This requires that the Mokolé have landed a blow with a bite attack on the previous round. The Mokolé can then snap his head back and forth, tearing chunks of flesh from an opponent's body. If the Mokolé's grip isn't broken, then he may use this maneuver each turn thereafter. The Storyteller may rule that a body part is severed or bones broken if enough damage is done.

Usable by: Suchid - Archid

Difficulty: 6 **Damage:** Strength + 3

Actions: 1

• **Swallow Whole:** This requires that the Mokolé have Huge Size, Disarticulating Jaw or both; it is usually impossible to swallow prey more than half the Mokolé's size in any case. The Mokolé must land a bite attack and then make an opposed Strength roll. If she succeeds, then she swallows the opponent whole. The opponent may continue to fight for a number of rounds equal to their Stamina, by which time he smothers. Of course, some enemies, such as fomori, may be toxic or dangerous to eat. Suchids are able to swallow fish, small animals, etc., but not human-sized opponents.

Usable by: Archid

Difficulty: Special **Damage:** Special

Actions: 2

• **Wishbone:** This maneuver usually requires either multiple heads or sufficiently large talons. The Mokolé latches onto his target in two (or more) separate areas, then begins to tug his victim apart. This is a continuous hold, and the Mokolé may continue to inflict damage until the target escapes by succeeding at a contested Strength roll.

Usable by: Archid

Difficulty: 8 **Damage:** Strength + 4

Actions: 3

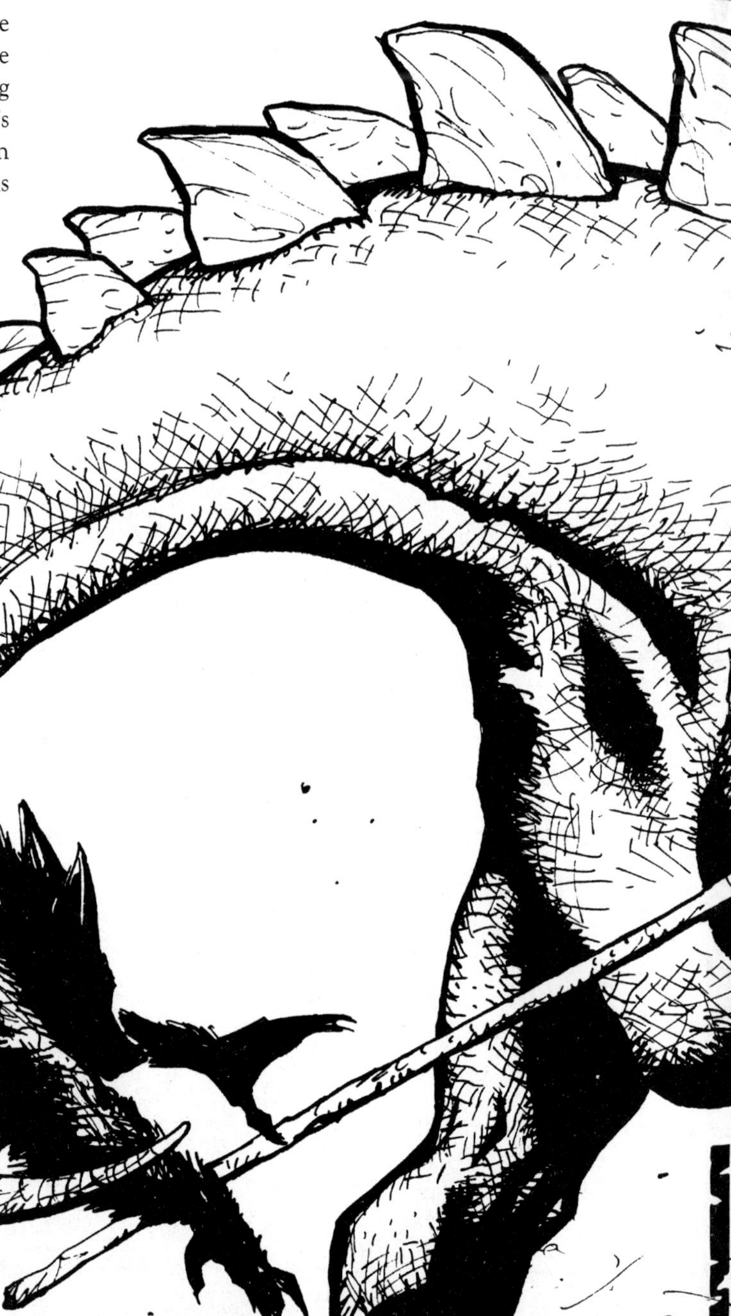

Mokolé Totems

A clutch usually shares a totem much as a Garou pack does. Totems attach themselves to wallows. The Rite of the Totem summons an Incarna, who decides whether or not the clutch is worthy. Mokolé generally cannot have mammalian totems (though Echidna's egg-laying breaks down barriers between Mokolé and herself); it's a gulf of identity rather than blood kinship. Totems common to Mokolé and Garou include Crocodile ("Iwai" to the Gumagan), Quetzal, Anaconda, Shark, Chameleon, Fog, Twister, Winds, Uktena, Rain, Raven, and many others. There are Mokolé who have remained Children of Turtle despite the fall of the Croatan, and claim that Turtle never departed, only withdrawing from the blood-mad mammals. The Gumagan say the same about Mu-ru-bul Tu-ru-dan the Bunyip. Note that Mokolé who share a totem with Garou would refrain from attacking them without cause, and might have some basis for communication. Indeed, Crocodile (in the **Silent Striders Tribebook**) demands that his Children leave Mokolé alone, or try to make peace with them.

Most Mokolé follow Dragon, a powerful Totem of Respect.

Dragon

Background Cost: 5

Dragon personifies the 150 million years during which reptiles ruled the earth. Dragon is great and fierce, burning all those who oppose him with his poisonous breath. He asks that his children succor his progeny, reptiles and birds, and preserve the memory of the Dinosaur Kings. Dragon has never yet accepted Garou as his Children.

Traits: Dragon gives the Gift: Dragon's Breath to those whom he favors; any one member of the clutch can use the Gift at a time. When his children are in true need, he may teach them the Gift of Dream Semblance, allowing them to appear as a true dragon for a scene.

Ban: No Mokolé may dishonor Dragon. Definitions of this ban vary, but violations of the Duties, betrayal of Mokolé secrets, or other actions endangering Dragon's Breed would qualify.

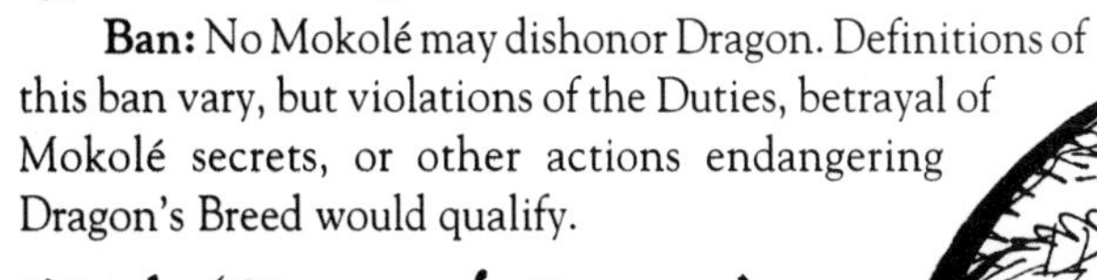

Finch (Totem of Respect)

Background Cost: 5

Finch is a wise totem who personifies adaptation and change. He revels in his ability to shift the shape of his beak, which

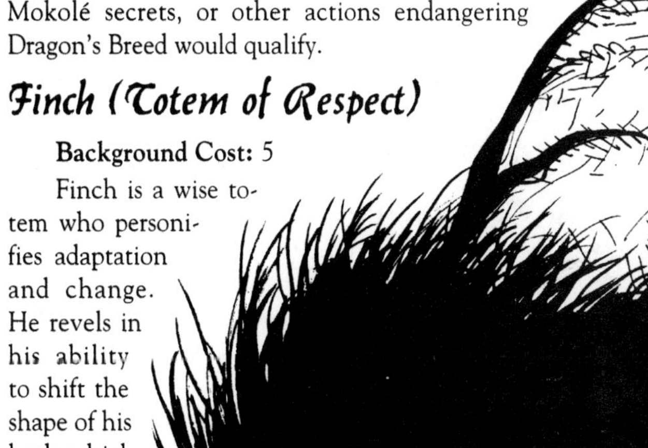

changes according to the place that he is in. Mokolé say that they can learn much from watching his beak change its shape and size. Finch is also known to the Corax, who try to learn the secrets of life from him. Finch and Horseshoe Crab do not like each other very much.

Traits: Finch, naturally enough, grants his children the Gift: Beak of the Finch. His children also receive one temporary point of Honor, and can draw on three extra Willpower points per story.

Ban: Finch's Children must adapt themselves to their environment. If they live by a river, they must eat fish. They must be content with what Gaia provides and ready themselves to take advantage of Her gifts.

Horseshoe Crab (Totem of Cunning)

Background Cost: 4

Horseshoe Crab is the ultimate conservative. This arthropod has hidden in the sand for two hundred million years, and has not changed at all in that time. He has thrived while the Kings rose and fell and plans to outlive human beings and the Apocalypse. He likes Mokolé for their rigidity.

Traits: Horseshoe Crab teaches the Gift: Become Log, and his children each receive an additional point of Willpower. To those who serve him well, he may allow an additional point of Mnesis.

Ban: Horseshoe Crab's children must oppose needless innovation and change — and it sometimes takes some persuading to make Horseshoe Crab see *any* innovation or change as anything other than needless.

Scarab (Totem of Wisdom)

Background Cost: 5

This totem is most familiar to Mokolé-mbembe, although a few clutches of the other streams know her as well. She is an attendant of Sun and rolls Sun across the sky. She chooses as her children Mokolé who honor Sun, who remember Khem and who dispel darkness wherever they find it.

Traits: To each of her children, Scarab gives the power to borrow the Sun dice of a clutchmate once per story. For instance, a Concealing Mokolé could exercise the sun dice of his companion, a Rising Sun, while taking the initiative. The clutchmate in question does not lose the sun dice for her own purposes.

Ban: Scarab asks that no corpse of her own children be left to rot, condemning the spirit to misery. All dead must be disposed of properly, such as by burial in sand, mummification, or other appropriate methods.

Snake Doctor (Totem of Respect)

Background Cost: 6

Snake Doctor is a Dragonfly-spirit, known best in the American South. He tends to the injuries of Mokolé and Nagah, "sewing them up" with his long tail. He does not like other shapeshifters and may "sew up their ears," deafening them, if they offend him.

Traits: Each child of Snake Doctor may, once per story, heal one health level of any type of damage if Snake Doctor may reach them — in other words, if they are anywhere that a dragonfly could be found. They also gain a temporary point of both Honor and Wisdom, and may draw on four extra points of Willpower per story.

Ban: Snake Doctor demands that his swampy homeland be preserved inviolate.

Whiptail Lizard (Totem of Wisdom)

Background Cost: 7

Whiptail Lizard is a totem of the American Southwest. The four known species of whiptail lizard contain no males: their eggs contain baby lizards that are genetic copies of the mother. In effect, whiptail lizards clone themselves naturally. Whiptail Lizard loves females who are strong and independent. She will never accept a clutch that contains any male of any species as her daughters.

Traits: To her daughters she gives the Gift: Whiptail's Clutch, a unique Gift enabling them to sacrifice three permanent Gnosis points to lay an egg containing a perfect infant replica of themselves. Furthermore, her clutches gain three extra dice to any Survival or Enigmas rolls. The Black Furies admire Whiptail Lizard and her daughters for their self-sufficiency, although they don't necessarily try to emulate them.

Ban: Whiptail Lizard forbids any daughter of hers to allow any male to rule over them for any reason.

The Last Ones

Background Cost: 5 and up

The cycle of life means that new species evolve into a position in nature, persist, and pass away. The Triat's work has adorned Gaia with millions of species over millions of years.

But some species pass before their time. Wiped out by disasters, the Works of the Dissolver, or human evil, they persist in the Shadowlands as ghost totems. Mokolé mourn these lost species, many known only to them, and can sometimes call on their power. To do so, the ritemaster must first go into a Mnesis trance and behold the species in life, and then perform the Rite of Summoning while the image rests in her mind.

Lost Ones include the dinosaurs and Great Beasts, the passenger pigeon, the dodo, the Great Auk, the elephant bird, the quagga, the snail darter, and many others. When called they stand silently looking at the world that destroyed them. While their wisdom is great, the sadness of beholding them means that any Mokolé who botches a roll falls victim to Harano when dealing with them. Their Traits and Bans vary widely are up to the Storyteller, but should be perilous — after all, these are spirits from a dead past.

Fetishes

Dragon Crystal

Level 1, Gnosis 6

This is a semiprecious stone or amber chunk polished into a lens, planchette, or disc and set into a necklace, etc. When activated, it reveals the presence of a true Mokolé; if the user looks through it at the subject, the subject appears in his Archid form, and if touched to a Mokolé's body, the stone shines with Sun's light. For this reason, the gems are sometimes worn as jewelry to a Gather.

To create a Dragon Crystal, a Sun-spirit may be bound to the stone, or an Insect-spirit may be awakened from insects preserved in amber.

Hatchling's Tail

Level 1, Gnosis 3

This fetish looks like nothing more than a dried lizard's tail, but when worn attached to a belt by a Mokolé (usually the young) it gives the wearer something extra when in Archid form. Upon assuming the battle form of the Mokolé, the wearer of this fetish grows a second tail, which has all the properties of the owner's actual tail. For example, the individual might gain a second tail lash attack (at +2 difficulty). All other actions involving the second tail have a +1 difficulty, but the Mokolé also gains a 50% increase in Archid swimming speed. This item is primarily used by hatchlings who have not yet gained experience in battle; most "grow out of" the fetish once they mature, passing it on to younger Mokolé. To make the fetish, a Glass-snake-spirit, a Palolo-worm-spirit, or a Father-spirit must be bound into the tail.

Scar Fetish

Level and Gnosis vary

Like the Garou, the Mokolé can and do bind spirits into scars or brands. They usually brand themselves with solid gold to make the wound stay open long enough to scar. Their scar fetishes are treated like the Garou's in all relevant manners.

Tray of the Teachers

Level 1, Gnosis 5

This valuable fetish is a tray carved of tropical marula-wood and decorated with the death-masks of the Crowning. Usually it is inlaid with bone, precious stones, etc. When used to store and process the teacher-plants of Gaia, the potency of the plants is increased by one level for each dot in the user's Rituals trait.

To create the tray, a spirit of visions must be bound into the tray, such as the awakened spirit of ayahuasca, acacia, or cannabis, or such a spirit as Tree Frog or Snake, who know medicines and poisons.

Egg Basket

Level 2, Gnosis 3

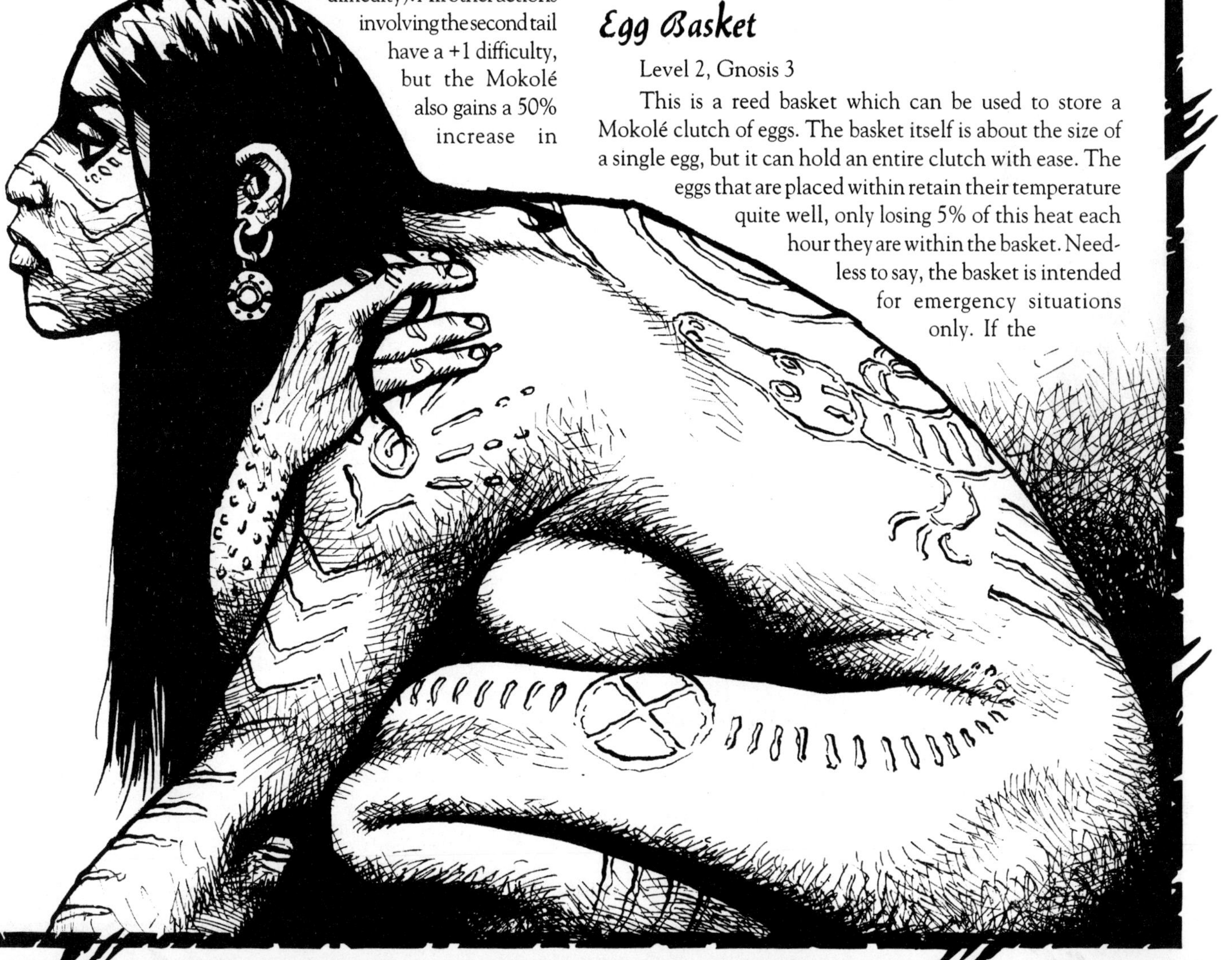

This is a reed basket which can be used to store a Mokolé clutch of eggs. The basket itself is about the size of a single egg, but it can hold an entire clutch with ease. The eggs that are placed within retain their temperature quite well, only losing 5% of this heat each hour they are within the basket. Needless to say, the basket is intended for emergency situations only. If the wallow is attacked or compromised, the mother typically uses the rite: Save Hatchling while concentrating on the basket. Of course the drawback is that the basket is as vulnerable to destruction as any woven basket, and contained within is an entire clutch. During the War of Rage more than one clutch was lost entirely when Garou warriors carelessly destroyed such baskets.

To make this fetish, the basket must be infused with a Weaverbird or Oriole-spirit.

Spirit Jar

Level 2, Gnosis 5

Akin to some vodoun paraphernalia, this fetish is a handmade pottery jar with the cover sealed on with tar or wax. It holds an imprisoned spirit. The owner can bargain with the spirit, promising it favors in return for the use of its Charms, such as Healing, Flood, or Create Fires. Favors which the owner might promise include giving the spirit Gnosis, allowing it to possess a medium, or setting it free. If the jar is broken, the spirit is freed. When freed, the spirit is usually fairly angry.

The spirit which is bound to create this fetish can be of almost any type. If the spirit is too weak, it will be no use. If it is too strong, it will probably free itself and attack the owner.

Mirror of Amaterasu Omikami

Level 3, Gnosis 4

This mirror is made of bronze, with a solar design molded into the back. There are only a few such mirrors, said to be cast from the shards of the mirror used to coax Sun from her hiding place long ago by the ravens. Though the face seems normal and reflects as does any other mirror, the reflection of the mirror contains the image molded on the back. In addition, the mirror can be used to store Sun's light. To do so, the Mokolé must expose the mirror to sunlight for several hours and expend a number of Gnosis equal to the number of hours. When he later speaks the name of Sun and activates the fetish, Sun's light shines out of the mirror as on a cloudless day for a number of turns equal to the Gnosis spent in storing the sunlight.

Sunstones

Level 3, Gnosis 4

These roughly egg-sized, smooth ovoid stones retain the sun's heat far longer than ordinary stones would. They are very useful in keeping eggs warm at night, or during periods of sleep. Also they can be used in combat against creatures that are vulnerable to sunlight. When touched by a Sunstone, a vampire or similarly solar-allergic creature suffers one health level of aggravated damage just as if exposed to sunlight; a hurled, activated Sunstone inflicts Strength + 1 aggravated damage to such a creature. In either case, this damage can be soaked with Fortitude.

A Sun-spirit must be bound into the stone to create this fetish.

Bowl of Mnesis

Level 4, Gnosis 5

This simple earthen bowl is sacred to the Mokolé. Even possessing knowledge of this artifact is a death sentence to any who are not Mokolé. This bowl can be used to preserve the memories of a fallen Mokolé or those of her enemy. First the corpse's intact brain is placed into the bowl, then filled with water and allowed to sit undisturbed in the sun for an entire day. With the setting sun, the liquid is then drunk by the chosen recipient of the corpse's memories. The Mokolé then makes a Perception + Enigmas roll at a variable difficulty and spends a Gnosis point.

Fallen creature	Difficulty
Mokolé	6
Mokolé Kin, Corax, Nagah	7
Other Bête, mortal, changeling	8
Mummy or true fae	9
Vampire, Bane, Wyrm-beast	10

The number of successes reflects the amount of memory that is salvaged from the fallen; in extremely rare cases (requiring at least 7 successes) the drinker can even retain a shapeshifter's Past Life trait. If the fallen was a Mokolé or Mokolé Kin, the drinker's Mnesis now functions through their ancestral lives as well. The Mokolé truly honor those chosen to have their memories thus preserved; this fetish is never used frivolously. In some cases the recipient of the corpse's memories has been driven insane; this was usually if the "donor" was a vampire, Bane, mummy or some shapeshifter other than a Mokolé. This fetish grants abilities similar to the Rite of Anamnesis, but can be used even without the knowledge of that rite. An Ancestor-spirit must be bound into this fetish.

Edge of the Sun

Level 4, Gnosis 6

This is a deadly weapon carried by the Noonday Suns for ritual duels and executions. "Dying under the gold" is a figure of speech for a lawbreaker's bad end. The machete is cast of solid gold and decorated with jewels. Ironically, it poses no threat to the Veil; any found by humans were melted down for the gold. Like Garou klaives, it must have a War-spirit bound into it, inflicts aggravated damage, and lowers the Gnosis rating of the Mokolé who carries it by one.

These weapons are rare in the extreme. The gold necessary to make one costs over fifty thousand 1999 US dollars. A Noonday Sun who owns one would need to be Rank 4 and Resources 4 to afford such a thing. Use of a Sun's Edge without the sanction of the Duties is itself a serious offense. To create a Sun's Edge, gold must be melted at sunrise and molded into the blade, ensorcelled to have the hardness of steel, then jewels must be set into the teakwood handle, and the whole invested with a War-spirit.

Spirit Tether

Level 4, Gnosis 6

A spirit tether is a mummified umbilical cord that anchors a Mokolé's mind to his body. When used for "going within" (Mnesis), one end must be tied to the Mokolé and the other to some object that is "of the now." Generally, this object can be anything created within the individual Mokolé's lifetime. When used in this fashion, the tether allows the Mokolé to go as deep into Mnesis as possible without fear of getting lost. It also allows the user to return from Mnesis with a perfect sense of his identity, totally eliminating the usual confusion that can follow such sessions. It lowers the difficulty of Mnesis rolls by one.

A second use for the Spirit Tether relates to the Rite of Lost Dreams. When tied to the subject being lowered into Oblivion and held by the participants of the rite, it allows the subject to tug upon the tether in order to signal danger. In this way, there is a chance the ritemaster can pull the subject out of the trance before he is consumed by whatever he sees there. The Spirit Tether must be fashioned from a Mokolé's umbilical cord immediately after birth. Along with the ritual mummification process, the spirit within the cord itself must be awakened. Note that because of this, the usual practice of wearing the Spirit Tether around one's waist like a belt tends to give the wearer a much stronger, almost Oedipan attachment to his mother. Also, a Spirit Tether must only be used by the Mokolé whom it was a part of, making it useful only for homid Mokolé. Using someone else's tether will cause the user to end up somewhere *else* after going within...

Blade of the Kings

Level 5, Gnosis 6

This is a weapon (sword, edged warclub, halberd, spear, axe, etc.) from the Mokolé of old. Occasionally elders sleep the Sleep of the Dragon with such a weapon by their side. The weapon causes aggravated damage and usually has a silver edge. It also shapeshifts to match its wielder; when the Mokolé changes to Archid, the Blade of the Kings changes to match. If the Mokolé has Grasping Hands, he can use the weapon in Archid form. These weapons are made by binding a shapeshifting spirit, such as Butterfly or Octopus, into the weapon as it is made. With each blow that shapes the metal or stone of the blade, the maker must call the spirit's name.

Blowpipe of Anamnesis

Level 5, Gnosis 7

This pipe is made of tropical ceiba wood, harvested without killing the tree, and carved with the signs of the Kings. It is used to administer the teacher plants by packing a dust made from them into the pipe, then blowing it into the nose of the recipient, one nostril at a time. It allows the Rite of Anamnesis to be made easier; the ritemaster can lower the difficulty by one for each level of Rites he has. A Poison-spirit is bound to create this fetish.

Talens

Arrows of the Sun

Gnosis 5

These are arrows containing the essence of Sun and decorated with gold. They are imbued with fragments of Sun-spirit. They cause aggravated damage, and any vampire hit by one suffers the effects of

full daylight for one turn. The arrow itself immolates and is gone in one turn after striking its target.

Cacao Moon's Chocolate

Gnosis 6

These beans are grown only in a small area of Soconusco, Guatemala, near the wallow of Cacao Moon, a Maya Mokolé chieftain who ruled Tikal for many years before retiring to become a mystic. He bred a variety of chocolate beans that are sought after far and wide. Anyone receiving the beans and brewing Aztec chocolate from them may share it with another. Any Gifts, rites, or Abilities that they share are learned twice as quickly while under the influence of this chocolate.

Note that the Mokolé of Soconusco Awaken the chocolate as they harvest it; Awakening chocolate from other sources will not work. Brand-name chocolate is *not* recommended.

Matre Medicine

Gnosis 3

This medicine is prepared from the emissions of crocodiles in the mating season. Its preparation is a distasteful business, and involves binding a Fertility-spirit. When applied before mating, the salve ensures conception, and adds 1% to the chance of true shapeshifter offspring. It is highly sought after by humans as well as Mokolé.

Quipu of the Amautas

Gnosis 5

The amautas were remembrancers of great skill in the Inca empire. This bundle of knotted cords serves to carry a Mnesis message. When tied in knots by a Mokolé-mbembe with the proper skill (which can be learned from a South American Mokolé, from a mummy of the Andes, or through Mnesis) along with the expenditure of a point of Gnosis, one memory can be bound into the cords. (The skill can be listed as Expression: Quipu). The quipu can be dyed, stained, etc., to retain further memory. When the recipient "reads" the knots by handling the cords, the memory passes into her mind. There are other forms of memory messages, such as coconut fibers, chalk drawings, etc., for other streams of Mokolé.

Snake Herbs

Gnosis 4

This is a bunch of powerful herbs from the deserts of Bandaiyan (similar herbs are known elsewhere). The herbs have the virtue of neutralizing snakebite and other poisons. For each bowl of herbs eaten or made into tea, one health level of Dissolver-taint or toxins can be healed. This even allows a Mokolé to eat poisonous flesh without sickening.

Swimmer's Medicine

Gnosis 5

This is the rendered fat from a Komodo monitor's tail, extracted after the lizard has died a natural death. When rubbed on the arms and legs it grants the recipient supernatural swimming prowess: he can easily swim up to half a mile underwater and remain underwater for 15-20 minutes. If he remains afloat (such as by holding onto something) he can swim many miles. A Lizard-spirit is bound to the fat to create this talen. The salve washes off in the water after use.

Fetishes of the Gumagan

Lungin

Level 1, Gnosis 5

This is a wooden pipe used for smoking tobacco, or a mixture of tobacco and pituri. A Fire-spirit must enter the pipe, although they are glad to do so if the owner of the pipe is a frequent smoker. When smoked, the pipe adds a die to dice pools for Gumagan rites. In addition, the smoker may smoke Awakened tobacco or pituri, and receive twice as much effect as usual.

Pearlshell of Healing

Level 1, Gnosis 4

This is an Australian pearlshell used to divine illness. When it is held over the body of a sick person, the medicine man or woman must make a Perception + Rituals roll, difficulty 6. The number of successes is the number of things that the Storyteller can tell them about the illness or injury: that it is contagious, that it is caused by magic, that it is fatal, etc. A Fish-spirit must inhabit the shell.

Kurdaitcha

Level 2, Gnosis 5

These are shoes made from emu feathers knotted together with human hair and stuck together with one health level's worth of the user's blood. The maker must bind a spirit servant of Tokampini the devil-bird into the shoes. When activated, the shoes prevent anyone from hearing the wearer's footfalls. Gumagan wear them when stalking an enemy.

Rangga

Level 2, Gnosis 5

This is a figure molded of clay or wax and used in hunting magic. It represents an animal, human, or Garou. A Perenty-spirit is bound into it. To activated it, the hunter speaks the name of the target softly. He then gets an extra die to one dice pool of his choice for the remainder of the hunt.

Tokoyanga

Level 3, Gnosis 6

This is a ball of goose down worn round the neck and imbued with a Bird-spirit. It dispels grief, and anyone who bites it cannot cry. In addition, nothing the wearer says is audible to a Suchid-form Mokolé or any other large reptile. At the Storyteller's option, activating this fetish may relieve the effects of Harano on the wearer for one scene.

Warshell

Level 3, Gnosis 6

This is a shell shaped into a triangle and sharpened. It can cut an enemy at a distance, at a range of 10 yards per success on the activation roll. The user slashes toward an enemy with the shell and makes a Dexterity + Melee roll, difficulty 7. The number of successes is the number of health levels of aggravated damage taken by the target (soakable if the target can naturally soak aggravated damage). A Snake-spirit must be bound into the shell to create this fetish.

Bret

Level 4, Gnosis 7

This gruesome item is a pair of hands or paws from a dead sentient being: human, Gumagan, Garou, or the like. A piece of the dead person's soul is bound into them. When wrapped in grass, dried and worn about the neck, the bret gives its owner as much Perception as the "donor" had. If the person had any perceptive Gifts, such as Sense Wyrm, the owner can use them as well. Of course, this fetish cannot be worn in most social circumstances; in addition, the relatives of the dead person will likely be angry and try to get the bret and burn it to release the soul.

Talens of the Gumagan

Bloodstone

Gnosis 7

This is blood extracted from a human victim by magic and preserved in a hollow tree. It congeals in a year or so into a stonelike substance. It is rubbed onto the skin or eaten. For each blood point of bloodstone used (the talen usually contains three "points"), the user can gain 1 point of Perception or of Primal-Urge for the duration of the scene. Blood-devils will offer much in order to obtain this item.

Message Stick

Gnosis 4

This is a stick carved and painted with symbols. It contains a message of as many words as the sender has Gnosis points. A Mynah-bird spirit enters the stick to deliver the message. If the recipient makes a Gnosis roll, difficulty 5, he understands the message and knows who sent it. The message then flies away.

Pituri (Plant Talen)

Gnosis 3

Pituri ("pitch-oorie") is a narcotic plant native to Australia. When un-Awakened, it suppresses hunger and thirst and induces a mild euphoria. Awakened, the plant can be chewed or smoked. It adds one health level of healing to all healing rituals. In addition, the user will feel no hunger, thirst or fatigue for one day.

Fetishes of the Makara

Beggar's Mantle

Level 3, Gnosis 7

Resplendent though they may be, the Makara also know the value of humility. This fetish, woven of rags and shed snakeskin, shields their true glory from the eyes of evil beings. When activated, the mantle makes the Makara completely invisible to vampires, Banes, fallen shapeshifters and other creatures of the Wyrm — they simply overlook the Makara. However, this mantle cannot hide a wearer in Archid form, and is very fragile and easily shredded. To create this fetish, a Snake-spirit must be woven into the mantle.

Mace of the Winds

Level 4, Gnosis 8

This uniquely Makara weapon appears to be an ornate, rounded mace made of brass-inlaid iron. When activated and wielded as a weapon, it causes Strength + 3 aggravated damage from its crushing power. However, the mace's true power becomes apparent when its wielder takes Archid form, for it hovers and swoops and attacks unaided as its wielder directs, always returning to hover by its wielder's head. It takes an action to direct the mace to attack (its attack pool being the Makara's Dexterity + Melee as usual), and the mace can fly for up to fifty yards away from its owner. Creating such a fetish requires excellent metalwork skills, and the cooperation of a War-spirit to empower the mace.

Talens of the Makara

Thunder Dart

Gnosis 6

This powerful weapon is as large as any lawn dart, but much more lethal. When hurled at an enemy, it strikes with the force of a thunderbolt, inflicting seven dice of aggravated lightning damage on the foe. To fashion such a talen, the Makara must craft it from the bone of a monster and fletch it with peacock feathers, then coax a Thunder or Rain-spirit into the dart.

Fetishes of the Mokolé-mbembe

Mask of Mnante

Level 1, Gnosis 5

This is a carved mask which can be worn as a necklace, over the face, as part of a headdress, or so on. It is a tool devised during the Wars of Rage to enable Mokolé to survive. When it is invoked, anyone trying to determine the Mokolé's Breed, such as through Scent of the True Form, has the difficulty increased by the Mokolé's current Gnosis, to a maximum of 10. If the observer fails, she considers the Mokolé to be a member of her own kind. If she botches, she sees herself and her hatred objectively, as in a mirror of the soul. This experience should be articulated carefully by the Storyteller, and may lead to profound personality change.

This mask contains a spirit of deception, such as Cuckoo, Chameleon, or Horseshoe Crab, or a Mirror-spirit.

Sword of Fever

Level 5, Gnosis 8

This sword of Entoban steel incarnates the wards of fever built by Mokolé-Mbembe himself around Entoban. When it is drawn, even a finger's width, from its scabbard, it cuts the Sickness-spirits free, and plague strikes. He who draws it may state the enemy's name, and they will sicken. An entire nation may be named. However, the Sickness-spirits cannot be contained. Sickness will spread as rapidly as it can, and many times, Mokolé have been prevented from drawing this sword, lest the plague slay their own Kin.

Spear of Mokolé-Mbembe

Level 6, Gnosis 5

This fetish may or may not have belonged to Mokolé-Mbembe himself, but the Congo Clutch swear that it is so. This weapon is in appearance an Entoban war-spear, but examination of the spear head will reveal that the metal is electrum. Furthermore, the singular purity of this weapon means that it affects shapechangers as if it were both silver and gold. Bête are rarely be able to discern the silver properties of this alloy (all rolls are at 10 difficulty). All difficulties in using this spear are increased by 1, but the weapon inflicts double damage when activated. This fetish is unique.

Fetishes of the Zhong Lung

Box of Rice (Debabako)

Level 1, Gnosis 3

This wooden box contains a Snake-spirit. It is full of rice for as many people as the number written on the top. If the number is washed off and a new number written, the box will contain that much rice the next day. It fills with rice only once each day; if the box is broken there will be no more rice.

Dragon Skin

Level 2, Gnosis 4

This is the shed skin of a Zhong Lung, which glows softly with five-colored light. It is an item of great prestige among clutches to have a fine shed skin. Of course, Eastern wizards and other hengeyokai will also wish to possess it. When activated, this skin grants armor equivalent to the Gift: Armor of the Tortoise. It must be shaped by a professional leatherworker, and a Sun-spirit must be bound into it.

Pearls of Flood and Ebb Tide

Level 5, Gnosis 9

These are pearls kept in the palaces of the Dragon Kings at the bottom of the sea and control the ebb and flow of the tide. They are imbued with Lune-essence and have Lunes bound into them. They can cause the tides to rise and fall: the activator may use the Gift: Call the Tide (pg. 83) with the same number of automatic successes as her Rank.

Talens of the Zhong Lung

Dragon's Spittle

Gnosis 4

This is the gathered spittle of a Zhong Lung. When prepared with the help of a Dragon-spirit, it adds Gnosis to other spirit workings. When the spittle is mixed into ink for mystic calligraphy, used in rock paintings, etc., allow one extra point of Power or Gnosis for the work.

Merits

Bird-spirit Companion: (1 point Merit)

A particular Bird-spirit has taken a liking to you and will sometimes materialize after you have fed (in Suchid or Archid form) to pick your teeth. It may bring you news, rumors, hints or the like, but these tidbits of information aren't guaranteed to be reliable at all.

Bite of the Monitor: (1-5 point Merit)

This Merit is common among Mokolé of the Ora varna. It makes the Mokolé's bite more dangerous. Any bite inflicted by the Mokolé can be healed as usual as the aggravated damage it usually is. However, after time the wound reopens. When this happens, the victim loses the same number of health levels they lost with the initial bite after soaking. The frequency in which the bite reopens depends on the strength of this Merit.

- Once a year (1 point)
- Once a season (2 points)
- Once a month (3 points)
- Once a week (4 points)
- Once a day (5 points)

The bite will open a number of times equal to the Mokolé's Gnosis, and after that will not reopen. It is up to the Storyteller exactly when the bite reopens. A being can suffer from only one "infected" bite at a time.

Manshape: (1 point Merit)

Your Archid form resembles that of humanity. You are essentially a "lizard person" — a human shape with a reptile head, roughly the size of a Crinos Garou. You will need to buy Bipedal and Grasping Hands for your Archid form to take this Merit, but this Merit allows you to use a greater variety of tools and fit in places you might not otherwise fit.

Mnesis of the Lost Ones: (1 point Merit)

You belong to a Mnesis lineage that, through cross-breeding, sharing of mates, or the Rite of Anamnesis being performed in the distant past, has some memories from an extinct Changing Breed, such as the Camazotz (werebats), the Khara (sabertooth Bastet) or the Grondr (boar-skins). This Mnesis will be fragmented, imperfect and difficult for you to understand. The Storyteller will convey to you what this memory contains, although you will not be able to use it as easily as Mokolé memories.

Terrible Footsteps: (1 point Merit)

When shapeshifting, the Mokolé can invoke this Merit by spending one Gnosis. The ground trembles, the trees sway, and the birds and animals flee. This is not connected to Delirium and the Veil, but is a function of Mnesis. The Mokolé is remembering the mighty tread of the Kings.

Yathamaya: (1 point Merit)

You possess the location of a Yathamaya, a memory realm in the High Umbra. This place may be a forest, an ocean, a temple or palace, or something unintelligible to human beings. It is a construct of living memory. If you possess the proper Gifts, you may be able to enter the Umbra and find it. The Storyteller will construct the Yathamaya, but will not reveal all of the information to you.

Retain Eggs: (2 point Merit)

This Merit is for females only. It allows them to delay labor or laying eggs for a period of time by spending a point of Gnosis. The mother may delay going into labor or laying eggs until she has reached a place of safety or has assured herself that no enemies are present. In rare cases, eggs may be retained until they hatch within the mother's body.

Retain Seed: (2 point Merit)

This Merit may be purchased by female Mokolé only. It allows them to retain their mate's seed for a number of years equal to their Gnosis. At any time during this period, they may spend a point of permanent Gnosis to produce a clutch of eggs (for suchids) or a baby (for homids) with the usual chance of being Mokolé or Kin. Suitable mates are rare, so this Merit enables more Mokolé and Kin to be born.

Temperature Control: (2 point Merit)

You can control your body temperature. You will never suffer from fever, heat exhaustion, heatstroke or hypothermia, save in the most extreme conditions. In addition, if you concentrate intensely enough, you can avoid being spotted by heat sensors. Your body temperature cannot usually go over 110° or under 65° Fahrenheit, however.

Farm Ties: (3 point Merit)

You are associated with an alligator farm at which crocodilians are raised to stock zoos, to restock the wild, or for human tourists to look at. The staff are usually Kin, and there may be other Mokolé at the farm. You have a reasonably sure supply of food and a place to stay. However, you have to work on the farm, probably including breeding. Also, the farm is a likely target for enemy attacks.

Sacred Crocodile: (3 point Merit)

Your suchid form is sacred to a human religious cult who honor you as the embodiment of divinity. You usually live in a pool near the temple. Your worshippers are mostly Kinfolk. However, they may not know that you are Mokolé. You do not get any money from them (after all, you are a crocodile) but you are provided with food (such as animal "sacrifices") as well as a secure place to live. Often you are painted or decorated with flowers, ribbons, etc., for religious festivals. You must not harm or offend your followers, or they may turn on you. This Merit is most common among Makara and Mokolé-mbembe. Please note that unless the worshippers are purchased as Allies, they will not do much except throw food to you and worship the "god within" you. They do not obey you, although they may listen to a priest who talks about you. Unless you also purchase the Kinfolk background, the worshippers and priests don't know that you are Mokolé, and will be frightened if you shapeshift, start to talk, etc. This Merit is particularly appropriate for historical games.

Supernatural Companion: (4 point Merit)

You have a friend and ally who happens to be some kind of supernatural creature: another shapeshifter, a mage, or perhaps a changeling. Your clutch does not know about this person, and might be upset if they find out about your friendship. If the ally is Garou, they will be extremely angry. The Storyteller will create this ally, but will not reveal all the details to you.

Gold Tolerance: (5 point Merit)

You can soak damage from gold, although it is still aggravated. If you choose to carry golden weapons, talismans or the like, your Gnosis loss is halved. Other Mokolé find this tolerance unusual and a little suspicious. This Merit is most common for Midnight Suns.

Eidetic Memory: (5 point Merit)

You forget nothing and can "photograph" scenes and texts into your memory with the appropriate effort. This Merit costs a lot more for Mokolé than for any other creature, for obvious reasons. Once any fact or scene has been recalled through Mnesis, the Mokolé can call it to mind again, although every single detail of an ancestor's life isn't available to him unless the ancestor also had eidetic memory. The player may ask the Storyteller for any fact or event that his character witnessed. The Merit makes learning anything memory-related cost half the usual experience points (although things that have to be practiced are as costly as usual). The Merit also brings respect, as other Mokolé appeal to the character to settle disputes and the like.

Backwards Mnesis (7 point Merit)

You can "remember" the future, although most of what you remember will be meaningless or useless to you. This is treated as normal Mnesis, although the Storyteller makes the roll and tells you what you see. Tragically, this Merit is useless for playing the stock market. This Merit is most common for Shining.

Color Change: (7 point Merit)

You can change color like a chameleon in your Suchid and Archid forms. This happens as quickly as blushing. You cannot change to any color of the rainbow, but you can become light, dark, or strongly colored. This usually makes you harder to spot, although the Storyteller can judge how much more difficult it will be. This Merit is most common among the caiman varna of South America.

Silver Tolerance: (7 point Merit)

You can soak silver, although it still does aggravated damage to you, and you only lose half the usual amount of Gnosis for carrying silver items. This is an extremely powerful Merit and is not to be taken lightly; there must be some explanation for your immunity, such as a pact or supernatural intervention. This Merit cannot under any circumstances be taken along with Gold Tolerance.

Step Sideways: (7 point Merit)

You can enter the Umbra without a Gift, just as the Garou do. This Merit is rare in the extreme and is dangerous to use, as it alerts Umbral beings who may be hostile to you. You may step sideways whenever you have a reflective surface, as per the **Werewolf** rulebook. You should present the Storyteller with a convincing reason as to why you have this Merit, and it remains wholly her discretion whether you are allowed to purchase it or not.

Veiled to Garou: (7 point Merit)

This is an extremely powerful Merit, available only to Mokolé. The Mokolé and the Kings hunted and slew the Garou and their mammalian ancestors for ages. There are a few Mokolé who retain that ancient aura of mind-shattering terror. The Mokolé with this advantage causes the Delirium in Garou, although not in other Awakened creatures. Garou react as per the Delirium chart according to their Willpower or Rage, whichever is higher. Garou, too, can make a Wits + Occult roll to move up the chart at the Storyteller's option.

Flaws

Albino: (1 point Flaw)

You have no pigment in any form. You are white-skinned and have pale pink eyes. In the sun, you will be burned within a few minutes. In addition, you receive two fewer dice on all social rolls because of your bizarre appearance. This Flaw is common among sacred crocodiles.

Deaf: (1 point Flaw)

You are mostly without hearing, like some large lizards. You are able to hear some things in your Homid and Archid forms, but are entirely deaf in Suchid.

Diurnal: (1 point Flaw)

You are strictly diurnal and sleep all night. You must spend a Willpower point to function with a full dice pool after the sky is dark. If there are lights as bright as the sun (Storyteller's decision) you may act as if it were day.

Migratory Urges: (1 point Flaw)

You have powerful inborn urges to migrate each year. Usually, you learn the migration routes immediately after your First Change, often through Mnesis from a migrating ancestor. The Storyteller determines your migration route, although she won't disclose every detail of it to you. If you are prevented from migrating, you will lose one die from your dice pools each day until you do so, as if you were wounded. Other Mokolé may join you in the migration or meet you at the end. Note that you have no special knowledge of the route. There may be all sorts of dangers that you do not know about.

Molt: (1 point Flaw)

You molt on a regular basis. When you molt, the scales, feathers, or fur of your Archid form slough off, and your Homid form loses all its facial and body hair. Your skin will shred and peel. You may lose tattoos, piercings, and scars, as well as suntan. Your Suchid form's outer skin will also shred and peel off. You are treated as Bruised during a molt and your armor or shell, if any, do not exist. Your Appearance is lowered by 2, although it cannot be lowered below 1 through molting. You itch horribly and are constantly scratching in all your forms throughout the molt. You may spend a Willpower point to stop scratching for one scene. The molt lasts as long as a sunburn, several days to a week, and occurs at least once a year. The Storyteller decides when you molt and informs you of the consequences. It is possible that stress, fear, or exposure to toxic chemicals could cause you to molt ahead of time or more than once. On the other hand, the difficulty of the Rite of Shedding Hide is lowered by 1 if you are molting.

Monogamous (1 point Flaw)

You are strictly monogamous (like several species of the Bird Kings). Not only can you not mate with anyone but your mate, you cannot even desire to do so. You may choose a mate, or one may be chosen for you from suitable Kinfolk. Note that your mate may also be your True Love (see the **Werewolf Players Guide** for this Merit). This Flaw does not guarantee that your mate will be monogamous, or that your mate is of the opposite sex. However, your mate will regard you favorably, at least at first.

Small: (1 point Flaw)

You are a small creature in your Archid and Suchid form and are probably smaller than normal even as a human. You have one less die on Social rolls and are not considered for leadership. You have normal Rage and health levels, but have less body mass, and subtract a die from your combat dice pools if you are brawling.

Scavenger: (1 point Flaw)

You are a carrion eater in your Archid form. This does not affect your combat abilities, but you cannot eat flesh that is not decayed. Fresh meat may even make you sick. You have bad breath (-1 die to Social rolls) and are unwelcome at parties and feasts. However, any flesh, even completely rotten, is nourishing to you.

Speechless: (1 point Flaw)

Due to a gap in your Mnesis, you are not fluent in the Dragon's Tongue and cannot converse with other Mokolé when in Archid or Suchid, save for primitive body language. You can eventually buy off this Flaw by learning the Dragon's Tongue over time, but be warned that it's a difficult business, and there are few Mokolé patient enough to give you the lessons you need at times convenient for you.

Slime: (1 point Flaw)

Your Archid form is slimy, and your human form sweats a great deal or has horrible body odor. Wherever you go, a trail of ooze follows. You receive -2 dice to Social rolls.

Bad Mnesis: (2-5 point Flaw)

Your Mnesis contains memories so horrible and tainting that any attempt to use the Memory is fraught with peril: you may retrieve false memories, remember something incorrectly, enter Harano or suffer Derangements. The more points in this Flaw, the more dangerous it is: three points means that there is a fair chance of any Mnesis quest ending badly, while five points means that using Mnesis for *anything* is sure to cause trouble.

Cold-Blooded: (2 point Flaw)

In all your forms, you have no natural ability to regulate your body temperature. In warm weather, you get +1 Dexterity, but after each hour of exertion you must rest or cool yourself (such as with water) or lose a health level. If it grows too hot, high temperatures alone have the same detrimental effects of exertion. In cold weather you suffer -1 Dexterity and -1 to Mental Attributes. In below-freezing weather you take one health level of damage per hour from the cold, and you continue to get colder until you fall unconscious. After a number of hours equal to your Stamina, you will die. You may reverse this by heating yourself, such as with heated coveralls or in a hot bath. This Flaw is most common for suchids.

Dream Hunter (2 point Flaw)

Your Mnesis contains a powerful and dangerous memory, called a Dream Hunter. This deadly creature was roused from slumber when you remembered the time and place wherein it lived. Whenever it gets a chance, it will attack you in Mnesis, trying to kill you or drive you mad. Your battles with it take place in Mnesis, using spirit combat rules. Unless you are able to kill it permanently by finding the place and time in the Memory whence it came and destroying it completely there, or by erasing Mnesis with the Rite of the Burning Library, it will continue to hunt you and anyone who inwits with you. This Flaw actually may include more than one Dream Hunter, but usually only one will appear at a time. More details on the statistics of these creatures are in the Appendix: Night.

Exclusive Herbivore: (2 point Flaw)

You are an herbivorous creature in your Archid form. Your bite attack is 1 die lower, and the taste of blood sickens you. The Storyteller may force you to spend a Willpower point to avoid retching. You may not eat or digest anything that comes out of an animal's body, including milk or eggs, in any of your forms; this will sicken you and cause you to lose one health level.

Infamous Elder/Clutch: (2-4 point Flaw)

An elder in your clutch, who has authority over you, has a bad reputation. Perhaps he has shown cowardice or broken the Duties. You may be insulted or shown dishonor on his account. You are three dice lower to dice pools for gaining Renown anywhere but your home clutch. Alternatively you may come from an entire clutch that is notorious for its words or actions. The Storyteller will develop the exact details of the dishonor but will not reveal everything to you right away.

Insane Elder: (2 point Flaw)

An elder in your clutch, one who gives you orders, has Bad Mnesis and is horribly mad. His mental illness may not be obvious to you. Indeed, you may not even know that he is insane. However, any information he gives you is suspect (the Storyteller may provide you with false information on the chronicle setting through him) and his judgments and sayings will be out of touch with reality. The other Mokolé you know will be more and more aware of his foibles as time goes by and will distrust you on his account.

Stench: (2 point Flaw)

You have a repellent stench which penalizes Social rolls by three dice in all your forms. Anything trying to track you by scent has the difficulty lowered by 2, and you cannot mask the scent with perfume or wash it away. Most mammals, such as horses and dogs, will be uneasy around you.

Sterile/Barren: (2 point Flaw)

For whatever reason, you are completely sterile. Unless you "buy off" this Flaw with experience points (such as by roleplaying a quest, magical gift, or operation), you will remain so. If other Mokolé know this, they may assume that you are diseased or Dissolver-ridden, or simply avoid you. You cannot gain Matre and are an undesirable mate: Mokolé and Kin who know of your "curse" will not want even casual intimacy with you, except perhaps for same-sex relations.

Wall Eye: (2 point Flaw)

Your eyes do not allow binocular vision in any form. You must turn your head to the side to look at something. You get two fewer dice on all visual-based Perception rolls.

Eyes of the Tyrant: (3 point Flaw)

Like Tyrannosaurus rex, you have difficulty seeing non-moving objects. You receive +3 to the difficulty of sight-related Perception rolls. If any enemy can remain perfectly still, you cannot see them at all.

Fallen Elder/Clutch: (3-5 point Flaw)

Whether or not you know it, the elder in your clutch has fallen to the Dissolver. The nature of the temptation and his weakness are not known to you automatically. The Storyteller will create the situation and reveal it to you in the course of the game. You may become aware of his nature through knowing of cannibalism, alliances with fomori or vampires, or other ghastly actions. If your entire clutch has fallen, you are in serious trouble. First of all, you effectively have no clutch. Second, your clutch will want to find you and either kill you or make you like them. Third, other Mokolé will automatically assume that you have fallen as well.

Hunted: (3 point Flaw)

You are hunted by human poachers, by Innocents in the Umbra, by the Noonday Suns, by other creatures, or by Garou. They will seek you out and try to kill you, or, worse, capture you. They are armed with silver or gold weapons and know about your abilities, even if they do not know much about the Mokolé. They are not constantly on your trail, but they will show up throughout the chronicle.

Limbless: (4 point Flaw)

Your Archid form has no useful limbs: you resemble a giant snake, though you may have flippers and a tail. You cannot manipulate anything and have no claw attack in Archid form; your land speed is reduced to a crawl (1/4 speed). However, Nagah may be favorably disposed toward you, should you ever happen to run into one.

Great Fossil Lizard: (5 point Flaw)

Your dreaming was warped by the beliefs firmly held by millions about prehistoric reptiles. You are not a real dinosaur in your Archid form, but the old-school image of one. You are cold-blooded, have a walnut-sized brain, are gray-green in color, and lurch along slowly dragging your long snaky tail. You are most comfortable living in a swamp and eating soft waterweeds. Your Mental Attributes do not change, but you have a tendency to think "slowly."

Merits of the Gumagan

Song Owner: (1 point Merit)

You have inherited knowledge of part of a mystic song of the Dreamtime. This usually concerns the ancestors and their deeds. You have gotten this song from your mother, uncle, or from a Mokolé in your clutch. You may be the only one alive who knows it. Each verse concerns a step of the great journeys made by the ancestors. You thus also "inherit" knowledge of a long series of desert trails, water holes, etc., although you do not own them. These places ritually belong to you, and to anyone else who knows any verses of the song. You have the right to sing this song and anyone else who shares even a single line of the song will treat you as a relative. You must pass the song on to your nephew, niece or some other heir or to your child if you are female. In addition, anthropologists might want to "study" you, leading to a useful source of cash and bizarre Weaver-trinkets.

Recommended Merits & Flaws

If the Storyteller allows players to take Merits & Flaws, the following from the **Werewolf Players Guide** are also quite appropriate for Mokolé:

- Psychological: Berserker, Intolerance (Garou), Territorial
- Awareness: Color Blindness, Hard of Hearing, Bad Sight
- Aptitudes: Jack-of-all-Trades (gained through Mnesis)
- Supernatural: True Love, True Faith (Sun), Banned Transformation (when the sun cannot be seen), Foe From the Past
- Physical: Bad Taste, Lack of Scent, Longevity, Huge Size, Strict Carnivore, Mute

Merits of the Makara

High Caste: (1 point Merit)

You were fortunate enough to be born into the Kshatriya or Brahmin caste, and thus are accorded a fair amount of respect among your society. You receive two extra dice to Social rolls when dealing with the humans of your homeland. Only homid Makara may take this Merit.

Ghar: (3 point Merit)

This Merit is for Gharials only; it indicates a swollen red lump on your Suchid-form snout. This adds two dice to Social rolls among other Makara, and allows the Mokolé to spend Gnosis to add to chances of siring a true offspring. For each Gnosis spent in mating rites, 1% is added to the chance of a true Mokolé being born.

Merits of the Zhong Lung

Same-Bito Kin: (1 point Merit)

You are Kin to the weresharks of the East. The Storyteller will create the Same-Bito school who are related to you, but will not divulge all this information to you; you may not know much about them. Should you meet any Same-Bito, they will likely respect you and listen to you.

Flaws of the Zhong Lung

Fear of Iron: (1 point Flaw)

You can be banished by means of iron. A hunter may throw iron into your pond, or strike you with iron. If his Willpower overcomes yours in an opposed roll, you must flee.

Fertile Essence: (1 point Flaw)

You are filled with life-giving essence, to the peril of anyone who knows you. If anyone drinks from the same glass as you, uses the same bathing pool, or even handles your clothing or utensils, they can have children who will resemble *you*. Even people who are sterile or barren might become pregnant because of you (Storyteller's option, and certainly not applicable to metis characters). This can become annoying, and cause some serious misunderstandings.

Stone Blind: (2 point Flaw)

You cannot see stones, or anything made of stone. If something is made of stone with other material added, such as mortar or paint, you know that it is there but cannot really tell what it is. You cannot read writings on stone tablets or markers and cannot see stones in your path, even if you trip on them. The Storyteller is urged to invent humorous uses for this.

Coming of Age in the Mesozoic

Peter and the two Mokolé sat by a fire, finishing a haunch of wallaby that Peter had run down into a two-perenty ambush. "So, how do you, uh, become Mokolé? The Memory tells me a lot, but it's got to be different from how we do it."

The Mokolé rite of passage is profoundly different from that of the Garou. Mokolé, like Garou, rarely have a Mokolé child. More often, Mokolé are born from human or reptile Kin. Although long ago Kin-Fetch spirits bound themselves to Mokolé during the hatching rites, attrition has naturally resulted in large numbers of "lost hatchlings." These unfortunates often have no one to guide them through the Change, but Mnesis means that no Mokolé is wholly lost.

The Mokolé may be aware of her heritage through being told of it, through tracing lineages, or through dreams and visions. Even if she does not know she is a Mokolé, she

will eventually undergo the dreaming. Exactly when this happens is up to the Storyteller. Mokolé do not kidnap their hatchlings as Garou do, though a trip away from human parents might be in order. Sometimes Mokolé elders take hatchlings on "camp-outs" or pilgrimages to teach them the Old Ways, or arrange for a "visit to relatives."

The hatchling falls into a deep trance. Sometimes the trance lasts only a single day. Rarely, it lasts so long that the Mokolé could be mistaken for dead. While entranced, she dreams of the past as Mnesis takes hold.

The exact nature of the dreams varies. In some cases, the dream consists of a series of scenes. In each scene, one of the characteristics of the Mokolé's Archid form is acquired through evolution. For example, Wind-Beneath-Her-Wings dreamed of being a primeval reptile with skinfolds, who leaped off a cliff to escape a pursuer and learned to fly. Kwame Wisdom of Sun was drawn by voices he could not hear to an ancient wallow, where Horseshoe Crab crawled up and introduced him to three animals, each of whom showed him one of the traits of his Archid form. In other cases, the trance is a story that teaches the hatchling important lessons. In still other cases, the dream is of the last ancestor who was a true Mokolé. When the dream is over, the Mokolé wakes, and has full shapeshifting abilities. However, she may still need to learn Mokolé lore and skills.

In game terms, this means that the Storyteller can create a story as a prelude for the character. Other players can play "walk-on" parts from the past, or the clutch can undergo their rite of passage together. Experience points from the story can fuel the acquisition of new skills or make the character stronger.

During the trance, the new Mokolé may be confronted by the Innocents, who will assume a shape appropriate to the setting and attack her or try to lead her astray. If she defeats them, they will not return to haunt her later. If not, then the next time she is in the Umbra, they will attack. Physically, Mokolé often end up moving towards a wallow or towards the location of a Sleeping Dragon. Consciously or otherwise, the hatchling will try to unite with Mokolé society. Great tales and songs concern hatchlings who crossed entire continents drawn only by urges that they could not explain, to be received with joy by their new clutch.

Come not between the dragon and his wrath.
— Shakespeare, *King Lear*

Sun and his allied spirits grant the Mokolé many Gifts. Mokolé can learn Gifts from each other, from spirits, or from Mnesis. The rules for learning them from another Mokolé or from a spirit are the same as for Garou, except that many spirits which help Garou are not friendly to Mokolé. Such spirits as Wolf, Bear, Porcupine and the like will not usually help Mokolé. However, the Mokolé may yet make some kind of deal with them — or failing that, threaten them in some way.

Gifts can be learned through Mnesis, if the Gift is present anywhere in the Mokolé's Mnesis line (Storyteller's option). The character must go into a Mnesis trance, then must spend as much time entranced as it would take to learn the Gift from another Mokolé. Then she must make a Mnesis roll and score a number of successes equal to the level of the Gift (she must, of course, be of high enough Rank to learn the Gift she seeks). If she succeeds, she learns the Gift. Experience point costs are the same as normal. To learn Mokolé Gifts, the difficulty of the roll is 8. With non-Mokolé Gifts it is 9 or 10.

A beginning Mokolé starts with two Gifts, one for her solar auspice and one from the basic list.

Generic Mokolé Gifts

• **Falling Touch (Level One)** — As the Garou Gift. Normally taught by a spirit of the Dinosaur Kings or Bird Kings.

• **Fatal Flaw (Level One)** — As the Shadow Lord Gift.

• **Find Land (Level One)** — By focusing his attention onto the balance of land and water, the Mokolé can locate the nearest fixed land amidst the waters of swamp or sea. This Gift is taught by a Turtle-spirit.

System: The player makes a Perception + Survival roll, difficulty 6. One success indicates the direction of the land. Three successes indicate the distance; five allow the Mokolé to tell whether the land is dangerous or contaminated.

• **Find Water (Level One)** — As the Gift: Find Land, save that the Mokolé can find any water within twenty miles, and likewise tell if the water is contaminated if he achieves enough successes. This Gift is taught by a Lizard-spirit.

• **Inspiration (Level One)** — As the Ahroun Gift.

• **Razor Claws (Level One)** — As the Ahroun Gift; needless to say, this works only in Archid form.

• **Scent of Sweet Nectar (Level One)** — As the Bone Gnawer Gift: Scent of Sweet Honey. It is taught by a Bee-spirit.

• **Sense Dissolver (Level One)** — As the metis Gift: Sense Wyrm.

• **Sense Moon (Level One)** — This Gift enables the user to detect a child of the Moon — usually a fellow shapechanger (save for Corax, Ananasi or Nuwisha).

System: The player rolls Perception + Occult, difficulty 7. With three successes, he can tell what kind of moon creature is involved; five allows a rough estimate of rank and abilities. This Gift is taught by a Sun-spirit.

• **Sense Prey (Level One)** — The Mokolé knows the trick of locating prey animals in a given area. An Alligator-spirit teaches this Gift.

System: The player spends a Willpower point, and rolls Perception + Primal-Urge, difficulty 7. Each success leads the Mokolé to enough prey for one meal: enough successes can feed an entire clutch.

• **Shed (Level One)** — By quickly shedding his outer skin, the Mokolé can escape an enemy's hold or slip through a tight area. A Lizard-spirit or Snake-spirit teaches this Gift.

System: By making a successful Dexterity + Primal-Urge roll (difficulty 7), the Mokolé can either automatically escape any grappling attack, or lower the difficulty of escaping restraints or slipping through tight squeezes by 2.

• **Sight of the True Form (Level One)** — As the Garou Gift: Scent of the True Form. This Gift is taught by a spirit of the Predator Kings.

• **Speed of Thought (Level One)** — As the Silent Striders Gift, save that the Mokolé must spend two Gnosis rather than one to activate the land speed.

• **Tailbiter's Mumble (Level One)** — The Mokolé may bite her tail in her mouth and roll any distance desired as quickly as her human form runs. This Gift is taught by Hoopsnake.

System: The Mokolé must be in Suchid or Archid, and spend a Willpower point; apart from that, the movement bonuses are automatic.

• **Talk (Level One)** — This Gift permits the Mokolé to speak any human language he knows while in Suchid or Archid form. This Gift is taught by a Bird-spirit.

System: No roll is necessary; the Mokolé becomes automatically capable of speech in all forms. With a successful Mnesis roll, difficulty 8, the Mokolé can also speak any of the other Bête's languages for the duration of a scene.

• **Axis Mundi (Level Two)** — By attuning himself to the land, the Mokolé can learn precisely where Sun is in relation to Earth. A Sun-spirit teaches this Gift.

System: The player spends a Gnosis point; the Gift automatically grants knowledge of the exact time, season, the Mokolé's placement on the Earth, and the direction that he is facing.

• **Sense Gold (Level Two)** — As the Ahroun Gift: Sense Silver, save that it detects the presence of gold.

• **Silver Claws (Level Two)** — As the Ahroun Gift. No common "Gold Claws" variant exists; the Mokolé have fought against other shapechangers much more often than they've fought against one another.

• **Stinking Breath (Level Two)** — The Mokolé can breathe out stinking gases that repel anything that breathes, making them flee. This Gift is taught by a Garbage-spirit or a Monitor-lizard spirit.

System: The Mokolé spends a Gnosis point and breathes on her enemies. Air-breathing creatures (obviously, the undead are immune) are repelled by the smell and try to flee the encounter, unless they successfully make an opposed Gnosis roll against the Mokolé's Gnosis.

• **Tides of Lust (Level Two)** — This Gift is most common among the Gila monsters and Mexican beaded lizards of the American Southwest, the Unktehi, who learn it from a Rooster-spirit. It gives them power over the tides within someone's body.

System: The Mokolé begins to dance and rolls Rites + Expression, difficulty 7. If the target already loves someone else the difficulty is 8, or 9 if the target is very old or attracted to the same sex. The number of successes determines the number of hours that the person will be unnaturally lusty. Impotence, if any, disappears, the target becomes fertile if ordinarily sterile (unless the target is metis, of course), and the target also becomes a little more open-minded about potential partners. Even so, the Mokolé must still seduce the person through roleplaying, as this Gift does not implant obvious desire — it merely removes barriers.

• **Waxwork Monster (Level Two)** — Brought to light recently by the Shining, this Gift lets a Mokolé take advantage of the fact that "dinosaurs are extinct" to hide in plain sight even in Archid form. Essentially, the Mokolé takes on the appearance of a model or dummy. A Tuatara-spirit teaches this Gift.

System: The Mokolé spends a Gnosis point and rolls Stamina + Expression. For each success, he can freeze in place for one hour unnoticed by anyone. In Suchid form, he appears to be a stuffed crocodile; in Homid form, he seems to be a mannequin or waxwork. In Archid form the Mokolé appears to be a life-size fiberglass or cement dinosaur model, but cannot cause the Delirium unless he moves or speaks. Some Shining will even carry around a small label designating the species of dinosaur that they are supposed to be. Of course, the "statue" will arouse suspicion if there is not supposed to be a statue in the place where the Mokolé is hiding. Whole clutches have concealed themselves this way as roadside attractions and the like.

• **Bark of the Mudpuppy (Level Three)** — This Gift allows the Mokolé to bark loudly at any one person or object, shattering glass, splintering light wood or even opening wounds on a living being. This Gift is taught by Mudpuppy.

System: The bark does one health level of aggravated damage, but automatically strikes its target. There is no actual cost.

• **Dragon's Breath (Level Three)** — This Gift allows the Mokolé to spit fire, as do the Dragon Kings. This Gift is taught by Dragon himself.

System: This costs one point of Rage per burst. To hit, the player rolls Dexterity + Brawl, difficulty 8; the flame does two health levels of aggravated damage. For each extra Rage point spent, one extra level of damage is done. Thus a Mokolé could spend four Rage and do five health levels of aggravated damage.

• **Dragonfear (Level Three)** — This Gift invokes an aura of menace so terrible that the Mokolé's Archid form is capable of inducing the night-fear in any creatures, supernatural or otherwise. This Gift is taught by Dragon.

System: The Mokolé spends a Rage point to invoke the fear for one scene; all witnesses become subject to the Delirium. Note that the other creatures may roll Wits + Occult to move up on the Delirium Chart as usual. However, creatures created to be immune to the Delirium, such as fomori, can still experience the effects of the Delirium when this Gift is used.

• **Walking Between Worlds (Level Three)** — Mokolé with this Gift are finally able to breach the Gauntlet and enter the Umbra. Most typically, they go into water instead of using a mirror in order to step sideways. This Gift is taught by any spirit who knows how to materialize in the physical world.

System: Once this Gift is learned, the Mokolé may step sideways just as Garou do.

• **Attunement (Level Four)** — As the Bone Gnawer Gift.

• **Cocoon (Level Four)** — As the Homid Garou Gift. Mokolé adepts often use the Cocoon to protect them when sleeping the Sleep of the Dragon.

• **View the Seed (Level Four)** — This Gift comes from the belief that all things are but a dream of the idea or object that birthed them. It allows the user to see the "seed" of anything, from the parents of a child to the mastermind of a plot. Note that some things result from the growth of several "seeds." A Mokolé looking at America, for instance, could see any number of things (John Locke in his study, Native Americans planting maize, Africans bought with Boston rum...). The Gumagan are most likely to learn this Gift, which is taught by Finch.

System: The Mokolé rolls Perception + Mnesis, difficulty 7. If the thing to be seen is outside the Mnesis of the Mokolé's line, the difficulty is 8. In the case of truly alien causes and effects, the difficulty could be 9 (Vhujunka plotting to sail into the Deep Umbra, etc.).

• **Grasp the Beyond (Level Five)** — As the Level Four Theurge Gift.

• **Song of the Great Beast (Level Five)** — As the lupus Gift. Usually the Dinosaur Kings will teach this Gift only to suchids, and they can use it to summon dinosaur Great Beasts. Note, however, that such monsters as sea scorpions and giant sharks also lie within Mnesis, and if the Kings decided to teach these Songs, then they could do so.

Gifts of the Gumagan

• **Songlines (Level One)** — This Gift covers the landscape with songs. The Gumagan can navigate from one end of Bandaiyan to the other using legends. This Gift is taught by an Ancestor-spirit.

System: The Gumagan sets out on a journey and begins the Song. He rolls Gnosis and adds to the number of successes the number of sacred songs he knows. The difficulty is 6 in his tribe's territory, 7 outside. In lands other than Bandaiyan it is 10. The number of successes is the number of times by which the distance is divided when calculating the length of the trip.

• **Dreamwalk (Level Two)** — The Gumagan may use her connection to the Dreamtime to lower the Gauntlet. A Dreamtime-spirit teaches this Gift.

System: The Gumagan must concentrate on the spirit world for a full turn; for the duration of the very next turn, the local Gauntlet is lowered by 2.

• **Bunyip's Boom (Level Three)** — The Gumagan may reach into Mnesis and imitate the mournful cry of the Bunyip. This Gift is taught by servants of Mu-ru-bul Tu-ru-dan the Bunyip.

System: The Gumagan spends one Gnosis and rolls Charisma + Performance, difficulty 7. Anyone who hears this roaring noise loses a number of Willpower points equal to the number of successes scored by the Gumagan. Many foes will flee on hearing the echoes of the land's past.

• **Landspeak (Level Three)** — The Aboriginal folk of Bandaiyan know the land as a series of interconnected songlines, the Ways of the Law. By listening carefully, Gumagan can hear the songs of the earth. A servant of Ngalyod the Rainbow Serpent teaches this Gift.

System: The Gumagan puts his ear to the ground or into a waterhole. He then makes a Gnosis roll, difficulty 6. The number of successes is the number of miles within which he can hear The Song. He will know what the Earth thinks of events on its surface within this area. If he makes a Mnesis roll instead, he can hear echoes of the past. Note that this Gift is not considered eavesdropping, but rather overhearing the Earth's commentary.

• **Nightmare Mnesis (Level Four)** — The Gumagan can overcome any foe with Mnesis, forcing them to remember the atrocities committed on the Aboriginal peoples and animals of the land. This Gift is taught by a Bunyip ghost.

System: The Gumagan looks into her foe's eyes and makes a Mnesis roll, difficulty of the opponent's Willpower. If she succeeds, the foe will remember lifetimes of slaughter, torture, rape and defilement. He must make a Willpower check, difficulty 7, or fall into despair (usually Harano). Many who have been struck by this Gift have harmed themselves or sought to atone for the crimes they recall.

• **Billabong Walk (Level Five)** —The Gumagan goes into any body of water suitable for his varna (fresh or salt for salties, waterholes or streams for perenty) and emerges from another. He must have bathed in the water where he plans to emerge before using this Gift. This Gift is taught by servants of the Bunyip.

System: The Gumagan submerges himself entirely and spends two Gnosis. He then reappears in the target body of water.

• **Bloody-Mindedness (Level Five)** — The Gumagan can "point herself" at a chosen goal or foe, a "life-enemy." She will pursue this goal until death and beyond. A servant of Mu-ru-bul Tu-ru-dan the Bunyip teaches this Gift.

System: The Gumagan spends two points of Willpower. Afterwards, she neither eats nor sleeps unless she wishes to do so. She may add two to her dice pools for any task related to her goal. The sheer intensity of her search will usually frighten anyone into helping her: Bloody-Minded Gumagan are often on the edge of frenzy every minute. She may not be persuaded to abandon her quest by any supernatural means (treat as the Merit: Iron Will). In combat against her life-enemy, she will gain one extra attack per round, with the difficulty of attacks against her target reduced by one. She may not dodge attacks from any other combatant, but her dice pool to soak damage is doubled.

Gifts of the Makara

• **The Thousand Arrows (Level Three)** — This Gift allows a Makara marksman to greatly multiply his missiles in mid-flight; an archer can send a swarm of arrows, and a machine gun spits forth a cloud of bullets. This Gift is taught by a Wasp-spirit.

System: The Makara spends one Gnosis and one Rage. Whatever firearm, bow, crossbow or hurled weapon he is using gains the benefits of firing full auto (**Werewolf**, pg. 230), but the difficulty to hit is raised by two rather than three.

• **Great as a White Hill (Level Five)** — As the Fianna Gift: Gift of the Spriggan. It is taught by a Monkey-spirit.

Gifts of the Mokolé-mbembe

• **Beak of the Finch (Level Three)** — This Gift is taught by Finch, the master of adaptation. Finch helps Mokolé adapt to new situations in order to survive. They do so by reshaping themselves into a form which can accomplish a goal.

System: The Mokolé spends a Gnosis point and rolls Mnesis + Survival. She then exerts herself toward the desired change. To grow fins, she jumps into water and starts paddling. To grow a long neck she would stretch. This Gift cannot create anything new, but can adapt existing body parts to new situations. Arms could grow into wings, but a new pair of limbs would not appear from nowhere. Likewise, lungs could become gills, but to breathe air again, the Mokolé would have to change back. The effects last for one scene per Gnosis point spent.

• **Heat Wave (Level Three)** — The Mokolé can bring the heat of Lord Sun to burn his enemies. Many can stand chill, but no living thing can stand endless heat. A Sun-spirit teaches this Gift.

System: The Mokolé dances the Steps of the Sun and spends 1 Gnosis. She then rolls Wits + Expression, difficulty 5 if it is warm, 6 if cool and 8 if cold. If below freezing, the difficulty is 9. The difficulty drops by 1 for each hour of dancing, and increases by 1 if the Mokolé cannot dance except with hand motions (due to injury or imprisonment). For each success, one mile of territory surrounding the Mokolé is heated to heatwave temperatures (130°F). Any creature vulnerable to heat will lose one die from their dice pools per hour. The effects last for one hour per point of Gnosis spent. They cannot last for more than one hour after sunset.

• **Walk into My Eyes (Level Four)** — This powerful Gift allows weakness to become strength. The Mokolé have been endlessly persecuted: under some circumstances, this can be an advantage. An Ancestor-spirit teaches this Gift.

System: The Mokolé stares into the eyes of a foe and rolls Mnesis. The difficulty is 5 for a relative (including Nagah, Corax and Kin), 7 for a being who shares even one common ancestor (anyone born human, any saurian, and any Changer), and 9 for some-

thing completely alien. For each success, the foe is overwhelmed for one turn by memory as he sees all of life from the Mokolé's point of view. During this time he will not attack the Mokolé (although he may defend himself if attacked) and will not be able to use any specific Gifts or powers of his own kind (such as Garou-only Gifts, shapeshifting, or vampiric Disciplines). After returning to himself, the target is often profoundly changed. Reactions vary: Garou have withdrawn into eternal Harano, while a Sabbat Priscus blessed by this Gift ended his unlife after seeing what he had lost centuries ago. The Storyteller should determine fairly what each target would do.

Gifts of the Zhong Lung

• **Chi'ih Ming (Level One)** — Chi'ih Ming is an old word meaning balloon, and using this Gift, a Mokolé may walk on air at normal walking pace. A Bird-spirit teaches this Gift.

System: The player spends a Gnosis point and rolls Dexterity + Athletics. One success enough to activate this Gift.

• **Shou (Level One)** — As the Level Three Philodox Gift: Wisdom of the Ancient Ways.

• **Serenity (Level Four)** — As the Children of Gaia Gift.

Auspice Gifts

Rising Sun (Tung Chun/Vasanta)

• **Bellow (Level One)** — The Mokolé can shake the swamps with his powerful voice, terrifying all who hear him. A Crocodile-spirit or Alligator-spirit teaches this Gift.

System: The player spends a Rage point and rolls Rage or Willpower. Difficulty is the target's Willpower: if the roll is successful, then the listeners react as per the Delirium Reaction Chart, using the target's Willpower minus the number of successes after the first as a guide.

• **Eye of the Raptor (Level One)** — By calling on her feathered cousins' talents, the Mokolé gains the ability to see for a number of miles as if the distance were a mere twenty yards or so. This Gift is taught by a Bird-spirit.

System: The user rolls Perception + Alertness, difficulty 8. The number of successes equals the number of miles the Mokolé can see clearly, although he cannot see through obstacles.

• **Paint the Meadows (Level Two)** — The Mokolé can utter pitiable moans to lure her prey. Usually used from hiding, this Gift is suitable for hunters and fighters. Blue Jay teaches this Gift.

System: The player rolls Wits + Expression as the character moans and whimpers. The difficulty is the target's Willpower or 5, whichever is higher. For each success, the target moves closer for one turn — however, the spell is broken if the target suffers any pain.

• **Sense Silver (Level Two)** — As the Ahroun Gift.

• **Dragon's Tongue (Level Three)** — This enables the Mokolé to call lightning down on a target. This Gift is taught by a Lightning-Bringer.

System: The player spends a Willpower point and rolls Strength + Intimidation, difficulty 6. Each success inflicts one die of aggravated damage on the target. The difficulty may be increased at the Storyteller's option if there is no storm, no clouds, the Mokolé is inside, or other unfavorable conditions are present.

• **Call the Tides (Level Three)** — This Gift makes the Mokolé able to bend the tides to his will. The Gift is taught by Tidekeeper.

System: The Mokolé must be in sight of a tidal body of water (ocean, sea, river estuary). The player then makes a Gnosis roll, difficulty of 8. The number of successes determines the result:

1	The tides come in or go out twice as fast as usual.
2	Tides can be reversed, and will come in instead of go out or vice versa.
3	High tide or low tide can be brought in one scene.
4	Unusual tides (spring tide or neap tide) can be brought in one scene
5+	Freakish tides (i.e. 30' tides in Florida) can occur in one scene.

• **Combat Healing (Level Three)** — As the Level Three Ahroun Gift.

• **Hot Ichor (Level Three)** — This Gift makes the Mokolé able to gain a pool of heat energy, increasing his prowess in hunting or battle. A Raptor-spirit teaches this Gift.

System: By spending Rage, the character gains a temporary "heat pool" of one point per Rage point spent. Beginning the next turn, the Mokolé can then spend the points in the heat pool to add to Physical Attributes; the bonuses last for one turn. The pool maximum is the Mokolé's Homid-form Stamina + 5.

• **Might of the Kings (Level Three)** — As the Get of Fenris Gift: Might of Thor.

• **Anger of the Wani (Level Four)** — As the Level Five Wendigo Gift: Invoke the Spirits of the Storm. Upon using this Gift, the Mokolé falls into a trance until Sun rises once more. He offers his dreams to the Dragon Kings as thanks for this Gift.

• **Scream of Gaia (Level Four)** — As the Get of Fenris Gift.

• **Jointsnake's Mojo (Level Five)** — This Gift enables the Mokolé to rejoin severed body parts without even touching them. A severed arm will twitch and quickly wriggle back to the stump, rejoining the 'gator's body as neatly as you could ask. This Gift is taught by Jointsnake.

System: To rejoin a body part, the player need only spend one Gnosis. The severed parts must be reasonably whole (i.e., not eaten or crushed) and they must be nearby for the Gift to work. This doesn't heal any health levels of damage, but a Mokolé with this Gift can spend a Gnosis to avoid receiving any Battle Scars.

• **Wall of Granite (Level Five)** — As the Philodox Gift.

Noonday Sun (Nam Hsia/Grisma)

• **Gold Claws (Level One)** — As the Ahroun Gift: Silver Claws, save that the Mokolé's claws become gold. This Gift is mainly used against fallen or undutiful Mokolé.

• **Sight of the True Form (Level One)** — As the common Gift.

• **Truth of Olodumare (Level One)** — As the Garou Gift: Truth of Gaia. This Gift is taught by a Sun-spirit.

• **Calm (Level Two)** — As the Children of Gaia Gift. This Gift is taught by a Tuatara-spirit.

• **Strength of Purpose (Level Two)** — As the Level Two Philodox Gift.

• **Tame Sunbeam (Level Two)** — Sun, whom the Mokolé call The Face of God, is opposed to evil and darkness. He teaches his children to call upon his aid when they need it. A Sun-spirit teaches this Gift.

System: The Mokolé must spend a Gnosis point, roll Intelligence + Occult, difficulty 6, and add any True Faith in Sun to the result. The effects last for one scene, plus one more scene for each additional Gnosis point spent.

Successes	Effects
1	Illuminate any dark area with ambient light
2	Sun can pierce clouds or trees with enough brightness point out targets or injure vampires

3 The sun's rays are as strong through water, glass, clouds or cover as from a clear sky.

4 Sun's rays can light fires or bring heat when it is cold, or appear inside windowless building during the daytime.

5+ Sun can shine at night.

• **Clear Mind (Level Three)** — This Gift allows fair judgment, no matter what the distractions. A Crow-spirit teaches this Gift.

System: The Mokolé may spend as many Willpower point as she likes; each point spent adds a die to the Mental dice pool of her choice. The effects last for the duration of the scene.

• **Dragon's Tongue (Level Three)** — As the Rising Sun Gift. The difficulty may be lessened, at the Storyteller's option, if the target is a Mokolé who has failed the Duties.

• **Eyes of the Cobra (Level Three)** — As the Galliard Gift.

• **Raptor's Gaze (Level Four)** — As the Fianna Gift: Balor's Gaze.

• **Serenity (Level Four)** — As the Children of Gaia Gift.

• **Strength of the Dominator (Level Four)** — As the Shadow Lord Gift.

• **Geas (Level Five)** — As the Philodox Gift.

• **Sleep of the Dragon (Level Five)** — This Gift allows the Mokolé to enter a state of estivation. She sleeps for a time limited by duration (for instance, "three moons") or condition ("when the lake fills with water"). In either case, she sets the waking condition herself. The Mokolé does not age as she sleeps, though she may dream. Usually the Mokolé buries herself in mud as she sleeps. The sleeping Mokolé is awakened by being moved or touched, but not by ordinary noises. A Dragon-spirit teaches this Gift.

System: The Mokolé may enter the sleep as an act of will. If she sleeps for longer than the duration of one story, then she regains all her spent Gnosis.

• **Wisdom of the Sun (Level Five)** — As the Stargazer Gift: Wisdom of the Seer, save that the Mokolé must gaze directly on Lord Sun's face.

Setting Sun (Tung Chun/Vasanta)

• **Mother's Touch (Level One)** — As the Theurge Gift.

• **Resist Pain (Level One)** — As the Philodox Gift.

• **Clap of Thunder (Level Two)** — As the Shadow Lord Gift.

• **Paint the Meadows (Level Two)** — As the Rising Sun Gift.

• **Spew (Level Two)** — The Warding may guard the nest with a spew of slippery ooze. He can drink a few gallons of water and spit it out as a slimy mess. This Gift is taught by Frog or Snail-spirits.

System: The Mokolé must have drunk quite a bit of water within the last 24 hours before using this Gift, although some drink oil as a precursor. The player rolls Stamina + Expression, difficulty 7, as the Mokolé spews out water and slime onto any surface. The number of successes determines the radius, measured in paces, of the area covered with slippery slobber. Any creature treading on the place must make a Dexterity roll (plus Acrobatics, if any) or slip and fall. Mokolé may also slime pathways with their vomit, urine or other bodily fluids, resulting in offensive odors as well as slippery surfaces.

• **Armor of the Tortoise (Level Three)** — This Gift enables the Mokolé to form a hard shell around his skin while in Archid or Suchid form, protecting himself even further from harm. The Gift is taught by a Turtle or Tortoise-spirit.

System: The player rolls Stamina + Primal Urge, difficulty 6; the Mokolé must spend a turn in deep concentration. The number of successes is the number of dice added to the dice pool for soak rolls. These dice are in addition to any armor already possessed, but the Gift can be activated only once per scene.

• **Combat Healing (Level Three)** — As the Ahroun Gift.

• **Might of the Kings (Level Three)** — As the Get of Fenris Gift: Might of Thor.

• **Clenched Jaw (Level Four)** — As the Ahroun Gift.

• **Hot Ichor (Level Four)** — As the Level Three Rising Sun Gift.

• **Halo of the Sun (Level Five)** — As the Children of Gaia Gift.

• **Fossilize (Level Five)** — This Gift allows the Mokolé to consign an enemy to memory — by fossilizing him for the edification of further generations. Paleontologists, needless to say, would probably be baffled by the results. A Death-spirit teaches this Gift.

System: The Mokolé points a bone at an enemy; the player rolls Gnosis, resisted by the enemy's Willpower. For each success, one health level of unsoakable aggravated damage cripples the target. If the target dies from the effects, he becomes a petrified fossil instantly.

Midnight Sun (Pei Tung/Hemanta)

• **Darksight (Level One)** — The Shining can draw on the ambient light of the Penumbra to see clearly in darkness. This Gift is taught by a Moon-spirit.

System: The player spends a Willpower point; the effects last for one scene. The Mokolé can see without penalty in all darkness save the complete absence of light, and even then he can discern a vague outline of his surroundings.

• **Lambent Flame (Level One)** — As the Silver Fang Gift. This is taught by a Fire-spirit or by a Sun-Spirit.

• **Sense Sun (Level One)** — As the common Gift: Sense Moon, save that it allows the user to discern the presence of Sun creatures such as Mokolé and Corax. This Gift is taught by a Moon-spirit.

• **Spirits of Laughter (Level One)** — This Gift allows the Midnight Sun to invoke Laughter-spirits which make everything seem funny. A Mockingbird-spirit teaches this Gift.

System: The Mokolé spends a Gnosis point and rolls Gnosis. The difficulty is 6 for friends, 7 for strangers, 9 for enemies. For each success, one remark that someone makes will cause everyone to laugh merrily.

• **Talk (Level One)** — As the generic Gift.

• **Dreamspeak (Level Two)** — As the Galliard Gift.

• **Breaking the Tomorrow Wall (Level Two)** — This is a foretelling Gift, taught by a Crane-spirit. It enables the Mokolé to remember the future, however inaccurately.

System: The Mokolé burns a bird feather; the player spends one Gnosis point and rolls Perception + Enigmas, difficulty 6. The Mokolé can then peer beyond tomorrow and learn one vague insight per success rolled.

• **Glib Tongue (Level Two)** — As the Fianna Gift. This is taught by a Parrot-spirit.

• **Become Log (Level Three)** — As the Ragabash Gift: Blissful Ignorance, save that the Mokolé must be on a forest floor, in a stream or lake, or in another environment familiar to his varna. This Gift is taught by an Alligator-spirit.

• **Invisibility (Level Three)** — As the Uktena Gift.

• **Open Sun Bridge (Level Three)** — As the Ragabash Gift: Open Moon Bridge.

• **Fool's Luck (Level Four)** — The Shining, being owed favors by many spirits of fortune, becomes largely immune to ill luck in all its forms. This Gift is taught by a Trickster-spirit.

System: The player spends one Gnosis and rolls Gnosis, difficulty 8. Each success allows the character to convert one botched roll into a simple failure; the player may choose when to invoke this special favor, but the effects last only for one scene.

• **Shadows by the Fire Light (Level Four)** — As the Galliard Gift, save that Mokolé often tell stories as sunshafts burn dazzlingly through the trees into the wallow's darkness. When this Gift is combined with Mnesis, the result is a unique art called inwitting, in which the teller sends her audience into the memory-dreams of the Dragon Folk. This enables a storyteller to set tales in the past as far back as the Mokolé who is telling the story can remember. A Shadow-spirit teaches this Gift.

• **Sleep of the Dragon (Level Five)** — As the Noonday Sun Gift.

• **Steal Shape (Level Five)** — This Gift is rare: only two lineages possessing it are known to have survived the Wars of Rage. It enables a Mokolé to study the shape of another being for a span of time, and then to take that shape as her new breed form. In this way, the Mokolé have survived millennia of evolution on Gaia's Face. This Gift is taught by a Lungfish-spirit.

System: The Mokolé must study the new shape for at least a year. At the end of that time, she may spend a point of permanent Gnosis and assume the new shape. The shape must be close enough to the old one that her soul will inhabit it. The Storyteller is free to rule on what will and will not work. Normally the Mokolé will then pass this shape on to her offspring, and they will replace one of her forms with the new. Only a few Mokolé have managed to make this work, but it is how a new varna comes to be able to incarnate shapeshifter souls, and is allegedly responsible for the rise of both the Corax and Nagah. Some loremasters say that all the Changing Breeds originated this way. However, this is unlikely.

• **Thousand Secret Faces (Level Five)** — This Gift is taught only to trusted friends. It allows the user to assume the illusion of almost any shape that she has personally seen. This is not true shapeshifting but is an almost perfect simulation. This Gift is taught by a spirit of deception.

System: The user must spend some times studying the shape she wishes to take. At the Storyteller's discretion, the difficulty may increase if she does not study it long enough. She then spends one point each of Willpower and Gnosis and rolls Manipulation + Subterfuge, difficulty 7. The effects last for one day per success; the user may dispel the illusion at any time. When trying to penetrate this illusion, such as by using Gifts, the difficulty is at least 9.

• **Take the True Form (Level Five)** — As the Level Four Philodox Gift.

Shrouded Sun (Sai Chau/Zarad)

• **Call the Rain (Level One)** — A power that has been responsible for more than one crocodile cult, this Gift allows the Mokolé to summon rain from a clear sky. It is taught by Rainbird or Rain-spirits.

System: The player rolls Expression + Rituals, difficulty 6. One success brings a spatter. Three bring a steady drizzle. Five or more bring rain. If rain is already falling when the Mokolé uses this Gift, it becomes a downpour. If a heavy rain is already falling, the result is a catastrophic flood.

• **Mother's Touch (Level One)** — As the Theurge Gift.

• **Sense Designer (Level One)** — As the metis Gift: Sense Wyrm, save that it detects Weaver manifestations.

• **Sense Dissolver (Level One)** — As the metis Gift: Sense Wyrm.

• **Sense Magic (Level One)** — As the Uktena Gift.

• **Spirit Speech (Level One)** — As the Theurge Gift.

• **Talk (Level One)** — As the generic Gift.

• **Breaking the Tomorrow Wall (Level Two)** — As the Midnight Sun Gift.

• **Dream the Matre's Mind (Level Two)** — This Gift, taught by human Ancestor-spirits or an animal spirit especially renowned for a long memory, such as Elephant, allows the Mokolé to leave her body behind as her spirit slips into the astral realm, or Deep Umbra.

System: The player must roll Gnosis, difficulty of the local Gauntlet rating. Successful use of the Gift renders the Mokolé's physical body unconscious while her spirit slips into the astral realm. Five successes indicates that the Mokolé may even travel into the true High Umbra, though she is still attached by a silver cord to her body. Failure means the character cannot leave her body and a botch casts the astral self to a random destination or breaks the silver cord. For more information on Deep Umbral travel, see the Sunset chapter.

• **Become Log (Level Two)** — As the Mokolé Gift.

• **Command Spirit (Level Two)** — As the Midnight Sun Gift.

• **Send the Dream (Level Two)** — As the Level Three metis Gift: Mental Speech.

• **Walking Between Worlds (Level Two)** — As the Level Three common Gift.

• **Call Water Spirit (Level Three)** — As the Uktena Gift: Call Fire Spirit, save that a Water-spirit is called. The Mokolé must have a water source. The water spirit will move water, dampen a foe, or short out a power system at the Mokolé's command.

• **Deeper Lungs (Level Three)** — The Mokolé may reserve air within himself, allowing him to live for a period of time without breathing. This Gift is taught by Turtle-spirits.

System: In the material world, this Gift allows the Mokolé to hold her breath for a number of hours equal to his Stamina. In the Umbra, the duration is the same number of days. In any event, when the duration expires, the Mokolé must be able to breathe air for a full five minutes before invoking this Gift again.

• **Exorcism (Level Three)** — As the Theurge Gift.

• **Open Sun Bridge (Level Three)** — As the Midnight Sun Gift.

• **Shadow Wings (Level Three)** — This Gift allows a Mokolé to fly through the "nothing" of the Umbra, ignoring the various paths and tracks in favor of a more direct route from Realm to Realm. This Gift is taught by a Sky-spirit.

System: The Mokolé must have the Gift: Walking Between Worlds to enter the Umbra, and must move to a place where "flying" between the Realms is possible. She may be using Dream the Matre's Mind. Should she be able to reach an Anchorhead, she may fly through the Deep Umbra as well. No roll is necessary: the Mokolé simply wills her wings to unfold.

• **Grasp the Beyond (Level Four)** — As the Theurge Gift.

• **Walk the Matre's Mind (Level Four)** — Similar to the Gift Dream the Matre's Mind, this Gift lets the Mokolé actually enter the astral realm, the Deep Umbra in physical form. Alternately, if she is already astral, she can remove her cord relatively safely. The use of this Gift is rare, as fewer Mokolé are versed in it, but it allows the Mokolé to enter the embodiment of Gaia's memory without leaving a helpless body behind and without a silver cord. Some Mokolé postulate that the silver cord becomes invisible, but is still there. This Gift is taught only by various spirits familiar with the Deep Umbra.

System: No roll is needed; the effects are automatic A Mokolé who has used the Gift: Dream the Matre's Mind and passes into the High Umbra may use Walk the Matre's Mind to remove her silver cord and continue. If she does this, she must make sure to return before her body suffers too greatly: her Stamina is the number of scenes that she will be able to voyage (at the Storyteller's discretion).

• **Recapitulate (Level Four)** — The Mokolé can attack enemies with their own evolutionary heritage, forcing them to retreat back down the tree of life toward the primordial ooze of Gaia. The foe is transformed into a lower form of life by force of will. A Designer-spirit named Haeckel teaches this Gift, and will demand a favor in return.

System: The Mokolé shouts the enemy's name and certain Words out of time. He then rolls Mnesis + Intimidation, difficulty 7. For each success, the enemy devolves through one stage of existence: one success makes him a primitive ratlike mammal, two make him a reptile, and so on. The effects last one scene.

• **Gorgon's Gaze (Level Five)** — As the Black Fury Gift.

• **The Malleable Spirit (Level Five)** — As the Theurge Gift.

Decorated Sun (Nam Hsia/Grisma)

• **Cooking (Level One)** — As the Bone Gnawer Gift.

• **Mother's Touch (Level One)** — As the Theurge Gift.

• **Persuasion (Level One)** — As the homid Garou Gift. This Gift is taught by a Snake-spirit.

• **Pilot Snake (Level One)** — This Gift allows Mokolé to summon the helpful pilot snake, a creature who knows how to get places. He can help find safe havens, drinkable water, wallows, and so on. The Gift is taught by a Snake-spirit.

System: The Mokolé calls on Pilot Snake and rolls Gnosis. The Mokolé must be in a place where there are pilot snakes (such as the American Southeast). The difficulty is 6 in wilderness, 7 in sight of human works, 8 in a park or suburb, and 9 in city areas. Near the Dissolver's works, it is 10. The number of successes measures the Gift's success; usually three is sufficient. Pilot Snake does not speak, but will guide the group anywhere within reason. He cannot provide guidance to things that he does not know about, such as Garou caerns. Once he is done, he departs.

• **Talk (Level One)** — As the common Gift.

• **Wind Beneath My Wings (Level One)** — This Gift, originated by a Pteranodon Mokolé, helps Mokolé travel more easily by marching or flying in formations. The strength of the whole group can serve to help each member. This Gift is taught by Goose.

System: The Mokolé assembles her fellow travelers in a line (for marching) or V formation (for flying) and rolls Stamina + Gnosis, difficulty 7. The number of successes is the number of travelers who can share the Stamina of the strongest member of the group (who will usually take the lead). If the formation is broken, the extra Stamina disappears. A botch reduces a group member to 1 Stamina.

• **Call to Duty (Level Two)** — As the Philodox Gift.

• **Dragon Drill (Level Two)** — This Gift allows the Gathering to organize her clutch into a potent work force. She can take an ability known to one clutch member and share it with all. The Gift can empower Kin as well as Mokolé. It is taught by Ant-spirits.

System: The Mokolé speaks of the Skill or Knowledge to her clutchmates in a sort of "pep talk." She then spends a Gnosis point and rolls Manipulation + the appropriate Skill or Knowledge. The base difficulty is 7, but the Storyteller can make it higher if the Ability is an unlikely one, such teaching lockpicking to suchids. The number of successes is the number of clutchmates who gain the Knowledge or Skill at the donor's level for one scene. This Gift cannot transfer spirit Gifts, rites, or other such advantages.

• **Walking Between Worlds (Level Two)** — As the Level Three generic Gift.

• **Long Running (Level Three)** — This Gift allows the Mokolé to reduce the travel time of a journey, whether on foot or in a vehicle. It is taught by a Sea turtle-spirit.

System: The player spends one Gnosis and rolls Dexterity + Athletics (or Drive) at the difficulty of the local Gauntlet. Each success decreases the travel time by 5%.

• **Reshape Object (Level Three)** — As the homid Garou Gift.

• **Infest (Level Four)** — As the Bone Gnawer Gift.

• **Strength of the Dominator (Level Four)** — As the Shadow Lord Gift

• **Calm the Flock (Level Five)** — As the Glass Walker Gift.

• **Obedience (Level Five)** — As the Shadow Lord Gift.

Eclipsed Sun (Sai Chau/Zarad)

• **Aura of Confidence (Level One)** — As the Shadow Lord Gift. This Gift is taught by a Dinosaur King or some other royalty.

• **Bellow (Level One)** — As the generic Gift.

• **Lambent Flame (Level One)** — As the Silver Fang Gift.

• **Razor Claws (Level One)** — As the Ahroun Gift.

• **Awe (Level Two)** — As the Silver Fang Gift.

• **Dazzle (Level Two)** — As the Level Three Children of Gaia Gift; it is taught by a spirit servant of Dragon.

• **Walking Between Worlds (Level Two)** — As the Level Three generic Gift.

• **Eye of the Cobra (Level Three)** — As the Galliard Gift.

• **Hot Ichor (Level Three)** — As the Rising Sun Gift.

• **Wrath of Dragon (Level Three)** — As the Silver Fang Gift: Wrath of Gaia.

• **Mastery (Level Four)** — As the Silver Fang Gift.

• **Sun Enfleshed (Level Four)** — This powerful Gift allows a Mokolé to embody Sun's holy fire. As the Mokolé prays to Sun, she appears to burst into silent, solar flames, lighting up the area as brightly as noon and burning her opponents with a touch. This Gift is taught by a Sun-spirit.

System: The player spends three Gnosis to call on Sun's radiance. Any vampires within line of sight react as if they were looking on the sun, and the Mokolé's claws, teeth and tail inflict one extra health level of damage. Finally, the Mokolé's touch inflicts damage as if it were gold.

• **Army of the Ancestors (Level Five)** — This rare Gift allows a Mokolé to materialize her Archid-form characteristics in an entirely different way. The Mokolé can call on the ancestors who gave him the shape he wears, bringing them out of the mists of the Memory to challenge his opponents. This Gift is taught by an Ancestor-spirit.

System: The Mokolé calls on his ancestor while indicating his bodily "gifts" that came from them. He then makes a Gnosis roll, difficulty 8. For each success, one ancestor appears. For example, a Mokolé with wings could call Pteranodon, while one with Huge Size could summon Apatosaurus. The ancestors are as intelligent as the one who summons them, and usually cooperate (unless the summoner wants them to do something stupid or ridiculous). The ancestors stay for one scene, then depart back to the depths of Mnesis. Depending on the scene into which they were summoned, they may not wish ever to return.

• **Dream Semblance (Level Five)** — This Gift may be exercised once in a Mokolé's lifetime. It allows the Mokolé to become a True Dragon for the duration of one scene. Once the confrontation is over, the dream will depart. This Gift is taught by Dragon.

System: The Mokolé prays to Dragon and makes a Wits + Mnesis roll with a difficulty of 7. The statistics of a True Dragon are up to the storyteller, but such a creature is extremely powerful. Its power is usually focused on the routing of Dragon's foes. The Gift cannot be invoked a second time, and often Mokolé who invoke it even once die after Dragon's foes are routed.

• **Stop Continental Drift (Level Five)** — This Gift invokes the spirits of the continents as they float across Gaia's Face and through the millennia. The Crowning can act as though continental drift did not exist, traveling as the Kings did. This Gift is taught by a spirit of the land (such as Mountain or Stone).

System: The Crowning sets out on a journey and rolls Stamina + Rituals, difficulty 7. The Crowning and her clutchmates speak and sing in the Dragon's Tongue as they travel. The number of successes needed depends on how far they want to go. However, the journey will be conducted as if the continents were still joined; a trip from South America to Africa could be a short walk of a few days.

Mokolé Rites

Peter sat thinking. "So, Jeffo, could just anyone learn those rites? It seems like you're teaching me an awful lot."

"Yer one of us now, mate. Not sayin' y' can't go home, but we're none of us afraid of you." He drew on the pipe; the tobacco/pituri mix filled the air with smoke. The coal glowed red as the sunlight that coppered all the pinnacles and towers of rock.

"What do you mean? You think I'm Mokolé myself now?"

"You are Mokolé, all but yer shape. You're come of the Kings same as me, and you've got the Memory. Yer Mokolé and egg-smasher both. You'd be the first we remember to be so."

I am both Mokolé and Garou. This is crazy.

This is the end of the Wars.

"So what else do I have to know, to be a dragon? I mean, they didn't exactly cover it in Career Day back at school."

Morwangu spoke once more, each word filled with centuries of meaning. How could a language, a thing made with the mouth, convey so much?

How could a man become a dragon?

Mokolé rites are ancient, some dating to the Time of the Kings. The Garou and Mokolé share the Rite of Accomplishment, hunting prayers, greetings to the Sun and in the case of Shining, the Moon, the Rite of Talisman Dedication, the Baptism of Fire, the Rite of Spirit Awakening, the Rite of Summoning, and the Rites of the Fetish and Totem. Other rites may also figure in certain wallows. The Mokolé have few or no rites connected with Umbral travel, as they seldom enter the Umbra because of The Innocents. They also have few rites of judgment and punishment, although some few practice the Rite: Eater of the Dead, which the Mokolé-mbembe taught to the Bubasti (see **Bastet**). They do have seasonal rites, which differ from those of the Garou.

Rites of Accord

Rite of Breeding

Level One

This rite is practiced by all streams of Mokolé. It consists of elaborate courtship protocols, exchanges of go-betweens, ceremonial singing and dancing, and mating. It ensures that Mokolé mate with a suitable Kinfolk partner and not with other Mokolé.

System: The Mokolé involved dances, sings, and otherwise celebrates, finally spending a Gnosis at the rite's climax. If the prospective partner is completely unsuitable (for example, sterile, horribly diseased, or another Mokolé) then the Mokolé will know. If not, then mating can take place.

Shedding Hide

Level One

This rite may be performed alone or in groups. It is usually done once a year. The Mokolé sheds her skin over a period of days or weeks, and at the same time sheds any Dissolver-taint accumulated through toxins or through contact with Dissolver-creatures.

System: The ritemaster rolls Charisma + Rituals as usual; the difficulty is 5 plus the number of times she has been Dissolver-tainted, such as by touching fomori or vampires, eating tainted food, speaking the words of the Dissolver, and so forth The maximum difficulty is 9. The number of successes gained indicates the number of levels of

Dissolver taint that pass away. The Mokolé will begin to itch horribly as the toxin works its way up to her skin. As she scratches, her skin peels off, revealing new skin beneath. Tattoos, scars or brands usually disappear during the shedding. This rite is highly refreshing to the celebrant.

Silence of the Oracles

Level Two

This merciful rite allows the ritemaster to protect a person from memories that would drive them mad. It is often used to protect survivors of torture, molestation, rape, or massacres. It allows the wounded person to live normally without going mad.

System: The ritemaster confers with the patient as she performs the rite. For each success, a memory may be sealed. The recipient will still know that his trauma occurred, but will not be injured by the memories and will be able to remember without pain. If the rite is used to aid a Derangement or Harano, the patient is allowed scene of rational behavior for every success on the ritemaster's roll.

Rites of Death

Last Communion

Level Two

This rite enables a Mokolé adept to receive Mnesis from a comrade. The two Mokolé must gaze into each others' eyes, and the giver of Mnesis will speak of a memory which he or she holds, or if unable to speak, will concentrate on it. She will then breathe out the memory, and the taker will breathe it in. Once the memory is passed, the donor has no more access to it. This rite is often used on battlefields to preserve the Mnesis of the dying, and is the only reason that so much Mnesis survived the Wars of Rage. Many highly emotional scenes have centered on Last Communion.

System: Either the donor or the recipient can be the ritemaster for this rite. If the giver is unconscious or dead, the taker can breathe in her last breath, but the Mnesis transferred will usually be confused.

Shed the Crocodile's Tears

Level Three

This rite shows a Mokolé's contrition for killing a foe. The Mokolé, before leaving a battlefield, weeps over the corpse of a fallen enemy (or friend). The length of time that she weeps depends on the depth of feeling involved.

System: The Mokolé must expend a point of Gnosis as she enacts the rite. Success indicates that the spirit or wraith of the person involved will not seek revenge on the ritemaster. If the Mokolé sacrifices a permanent point of Gnosis, then even the kin and allies of the fallen believe that the Mokolé was not a crazed killer, but was only doing what was necessary.

The Bones of Time

Level Five

This rare rite is known to a few Mokolé of the Americas and China. It allows a ritemaster to retrieve Mnesis from remains of the dead, including "dragons' bones," fossil dinosaurs, and similar items. To enact the rite the ritemaster must caress the remains while chanting the Song of the Bones, which lasts for many hours if all its cantos are sung. Other Mokolé sometimes dance as accompaniment to the ritemaster's song.

System: The ritemaster rolls Charisma + Rituals as usual, difficulty 7 (if the remains are mutilated, such as a lizard-skin coat, the difficulty is 9). When the Song is done, the Mokolé may enter a Mnesis trance for one day. He may then add the number of successes gained on the rite to his Mnesis roll. The Storyteller will determine what memories could be gleaned — the dragons' bones of Chinese medicine shops or the dinosaur fossils of the Smithsonian might possess some interesting memories indeed. Any number of Mokolé may attempt to gain memories from the bones, but if more try than the ancestor's Gnosis score (or more than one, if the ancestor was not Mokolé), the remains will crumble.

Mystic Rites

Rite of the Stone

Level Three

This allows the Mokolé to attach a mystical stone to his body. The stone can be a belly stone, giving strength, or a skull stone, giving wisdom. A belly stone must be heavy, smooth, and properly shaped — the search for the perfect stone can last a long time.

Skull stones (carbuncles, or "dragon stones") are much harder to find, as they must also be perfect, flawless jewels. The jewel must be cut by an artisan with stonecutting skill, then heated to searing heat, such as in Sun's fire, in a forge or in volcanic heat. The stone is then burned onto the Mokolé's forehead, where it is visible in Archid form (in some Mokolé, it is visible in Homid form as well).

System: During the rite, the Mokolé must fill the stone with Gnosis by meditating in Sun's light (save that Gnosis goes into the stone instead of into the Mokolé). The stone's maximum Gnosis is equal to the ritemaster's current Gnosis. The stone is then swallowed, if a belly stone, or branded into the forehead, if a skull stone. In hunting or battle, the Mokolé may spend the stone's Gnosis on a one-for-one basis; belly stones add to Strength for one scene, and skull stones may add to any Mental Attribute. Once the stone's Gnosis is expended, the stone is absorbed fully into the Mokolé's body.

Garou who hunt Mokolé sometimes seek these mystic stones, and use them to store Gnosis. In addition, when an ancient Mokolé dies, her stone can be passed to a younger Mokolé without losing its Gnosis. Mnesis records more powerful stones, and sleeping elders often have a mighty stone from a past age.

Boat of the Sun

Level Four

This rite allows the ritemaster to borrow Sun's boat for a time to transport himself and colleagues to any destination under the sun.

System: The ritemaster must behold Sun's Face, then assemble the boat's crew, who must sit as if in a boat and hold their hands as if paddling. He may take as many passengers as he has current points of Gnosis. The ritemaster declares the destination, which along with the port of departure, must be in Sun's light. He must know the destination through having been there, or through a Mnesis roll (Storyteller's discretion). He then calls out the strokes for the paddlers and enacts the rite. The difficulty is 6 for a destination that the ritemaster has seen and 8 if he has only Mnesis to guide him. For each success, one person reaches the destination. The others are left behind. If he botches, then one passenger per 1 rolled is unharmed, but stranded in between the two places.

Burn the Library

Level Four

This rite erases memories. It is named for the day when the Library of Alexandria burned, and two Mokolé were the only ones left with its knowledge. The rite was first used when Ancient-My-Enemy, a Mokolé warrior, erased his mind to prevent Garou from locating his clutch.

System: To perform this rite, the ritemaster may name the memories that will be destroyed and then speak Unmaking Words, which are perilous to hear. The Words will seek out the memories and destroy them. For each success, one memory is destroyed. The ritemaster may use this to erase his own memories, although a failure means that he erases his knowledge of how to perform the rite. A botch indicates that *all* his knowledge is gone.

Walking In Your Footsteps

Level Four

This rite enables a Mokolé to follow those who have gone before her. The ritemaster locates the footsteps of a past Mokolé; these may be made the day before, a hundred years before, or be fossilized. However, the footsteps must be visible. As the Mokolé enacts the rite, she stands in the footsteps of the ancestor and calls for the ancestor's aid. If successful, her forebear's ability is passed on.

System: In addition to the ordinary rite roll, the ritemaster must make a Mnesis roll or have a remembrancer make one for her, in order to know what the ancestor did, or could do. The Storyteller makes this roll and keeps the result secret. If the rite is a success, one Ability owned by the ancestor, including Mnesis is made available to the ritemaster for the duration of the story. However, if the Storyteller determines that the Mnesis roll failed, or that the ancestor did not have this ability, then another attribute possessed by the ancestor, such as arthritis, could come to the ritemaster. If the roll is a botch, the number of 1's rolled is the number of permanent points lost by the ritemaster in an area of the Storyteller's choice.

Rite of Anamnesis

Level Five

This rite enables a Mokolé to communicate Mnesis to another directly. The Mokolé who wishes to do so can pass on visual impressions, thoughts and feelings. However, the communion is imperfect.

System: The remembrancer and the subject must share one of the teacher plants of Gaia (a hallucinogen). The subject automatically takes one health level of damage from the noxious drugs. The remembrancer must succeed in a Mnesis roll to find the desired memory, and then make a Gnosis roll against a difficulty of the subject's Willpower. In the case of non-Mokolé subjects, the difficulty is 9. The number of successes determines the extent of memories communicated. In unusual cases, the rite can be performed more than once on the same person, resulting in one person with vast amounts of Mnesis. The memories of lost clutches and bloodlines have been saved in this way. However, if one person receives the Mnesis of more people than he has points of Willpower, then he will almost certainly become insane. The Mnesis given may then be passed on to the descendants of the recipient as with any other Mnesis.

Rite of the Eidolon

Level Five

Mnesis is powerful: it is a direct exercise of the Mokolé's purpose as the Memory of Gaia. The Rite of the Eidolon allows the images (eidolons) contained in Mnesis to take shape. It is different from the Shadows by the Fire Light Gift in that the image is not merely "backdrop"; it is as real as the mind of the remembrancer who imagines it.

System: The rite may be performed alone or by a group. The ritemaster goes into a Mnesis trance, focusing on a person or thing of the past (such as an Egyptian inscription, African statue or a long-lost ancestor) and meditates for a number of hours equal to his Mnesis score (which must allow him to behold the period of history that the eidolon is from). He then spends one Gnosis to materialize the eidolon for one scene. To preserve it for another scene, he must spend another Gnosis point. The number of successes on the rite roll is the number of things that the eidolon is capable of:

Successes	**Eidolon's strength**
1	The eidolon is visible as a vague outline to observers.
2	The eidolon can be seen clearly.
3	The eidolon can answer questions by nodding, shaking its head, or gesturing, but cannot speak. If the image is of a nonliving thing, it can be seen clearly enough to answer any questions about its appearance and is three-dimensional.
4	The eidolon can speak in response to a question, but cannot say anything that the remembrancer does not already know.
5+	The eidolon can access the deepest recesses of Mnesis and can speak as if it were the living thing which it once was. If an object, it can be touched and handled as if real.

Note that the eidolon is a memory, not a ghost. It does not come from the Shadowlands and it probably does not know any cosmic secrets. The storyteller can allow this to become a voodoo-like 'summoning' with dark implications if he wishes to do so, or allow it to be a glimpse of lost glories.

Rite of Lost Dreams

Level Five

This rite allows any person to be lowered into the Sea of Shadows with the express purpose of regaining memories that have been lost on account of a whole clutch being destroyed. The person who goes does not have to be Mokolé. This is more than just a dangerous form of Mnesis; it allows the recipient to make those memories a part of them. In a sense, it brings a dead clutch back to life. The reasons for doing this are varied, but are always serious; this rite is a deadly affair.

System: The ritemaster first summons spirits of War and Time, who will accompany the quester. The ritemaster must find some way to compensate them. The storyteller should keep track of the spirits and their nature and powers. When being lowered into the Sea of Shadows, the subject of the rite will first fall blindly into the Abyss. If all goes well, the spirit guides will protect the subject from the ravenous Dead who lurk there. This won't prevent them from vainly clawing, screaming and threatening the subject. They can also offer to grant him favors, or offer to "spare" him from harm. They are usually lying, of course. Occasionally, a powerful monstrosity may come along, and unless the quester can climb out of the Abyss very soon, he will probably die, as he will have to fight the attacker without being able to see it. He will also risk losing his mind from the madness that these infernal beings carry or from fear. If you have **Wraith: The Oblivion**, use rules for Spectres. Otherwise, assume that the attackers are Dark Umbral spirits roughly equal to the traveler in power. If he passes these spirits, he then goes into the Sea of Shadows itself.

If the subject goes deep enough into the Sea, he will experience some part of the memories sought, and will incorporate them into himself. As such memories would otherwise be lost, this is one of the most honorable feats a Mokolé can perform.

Rite of the Sleeping Dragon

Level Five

This rite enables the ritemaster to send another into the Sleep of the Dragon; the effects are much like those of the Gift of the same name).

System: The ritemaster must lay the sleeper down and cover her (in mud, in a hill of stones, in a mummy case, etc.) while reciting the Chant of the Dragon. If the sleeper resists, the difficulty is her Willpower. The sleeper can be awakened by being moved or touched, or by a condition set by the ritemaster. The ritemaster can use this rite to put himself to sleep.

Seasonal Rites

Rite of Sunreturn

Level Three

Each winter solstice (December 21 in the Northern Hemisphere, June 21 in the Southern), Sun is at his weakest. Darkness is strong as Gaia turns away from his heat and light. The Mokolé usually gather at such times and perform the Rite of Sunreturn to strengthen him. The rite takes many forms among the different streams: the Mokolé-Mbembe light candles and give each other presents of cakes and sweets baked in circular shapes. They keep watch all night long with songs and bonfires until Sun shows his face again. The Zhong Lung meditate, asking that the Wheel turn uninterrupted. The Makara, who call this festival Diwali, illuminate the night with lamps and burn incense to show Sun the way to come back. The Gumagan stage mock battles in which one party represents Sun and the other darkness. Adepts among the Gumagan also enter the Dreamtime before Sunrise and face Sun's enemies, daring them to show their faces.

System: The ritemaster first oversees the preparations for the rite, which take different forms. She then participates (eating cakes, drinking rum, singing songs or similar activity) all night long. The rite's difficulty is 7 for normal circumstances, 8 for a bleak winter. For each success, one of the celebrants gets one additional die to use once before the next winter solstice.

Failure means that Sun rises in a black cloud and the ritemaster loses her sun dice until she beholds her Sun sign again. A botch may be interpreted by the Storyteller to mean that Sun does not rise or that some other disaster befalls.

Wallow (Caern) Rites

Feed The Wallow

Level One

This rite takes a small amount of food and increases it to provide food for many.

System: The ritemaster blesses the food and divides it while performing the rite. The number of successes is the power by which the food is increased. A dinner for two would serve four if there were two successes, and sixteen if there were four successes.

Rite of the Illuminated Wallow

Level One

This rite is very similar to the Rite of the Opened Caern, save that Sun's light must fill the wallow with its blessing. For Midnight Suns, a night sky is appropriate to "illuminate" the wallow with darkness. Note that the ritemaster must please not only the spirits, but the sleeping elder, if there is one. The method for which these creatures can be bested varies from wallow to wallow. For example, if the elder was a mancala player, playing a riotous game in the wallow's sands might illuminate a wallow of laughter, while an elder who had fought the Garou all her life might demand a much darker ritual...

System: As the Rite of the Opened Caern.

Rite of the Nesting Mound

Level One

This rite enables a mother to pile up earth and vegetation to create a protective nest for her eggs. Although this is common behavior among crocodilians and monitors, the ritual version grants the eggs an extra measure of spiritual protection.

System: If performed properly, the rite keeps the eggs at optimum temperature until they hatch. The eggs will either hatch twice as quickly or twice as slowly, depending on how the mother performed the rite and built the mound; some mothers try using this rite to ensure a certain sun auspice for their children.

Save Hatchling

Level One

Over 90% of potential suchid Mokolé and other reptiles die in their first year of life from disease and predation. This rite creates a link between parent and child, allowing the parent to know any one child's condition at any one time.

System: Once the rite is performed, the parent need only concentrate for a turn on a given hatchling and the child's relative condition (safe, in immediate danger, wounded, and so on) is revealed.

The Gator's Burrow

Level Four

As the Garou rite: The Badger's Burrow; naturally, this rite is used to protect a wallow.

Open Sun Bridge

Level Four

This rite enables Mokolé to open paths from one place to another "through the heart of the sun." The Sun Bridge can be invoked when Sun's brilliance dazzles the eyes, and carries Mokolé from one wallow to another. A normal means of using a Sun Bridge is to pass at sunrise or sunset, allowing the "sun path" created by the motion of light in water to serve as a highway across the world. Travel is instantaneous or nearly so. The wallows involved must have a pool or body of water to allow passage into the Umbra. This water must be blessed with the rite at least once in living memory (not once a year as with a Moon Bridge). This means that as long as a sleeper remains who enacted the rite, Mokolé can open a way through the Sun Bridge by using the Gift: Open Sun Bridge or the Rite of the Illuminated Wallow. However, to create a Sun Bridge, to decide the destination to be reached, or to ascertain the safety of the passage, this rite is necessary.

System: The participants meditate as the ritemaster performs the rite; the difficulty is 8 minus the level of the wallow. The number of successes must equal the level of the target wallow. There need to be three more successes if no true Mokolé are watching at the other end (i.e., if a wallow destination is tended only by a sleeping elder).

Citadel of the Dragon

Level Five

Through chanting that helps her dig into her Mnesis while guiding a group of artisans, this rite allows the ritemaster to direct the carving of stone structures with images of the Dragon Kings. These images are so horrific that they tap into the terror that the Mokolé cause in mammals. This rite once allowed Mokolé to construct stone citadels hidden from mankind.

System: To perform the ritual, the ritemaster must make a Charisma + Rituals roll, and the least talented of the artisans must make a Dexterity + Crafts roll (substituting Expression or Repair if the Storyteller prefers), the difficulty being 7. The Storyteller will determine the number of successes needed depending on the size of the structure: a small shrine will take fewer days than a castle. If the rite succeeds, the building will cause the Delirium.

Unfortunately, Mokolé know that fear engenders hatred, and occasional hunters are strong-willed enough to fight instead of fleeing, especially if they attack at night when the stones can't be seen clearly.

Rites of the Gumagan

Djunggawon

Level One

This Rite of Renown is a rite of passage for Kinfolk and Gumagan. It takes place when they are young. The mob will assemble at a waterhole or sacred site. The men (for a boy) or women (for a girl) go off together. They then tell the child about the Gumagan and the spirits of the Dreamtime. The rite involves body art: painting, circumcision, or the removal of one tooth. For Kinfolk, this is the moment at which the adolescents become adults. Gumagan usually pass from the ceremony into their great trance in which they dream their Archid form.

System: Men and women who bear the scars of this rite will be recognized by anyone else who is also initiated this way, and receive an extra die on Social rolls with any native people of Bandaiyan. Thereafter they may learn the rituals and songs that they are in line to inherit from uncles, aunts and other elders.

Suchids perform this rite as well, but the Mokolé themselves initiate the young one by biting them.

The Oknanikilla

Level One

The Gumagan, Australia's native Mokolé, originated this rite and allowed their allies, the Bunyip, to share it. It is performed alone. The ritemaster, who must be a gravid female, makes a journey along the "paths of the ancestors" (songlines) to an oknanikilla, a place where a totem has manifested. Usually this place will be a wallow, or it once was one. (Of course, many oknanikilla are now wallows of the egg-smashers). The totems give special favor to anyone born in their sacred sites.

System: After performing the rite, the mother-to-be spends one or more Gnosis points, and lays her eggs or gives birth on the site. She remains there until the eggs hatch (if suchid) or until she is able to walk after the birth (if homid). The number of Gnosis spent is the number of additional dice that the child may roll, when an adult, when trying to call the totem of the sacred place.

Songs of the Dreamtime

Level One

This rite is associated with spirit songs. The ritemaster must sing the song for a place (such as a songline) or a thing (such as a tjurunga; see below). He is then able to use the songline to travel or read the memories of the ancestor, usually via the Gifts of the Gumagan.

System: The roll is Manipulation + Rituals, difficulty 6. However, to learn the rite, you must inherit the right to do so.

Into the Waterhole

Level Two

This rite allows the soul of a dead person to be free. The body is disposed of by exposure, cremation or burial. The ritemaster then sings and dances and burns the dead person's possessions while calling their name. The soul passes on into a waterhole to be reborn, and does not haunt the living anymore. Most souls welcome this rite. Some, frighteningly, do not...

System: Like other Rites of Death, the roll is Charisma + Rituals.

Tjurunga

Level Four

This Rite enables a Gumagan to put some of their Mnesis into a carved and painted board, a tjurunga. The Mnesis can be accessed by anyone who knows the spirit songs.

Gumagan mobs often trade tjurunga. This is a common way to establish alliances and unify the people. The hereditary owners of tjurunga are very choosy about whom they exchange them with, or at least they used to be. Tjurunga are

exchanged across thousands of miles among mobs who know each other well.

There are said to be three tjurunga left which were made by the Bunyip before they perished. No one knows where these mystic spirit boards are located, but the Gumagan are looking for them. They hope to find them before the European Garou do.

System: The ritemaster must sacrifice a point of permanent Gnosis and carve and paint the board during the rite. The tjurunga is then stored in a sacred cave or other such place. Anyone seeking to read it must sing and make a Expression + Rituals roll, difficulty 7. The number of successes is the number of memories that emerge.

Rites of the Zhong Lung

Shedding Bones

Level Five

This powerful rite allows the Zhong Lung to prolong his life. He must first prepare a medicinal potion of herbs to restore the balance of yin and yang. This takes some time. He may also engage an herbalist to make it for him. He will then identify his weakest and oldest bones, and push them out through his skin. As he does so, his youth returns to him.

System: As the rite is performed, the Zhong Lung must sacrifice a permanent point of Gnosis to grow a new bone for each bone expelled. For each point of Gnosis thus sacrificed (and each bone renewed), five years of physical age return to the ritemaster. The cast-off bones are valued by wu-magicians, herbalists, and paleontologists.

What's the race? Call again
in some millennium
Memory is dynastic.
— Gill Holland, "Guessing the Alligators at the Charles Towne Landing"

Morwangu said, "No Mokolé will trust a wolf. We remember you all too well. To you, the Wars of Rage were a long time ago. To us, it's like yesterday. You saw it yourself."

Peter inhaled deeply before answering. "Yeah. But, Morwangu, the Mother-Cow is dying. And, as much as you hate the Garou, we're fighting to save Her. Isn't that what you want?"

"Yeah. But The Memory says—"

"I know. I remember the Wars of Rage too. Maybe not as well. But Trees Dream gave me The Memory. And — and there's everything in there. There's all that hate and bloodshed, but there's a time when we were one, too. You remember the First Times. I know you do."

The black eyes narrowed to slits under the akubra. "Yeah."

"Then Mokolé and Garou can live in peace. You know we can. It's in Mnesis. Morwangu, we have to try this. The Mokolé know too much. You have to help us save the Mother!"

"Well. You're not just blowing smoke. Let's see what the clutch says."

They walked toward the waterhole where dragons and Kin waited.

The Clutch

The clutch is the first social unit of Mokolé and Kin. It consists of two to thirty Mokolé and their Kin, who usually number a few dozen to a hundred or so. Not all Mokolé belong to clutches: a few are solitary by temperament, a few more because there is too little prey to support many Mokolé, and some because no other Mokolé live where they live. Mokolé without a clutch are not reviled or pitied (if there's a legitimate reason for them to have none), but there are a lot of things that they can't do. Most Mokolé belong to a clutch and work to further its goals. The term comes from a clutch of eggs, and in the Time of the Kings, a clutch of many Mokolé would often hatch from one nest. As opposed to a pack, a social unit which originated from the cooperative hunting of wolves, a clutch originates at birth, from the fact that eggs are safer in their nest and nests are safer when guarded. The term persisted through the Age of Sleep and to the present day. The title is important. To "clutch" is to hold closely. Mokolé don't always love their clutchmates, but they know to stick together.

A clutch is not a pack, and it's not a family. It is Mokolé united as if the same eggs had hatched them (which is sometimes the case). The members are interlocking and interconnecting parts of a whole. The clutch is more than the members, because they combine to make something greater. The clutch is effectively immortal. As Mokolé die or are killed, more can hatch and the clutch can go on. Elders can enter the Sleep of the Dragon and awaken millennia later. There are clutches which literally date back millions of years as single entities. The connecting factor is Mnesis. If each member of a clutch can recall a thousand former lives by the same river, a sense of belonging can extend through time as well as space.

Note that by sleeping for many years at a time, Mokolé can make themselves almost immortal. Many clutches have sleeping elders who stretch out their lives by sleeping nine years of every ten, aging only a decade as a century passes, or sleep even more than that. They are able to plan and plot as mummies and vampires do, although there are few Mokolé able to sleep the Sleep of the Dragon. In many cases, these "Nomads of Time" cooperate, leaving messages for each other on stone tablets in the Dragon's Tongue. Sometimes they fight centuries-long duels with immortal foes such as mummies, pursuing each other through time. Their mortal Kin guard and revive them through the years, many living and dying without seeing the sleeping dragons. The true number of sleeping Mokolé is unknown, but may be large enough to yet provide some hope — many elders' locations were lost in the Wars of Rage.

Creating a Clutch for Players and Storytellers

The offering of jokes he had left might have placated the technospirit. Anyway, he had to try. Peter took out the cellphone and called Aunt Penny's number. She picked up on the fourth ring. "Hello?"

"Aunt Penny, it's me, Peter. I'm—"

"Peter, where have you been? The sept has been worried sick! We thought — well, we thought you were gone."

"I'm okay. I'm, uh, in Australia. Near Darwin. I've been staying out here. I'm, uh, learning a lot." Like how not to remember, *he thought.*

"Australia? Peter, what are you doing down there? We need you here. The cadavers have been taking Kin. Your cousin Don's in the ICU at Mercy from blood loss. When can you come back?"

"I don't know. There's some, I guess, serious business down here."

"The People's business?" There was no other kind that *mattered, her tone said louder than words could.*

"No, Aunt Penny. Look, I'll tell you right off. Don't be upset. There are Mokolé here."

"What? Those monsters that used to hunt Garou? Aren't they extinct?"

"Please, please listen. There are Mokolé here, for real. Real dragons. They're not of the Wyrm. And I'm okay, okay? They're my friends." Oh. That had been the wrong thing to say.

"What? Come back here, Peter. This doesn't sound good."

"Aunt Penny, please listen. There were some Mokolé still alive after the Wars of Rage. I know you and Mother always said they were all gone. But there are some here. And this... this is important. They used to say that the Mokolé remembered everything, and we thought that was just a story. But it's not, okay? It's real. There's an ancient Mokolé here who remembers the dinosaurs. And... and they want to make peace with the People. This is really important. I think I could really make this happen."

"This is serious, Peter." Her tone had changed. She hadn't lived to be the oldest Garou in the protectorate without having sound judgment. His mind's eye saw the sept assembling. What would they judge? What would they do?

"This is serious. I want to go through this with them. They tell me that they want me to understand what being a Mokolé means. Because they need us. They need peace with us, because...because the Apocalypse is coming, and... we need them. We need the Mokolé. They are the Mother's Memory. If we can get them to help us, we can restore Her, make the world like it was. They're the hope of Gaia."

"You believe this." She was neutral. How many generations of wild cubs had she been so dispassionate to? No one knew how old she was.

"We have to try. Listen, I'll, I'll call you a little bit later. I'm learning a lot now. I might be able to get back soon."

"Peter, don't stay away too long. I must go."

"Good-bye, Aunt Penny."

She hung up the old rotary-dial phone in her parlor in Toronto, and in Arnhem Land that had been Ulungan, Peter closed the phone.

Mamu of the Talons heard the Weaver-thing say that the traitor-wolf was done talking to his dam's littermate. He told the Weaver-spirit that had relayed the call to go eat itself, and it vanished with a pop. His Hispo shape towered over the dingoes at the waterhole. He threw back his monster head and howled Gather To Me *over the red outback.*

The pack began to assemble. Mamu addressed them.

"Sibs, I smell the urine of a traitor, a fallen wolf who wears a two-legs' shape. This thing calls itself—" and his dog-snout shaped the words Peter Ward. *"It is lying among bushes that the Wyrm pisses on. It speaks to the dragon folk, the very image of the Wyrm. My spirits have brought its words to me. Your snouts can sniff for foulness in the deserts of the north. Follow me and we will take two quarries at once: this thing that was once a wolf and its Wyrm-beasts. Are you with me?"*

The pack's Half Moon answered, a smaller dingo with brown and black fur. "Leader, what is their crime? What are these Wyrm-beasts?"

"They are Gumagan," Mamu said, hating even to say the word, "worse than Black Spirals who were once Garou like us. These things do not only serve the Wyrm — they take its shape!" Talons and Kin alike growled at their leader's words.

The Half Moon, Rears-and-Rends, spoke again. "Leader, I have heard of the Gumagan. Tales of them fill the night at moots. They are two-legs who sing themselves into a crocodile's skin. If they are anything but a story, they can't be any harm to us."

"This is weakling's talk! When Talons came to Fire-Country, scorning weak Garou with the ways of two-legs and the hearts of rats, we found the Bunyip here, things that were Garou once and became hopping beasts like kangaroos! Gumagan were here too. They betrayed Talons at Red Sands, left us to fight the Banelord alone. We slew their pack at Greatrocks for that deed, but ten Talons died. Then my ancestor, Splits Mountains, vowed that no Gumagan should walk Fire-Country's sand. For many seasons they hid. Now we have found them. Now we fulfill his vow. Let us kill, and rise to kill again."

There were barks and howls of assent. Mamu and his pack set off loping across the empty red sand. There was a long way to go.

There are several ways to handle the possible existence of a Mokolé clutch in the course of the game.

- A clutch may already exist when the game begins, and the players may know about it.
- Another approach is to take the player characters through their form-dreaming, alone or together, then have them find each other. They can spend a story or two finding a clutch and seeking a place in it. As outsiders, they may have a hard time.
- You can certainly rule that there is no clutch in the area of the game and have the players create one themselves.
- Lastly, the player characters may find some other home base, such as by associating with a Bata'a temple or a pride of Bastet.

The players and Storyteller should think about the clutch and its nature. The players may do this while they are talking to the Storyteller before the characters are created, or when the characters have passed through their Rite of Passage but before the story proper begins. You might also want to ask yourself these questions when planning the game:

- Where is the clutch going to be? Mokolé tend to stay in one place. Nesting grounds, suitable prey, and places of strength (wallows) are not common. The choice of location can be important. Is it a wilderness park? A rainforest under threat? A coastal village? A remote island? An urban slum? Outside the tropics altogether? Is there a wallow? If not, where will the Mokolé worship and perform rites? Is the wallow known to Garou or mages, who might want to take it away?
- Is the clutch dedicated to a purpose? Many clutches have always guarded their wallow, or have always planted and replanted a forest valley, or have always taught the Old Ways to the local village. Some clutches do not have a purpose (except to survive). There are war clutches, teaching clutches, guard clutches, nest clutches, and many others.
- How complete is the roster of Sun auspices? Is it a perfect clutch? Is there a Crowning? If not, who is the eldest? The most respected? Who sits at Gathers as the Sun rises? Who judges when the Sun is at noon? Who remembers when the Sun sinks, or revels when it is dark? If there are

empty places, are there Kin who are trained to fill them? If not, could they be trained?

• Who is the clutch's totem? What is her nature? What does she want? Note that individual totems are very rare, because totem spirits don't bother with individuals. Usually only a clutch group can muster enough spirit power for a totem.

• Whom does the clutch remember? Who are notable figures in their Mnesis? How far back does it go? Were the Kings involved? Are there famous reptiles or humans in the lineage? What non-Mokolé memories are involved?

• Does the clutch have notable enemies or allies? Who are they? How powerful are they, and what do they want?

• Is there actually a sleeping elder? Who is she? How powerful is she asleep? How powerful would she be if awakened, and what are the awakening conditions? How much of all this do the players know? Note that many elders leave instructions to be wakened when certain events happen or use the Gift to awaken themselves.

After rainy season comes dry season. After dry season comes rainy season. We are patient. Our time will come again.

— Swims-In-Mbembe's-Wake, Crowning the Congo Clutch Mokolé

Matre

The Mokolé recognize a mystical power in fertility, which they call Matre (MOTT-ray). A Mokolé female mates every year, but lays eggs, or births babies, if Homid, every two or three. For each egg hatched or baby birthed that is Mokolé, the mother gets one permanent die to add *anywhere*. These are her Matre dice. Once Matre dice are distributed, they cannot be changed, although the mother can gain more by birthing more true Mokolé.

Alligators and crocodiles lay perhaps a dozen eggs in each clutch, and each clutch has a 10% chance of containing one Mokolé. No matter how many eggs a suchid female lays, there is still only a 10% chance of one Mokolé appearing; multiple Mokolé from the same clutch are so rare that they're legendary. It is therefore impossible to gain huge amounts of Matre "instantly" by laying a nest full of eggs. However, the skill: Brood Kenning, and the merits Retain Seed and Retain Eggs make breeding easier. In the present day, as Mokolé lands shrink and the Dissolver poisons the world, Matre is not the never-ending fountain of power that it might seem. Player characters who wish to gain Matre must roleplay courtship and safeguard their offspring. Mokolé have great affection for children, using the Rite of the Nesting Mound to safeguard them.

It might seem that only female Mokolé can gain Matre dice. However, if a male directly fathers a Mokolé (rare, for the gene is quite recessive; most often the birth is due to a recessive gene), he, too, can gain a Matre point at the Storyteller's discretion. Since Matre is a connection to Gaian fertility, the male will know when he is a true sire if he gains Matre.

Kin are sometimes spoken of as having Matre. If a Kin character has a true Mokolé child, then the Storyteller may allow a point of Matre.

Shapeshifting and Reproduction

What you had to visualize was an already pregnant woman strolling around on her daily foraging round. Suddenly she steps on a couplet [of the songlines], the spirit child jumps up… and impregnates the foetus with song.

— Bruce Chatwin, *The Songlines*.

Mokolé carry out courtship rites, which vary from clutch to clutch and from ripple to ripple. Mating, even if carried out every year, only brings children every two or three years. The Rites of Breeding ensure that two Mokolé of the opposite sex do not mate. Homids mate when possible for them, while suchids will be interested in mating only during their mating season. Some varna are affectionate at other times of the year, but most suchids are not. Same-sex love is familiar to both homid and suchid Mokolé, although most Mokolé are not so oriented. As same-sex relationships cannot produce children, they can be more affectionate and permanent than opposite-sex mating (as the relationship is obviously existing for its own sake), and often are.

Females say that they "know" (allow a Gnosis roll, difficulty 7) when they are "heavy" with eggs or a baby. They also "know" if one is a true Mokolé (although the difficulty for this roll is 9). Note that eggs are usually in the suchid mother's body for only a few days before they are laid.

When gravid, a female may shift into Archid and back. The larger body shape can contain the child safely. However, shifting beyond Archid is dangerous. A homid who tries to shift into Suchid form after the first trimester is unable to do so. A suchid trying to shift into Homid form while gravid will fail. If she uses a Willpower point to succeed, she will lose all the eggs save one in the shift.

A pregnant Mokolé who uses Rage runs the risk of her eggs breaking or of her human baby being harmed. Each time Rage is used, allow a Stamina roll, difficulty 6. Any success means that the child is safe. A failure means that the power of Rage sends her into labor prematurely, and either she births a premature baby or lays her eggs early. The Storyteller should determine whether or not a human child could survive — usually before the third trimester, the child won't be able to live outside the womb. If she botches, the child dies and she loses one health level from the miscarriage or eggbinding. Note that premature children can survive, if properly cared for. Matre is lost if a child dies. If the Mokolé was especially foolish, 1 point of Wisdom may be lost as well. Any Mokolé who deliberately causes a child's death is a criminal and a murderer in Mokolé society, while any who causes the death of their own child is considered dangerously insane.

Pregnant Kinfolk or Mokolé are zealously guarded by their own clutch; in fact, any Mokolé would consider it his duty to do so. The laws of sanctuary require that any of the

Dragon Breed give aid and shelter to a mother with child. The laws are so strict that a murderer may take shelter with her victim's family if she requires it. The No-Suns spin many tales of heroism and sacrifice centered on the pressing need for reproduction.

Mokolé and the Umbra

The Dragon in Flight

Many Garou believe that the Mokolé are inept at Umbral travel or ignorant of the Shadow. However, the Mokolé simply frequent different regions of the spirit world. As the "memory" of Gaia, the Mokolé are most interested in the Deep Umbra, also called the High Umbra by mages. Here ideas and thoughts take spiritual form, and here the Mokolé seek to gather those memories that have escaped them or been forgotten. They even search for knowledge of the lost times of the WonderWork, although such searching can lead to Harano and death.

The Middle Umbra

Mokolé do not normally like to travel the Middle Umbra. It is the realm which the Garou prowl. Indeed, it requires the Gift: Walk Between Worlds, for a Mokolé to be able to step sideways, as well as a body of water to serve as a gate. Few of the children of Dragon risk the trip. The Garou are just as hostile to the Mokolé in the Umbra as anywhere else. In addition, the Innocents attack any Mokolé they see.

Some Umbral paths lead to Pangaea and the Land of Dinosaurs. Concealing differ on the question of whether the Land of Dinosaurs is located in the Near Umbra or in an Inner Umbra "Lost World." However, Pangaea is "Gaia as She was," and at least one Mokolé has slept there since the Realm came into being. Spiteful Mokolé travelers sometimes go there to ambush Garou hunting parties and eat

The Innocents

Father?

Yes, son?

I want to kill you.

— Jim Morrison, "The End"

Mokolé have no metis and never will. While a Garou wears a war form that has been the same since the Last Times, every Mokolé's battle form is different and must be dreamt into being. A Mokolé with two Mokolé parents would have to dream her Archid form in the shell, which is impossible. The result of Mokolé-Mokolé mating is a deformed fetus (or a clutch of horror-eggs with monstrous embryos inside) constantly shifting shape. The Mokolé mother usually has to shapeshift to Archid form to avoid being ripped apart by her freakish offspring, who sometimes claw their way to Sun's light through her body.

Should the offspring survive hatching or birth, they appear in the mother's breed form, but soon die. No such child has ever reached maturity. The child dies, unable to maintain a stable shape, and becomes an Innocent. It is said that No-Face, child of Night's-Fire, was the first. These hungry ghosts prowl from the Shadowlands to the Near Umbra and back, without memory of who and what they really are.

Generally, the Innocents are treated as spirits, with statistics of the Storyteller's discretion; some are little more than Gaffling-level strength, while others have transcended the upper limits of a Jaggling's power. Instead of the usual Charms, the Innocents have dark powers of their own. These can include the following.

• **Dark Whispers:** The Innocent can speak to the living.

• **Umbra Passage:** The Innocent can use a weak spot, or Depression, in the Dark Umbra to enter the Middle or Deep Umbra, usually in pursuit of prey.

• **Mnesis Travel:** The Innocent can enter the Mnesis of other Mokolé to haunt them.

• **Materialize:** As per the spirit rules.

• **Take Homid Form:** The Innocent can take Homid shape, effectively passing as an ordinary wraith.

• **Take Suchid Form:** The Innocent can appear as the wraith of a crocodile.

• **Give Power:** Can give Gnosis to another spirit.

• **Take Power:** Can steal the power of another spirit. The difficulty is the target's Willpower.

• **Steal Mnesis:** The Innocent can take Mnesis away from its owner. She comes into contact with the target's mind and rolls Power vs. a difficulty of the target's Willpower. The effect depends on the number of successes:

One success: a memory within Mnesis becomes confused.

Three successes: A minor memory is gone.

Five successes: An ordinary memory is gone, or a great memory is blurred.

Seven+ successes: A great memory is destroyed.

• **Corrupt Mnesis:** The Innocent can change Mnesis into Bad Mnesis, warping the dreams of the Mokolé. The system is as above, save that instead of being gone, the memories are altered — a kind friend becomes an enemy, or a skill learned is guaranteed to backfire. The damage done can be healed by Gifts, by a Mnesis quest, or by pilgrimage to the Deep Umbra.

• **Arcanos:** the Innocent can use the powers of the Restless Dead, called Arcanos. These resemble Gifts but have somber effects. A Storyteller can use appropriately nasty Gifts, or can use the rulebook for **Wraith: The Oblivion**, equating Pathos to Gnosis.

them. They consider this a hunt for the "most dangerous game" and revel in the challenge. Most of the other Middle Umbra realms are not accessible to Mokolé or would not interest them, such as Wolfhome. In the Summer Country, Mokolé say that they meet Garou who are not hostile to them. As no one can reliably enter the Summer Country to verify this, the truth remains unknown.

The Deep Umbra

The Deep Umbra is the portion of the spirit world that reflects the Mind of Gaia. Its relation to the Realm is defined in a manner similar to that of the Middle Umbra, but a different way of seeing is necessary to understand it. Simply stepping sideways usually will not suffice to enter the Deep Umbra. A special path into it is necessary, although several wallows know one or two such roads. Many Mokolé and most magical practitioners must restrict themselves to traveling astrally along the shores of Gaia's Mind, as they are unable to advance further. Further away from the Realm, the depths of the Deep Umbra are home to Gaia's thoughts and the spiritual representations of beings from the Realm. This is the goal of the Mokolé spiritualist, to sail into Gaia's thoughts in search of the memories that she has forgotten and the enemies that seek to corrupt her mind. Because of their different goals and methods, mages will see Gaia's mind differently. Astral travel, which is a discipline developed by the Mokolé using the same mental tools that they use to voyage through Mnesis, has its own laws of reality. Generally, the astral self is connected to the physical body by an ephemeral silver cord. The traveler is unaware of the condition of her physical body but can use the astral cord to return to her form at any time. Depending upon her personal beliefs, a Mokolé may view the silver cord as an umbilical cord to the Mother Gaia or as the protecting tail of Dragon.

Astral form Mokolé may travel at great speeds; storytellers are encouraged to use 1,000 miles per hour as a general guide. Astral travelers cannot interact with the physical world except in very limited fashion. By spending a Willpower point, an astral traveler can manifest as a ghostly shape and even speak. Mortals viewing a Mokolé doing this in Archid form will be subject to the Delirium. Two astral forms meeting one another may react as if they were physical. They could speak, touch or even fight. However, since they have no physical bodies, their astral selves' attributes are derived from their minds. Wits replaces Dexterity, Manipulation acts as Strength and Intelligence operates as Stamina. The only way to do true harm to an astral traveler with a silver cord is to cut the cord. Treat the Mokolé's Willpower points as health levels. When all Willpower is lost, the cord is severed. Mokolé physically present in the astral realm fight using their normal physical attributes and health, however they suffer the standard plus one penalty to physical combat difficulties that all Changers face in the spirit realms.

A being whose astral silver cord is cut is stranded in the Umbra. Their bodies begin to die and their natures change. Allow one hour per health level until the astral form withers into a ghost and one day per health level

Mages and the Umbra

If you're a regular **Mage: The Ascension** player, and you're getting a touch confused, remember that there's a difference of terminology between Mage and Werewolf. What mages call the *High Umbra*, werebeasts call the *Deep Umbra* — they're both talking about the same thing, which is the realm of abstractions.

What mages call the *Deep Umbra*, shapechangers call "outer space." As **Werewolf** doesn't presume that reality is consensual, it's assumed, for simplicity's sake, that outer space is as physical as Earth. Don't freak out about it, though. It's not as if spaceships are a common theme in the World of Darkness, anyway; what are the odds that the truth is actually going to matter?

before the Mokolé's body dies, unless the Mokolé is somehow fed or otherwise sustained. The unfortunate becomes a ghostlike creature, essentially an astral wraith, over time. They forget their former lives and revert to mere shells of their past hungers and longings. Their astral attributes are the only ones they have.

Mokolé usually avoid the few mages to be found in the Deep Umbra; the two groups have little in common and don't care for each other much. Any real combat is usually a disaster for both sides. Those few mages who do get along with the Dragon Breed are usually shamans of various traditions.

Within the Umbra, there are byways and portals to other regions. It is known for example that certain dark areas, called Depressions by some Mokolé, touch the Shadowlands. This is how wraiths skilled in Argos and hideous Spectres slip into the mind of Gaia. Spectres often pose as Banes or are seen as Banes when they enter the higher realms. Mokolé seeking to enter the realms of the dead should be wary of the souls that lurk within the Depressions. They range from Spectre life-eaters to dead mystics who seek to draw the living down into the Dark for their own nefarious purposes.

Silver portals, known as Eyes, lead into Lunar shards in the Middle Umbra. They can be seen far off by their gentle glow. These are the areas where one is most likely to meet with Garou or sorcerers traveling from the Middle Umbra. Lunes and Glade Children sometimes lurk here, though they usually fear to leave the confines of the Eye, as they sense the danger to their being. Finally, the common occurrence of bright lights reaching into the Deep Umbra are called Ascensions. It is believed that these usually temporary places are charged with the thoughts of great intellects and powerful thoughts creating a conduit from the minds of the Realm straight into Gaia's mind. Mages experiencing epiphanies, powerful dreamers and mighty thinkers may be found within these conduits, either in person or through some sort of idea which represents them, such as Beethoven's Ninth Symphony or Newton's Principia. Though they can be dangerous, these are the features most likely to attract the Mokolé.

As travelers leave the portions of Gaia's mind where the physical realm still holds some sway, at least in determining the shape of the landscape, they travel into the Deep Umbra. The experience can be likened to plunging into the sea from a shallow beach — cold and deep. Suddenly the silver cord becomes thin, and those who carry on often feel vulnerable or even claim that the cord seems to want to draw them back. The most common way for a mystic to reach the Deep Umbra is by passing through one of the various portals, such as those provided by the Ascensions. Those travelers skilled enough to have reached this point have often done so physically without a silver cord, but there are others who have the skill to remove the cord and travel onwards undaunted. An astral traveler who cannot remove her cord can still enter the Deep Umbra, but she is at great risk. A portal may move great distances and require her to spend incredible amounts of time trying to return to her body. Sometimes a portal may even close, cutting the cord and stranding her in the Deep Umbra as her body begins to die, or attract some entity intent on tracking the cord to her current whereabouts. Typically, Mokolé enter the Deep Umbra in search of lost memories, which in the Umbral realms can take the forms of spiritual ideals or beings.

The Makara of India hypothesize that memories cannot truly lose themselves. The Pratigata, the lost dreams of Gaia, are their goals. They seek out these ancient spirits, who are often seemingly worn to near-nothingness by ages of disuse, who flit about so chaotically that none can catch them or who are so obscure and cryptic that no one can understand them. The Makara say that the Pratigata are the forms of all of Gaia's "lost memories;" if the Mokolé can just find all of the Pratigata the balance will be restored, for they will know the original mind of Gaia. Of course the Deep Umbra is an unimaginable array of ideas, ideals, spirits, magical places, enigmas and puzzles. Some of these are no more than loose thoughts and are small or weak. Such a presence might be no more than a single idle joke half-remembered over morning coffee with no more power to even cause the Mokolé to chuckle.

Tremendously potent ideas, it's said, come from the beliefs of entire cultures. It's said that divinities from ancient mythologies can be found here, but who can say for sure? The Mokolé are not pilgrims in the Umbra, but are there for a reason. If there are Incarna claiming to be gods hanging about in the Deep Umbra, the Mokolé don't have time to play supplicant.

The Mokolé often visit the memory realms, which they can enter through dreams or by trekking through the Shadow to these Deep Umbra locations. The memory realms appear as caves, palaces, or even spheres floating in the Shadow's sky-ocean. When approaching a memory realm, voyagers can usually behold the nature of the memory through windows, refracted in the bubble's surface, and so on. To enter requires a Mnesis roll against a difficulty that the Storyteller can set. To enter a total stranger's memory of a trip to the supermarket, the difficulty would be 9, while to access the last thoughts of a Bosnian in a death camp might be 10. Memories such as the Civil War, which are familiar to many, would be only a 4 or 5 — but specific memories of subtleties are harder.

When Mokolé enter the memory realms, they can effectively enter any memory accessible to any Mokolé. Of course, their own memories are most easily accessible. If they enter a memory, the Storyteller may simply allow them to enter the story that the memory relates, with each Mokolé traveler playing a part. If they succeed in finishing the story, the memory enters their own Mnesis.

Occasionally, Mokolé try to change the contents of a memory. The Storyteller should allow them to roleplay their way through this process, in which the strength of the story opposes their own Mnesis and will. Stories, even the Mahabharata, Iliad, or Odyssey, are not immutable, but the Storyteller should emphasize their strength. No single Mokolé, not even mighty Mokolé-Mbembe himself, has the power to rewrite history by saving Martin Luther King from death or overthrowing Set before he could banish the Silent Striders. To change history so dramatically, an army would be needed — and even then there's no guarantee of success.

If the Mokolé succeed, they will find that the memory they came across is different when they return to the physical world. Reality itself might seem to be unchanged — or then again, maybe not. After all, time is a powerful thing, so powerful it governs Sun and Moon. And if time is upset, it rights itself eventually.

Two spirits of particular interest to the Mokolé are the Pranastajjanika Pratigata and the Smrtihara. Pranastajjanika is the word the Makara use to describe a Mokolé who has lost all knowledge or memory; this personal oblivion is a fate worse than mere death, for the memories can't pass on. Given the Makara assertion that a Pratigata exists for every one of Gaia's lost memories, it is believed that there is a Pratigata for each Pranastajjanika. This creature is the Mokolé's lost memories. If the two can be rejoined, they will become one once again.

Smrtihara are spirits found in the Deep Umbra that apparently seek to destroy Gaia's memories. The memory-seizers are believed by certain Makara to be the Daughters of the Demoness of Sorrow, embodiments of the suicidal impulse that has entered the mind of Gaia through the Imbalance. The Smrtihara hunt and attack other denizens of the Deep Umbra and destroy memory: they can make something "never have been" by eating its ideal form in the Astral Realm. Of course, the spirits that they defeat generally simply enter slumber, and eventually awaken, but the Smrtihara are still incredibly disruptive and are quite possibly responsible for the fleeting nature of many Pratigata. The Makara consider it their duty to bind or destroy the Smrtihara.

Many spirits within the Deep Umbra know the Mokolé and respect their duty to the Mother. There are treaties made with the memories of Gaia by the Dragon Kings, resembling the pacts made with the denizens of the Middle Umbra by Garou. To reflect this the Mnesis of the Mokolé acts as a bonus to Social rolls with most denizens of the Deep Umbra. Obvious exceptions are malevolent thoughts such as the Smrtihara.

The Mokolé have walked the Deep Umbra so long that they possess many way stations and realms there. These are called Yathamaya — "As Fixed in the Memory" — by the Makara. The Mokolé-mbembe refer to them as "memory palaces," and insist that each and every tree, room, seat of marble, etc., is a memory within the great scheme of things. There are wallows where tired and wounded Mokolé can rest, temples and pagodas where they can contemplate the nature of the Pratigata and meditate upon the bond between their mind and that of Gaia, and libraries with scrolls and maps representing the memories that the Dragon Breed protect. The spirit-books and tablets often contain text in the Dragon's Tongue, and in lost human languages only Mokolé can read. The Caves of Memory, long known to mystics, are also Yathamaya.

The Storyteller can assume that these Umbral refuges are inhabited by wandering Mokolé and possibly by spirits which reflect the nature of the place. An idea for storytelling is to have Yathamaya which depict memories associated with the chronicle: one room could be full of "books" which are the Mnesis lineage of a specific character, while a shrine could be decorated with mosaics of the heroes whom the clutch remembers. The Storyteller can assign a Yathamaya a number of points, similar to a caern or wallow, to reflect its importance and the number of memory lines there.

•	One memory lineage
••	Two memory lineages, or one with famous or powerful memories.
•••	Three lineages, or one major and one minor lineage.
••••	Four memory lineages, or one very powerful lineage.
•••••	The greatest and most powerful memories are housed there.

Stories could revolve round the clutch's search for a Yathamaya, their struggle to understand its mysteries, and the rewards that comprehension of such a place can offer.

More Mage Business

Is it in fact possible for Mokolé, the travelers most experienced in communal remembering and memory realms, to enter the Akashic Record — the "Mnesis" of an entire tradition of mages?

Maybe.

Interesting thought, eh?

Mnesis: A User's Guide.

"We Mokolé have a saying: No Mokolé dies until all the lives it has touched are gone, until all the good it has done is destroyed. Our clutchmates will live so long as we keep the memory of Gaia."

— Stands Against the Tide, Warding the Clutch of Towers above the Kings, Remembering the Clutch From Across the Blue Waters.

Mnesis is the direct exercise of the Mokolé's function as the Memory of Gaia. Living and dead, the Dragon Breed

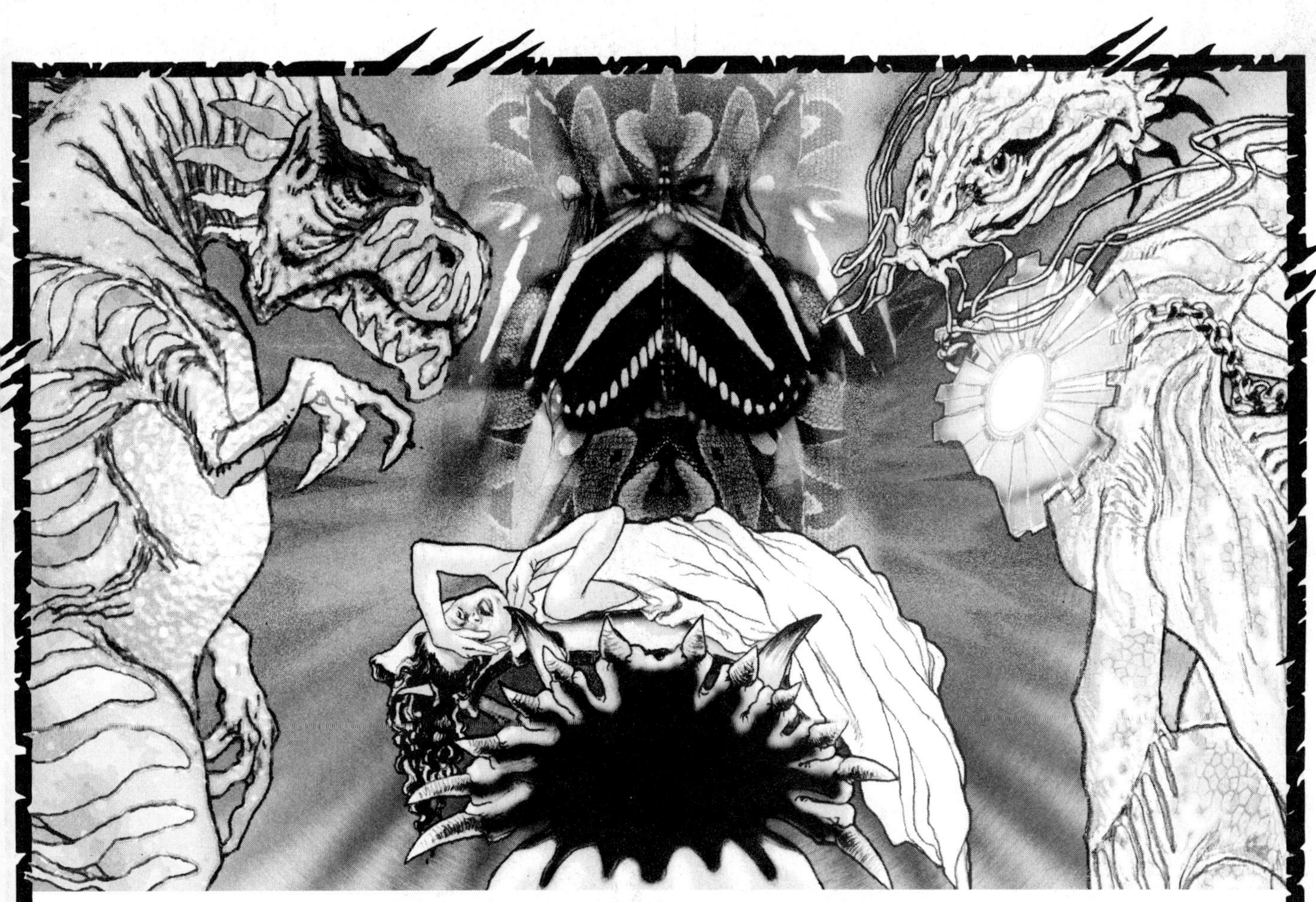

contain Her past. Mokolé have never cared much for the sentimental notion of the afterlife that is expressed in myths like those of the "Happy Hunting Grounds." Death is not frightening or hateful to the Mokolé, because they progress to become part of Gaia's Memory.

The Shining are the guides of the dead, both in this life and the next. At the deathbeds of the Dragon Breed they are sometimes visible when they arrive to escort the soul to its destination. The Midnight Suns tell of a dreamspace built out of the barrier-range between the Middle and Dark Umbra, a Greek amphitheater into which pilgrims can enter to consult the Memory. Mnesis trances sometimes work like this.

The pilgrim stands on the stage. In the first row sit his parents. Behind them are the grandparents. Mokolé in the family tree are in their Archid form, while others are humans or reptiles. Non-Mokolé ancestors often have less to say. As each person dies, they are conducted into the tiers by Shining spirits. Each generation's bench is twice as wide as the one below it; in the distance are the plumed, horned shapes of The Kings. The level of Mnesis possessed by the pilgrim determines how far he can see. The questioner may ask any question, but the answer depends on whether an ancestor could have known this and whether the distant memory traces can be found and read.

Rarely, the ancients will speak of their own volition, and when they do, Mokolé are advised to listen closely.

Mnesis Quests

Learning is nothing but remembering.

— Plato, *Phaedo*, 72e

Mnesis quests are dangerous. The Storyteller can emphasize this by being mindful of three kinds of peril.

The passage within has its terrors for the remembrancer. The realm of Mnesis is inhabited by Dream Hunters — memories so savage and clever that one past cannot hold them. The Dream Hunter emerges when the Mokolé remembers a scene containing something dangerous. It may well bide its time, attacking when the Mokolé is deep into remembrance, shattering the illusion of the past like a bloody John Wilkes Booth jumping onto a stage. If defeated, it must wait until the Mokolé or one of her descendants again remembers the scene whence came its shape.

There are three doors that Mokolé cannot open: the start of the Wars of Rage, the First Changer, and the WonderWork of the Wyrm. To approach any of these is to invite madness or death Within. There are many, many other perilous memories. Breaks-The-Chain, a remembrancer of the River of Grass clutch, delved for memories of the slave trade and upon emerging, took her own life in horror at what she had seen. In game terms, the Storyteller may rule that a Mokolé beholding a scene of great evil and horror must make a Willpower check. Failure means the Mokolé must spend a Willpower point to avoid Harano or Derangement.

The third kind of peril is much subtler. The past contains horror, but also endless beauty and joy. Too many Mokolé love Mnesis so much that they prefer it to their own lives, spending months on end reliving the glories of the past while Gaia dies. There is no actual rules system for this, but the Storyteller can fill Mnesis trances with hints and lures to draw players further and further in, all the while promising more and more power and knowledge. Botching a Mnesis roll is extremely dangerous. The Mokolé who does so is liable to misremember important facts or to remember things that did not happen. In the case of important rolls, the Storyteller can make them and then give the player the information. Another option is to allow an attack of Dream Hunters.

Remembering Non-Mokolé Memories

What we had witnessed, he said, was not the real Lizard song… the real song would have named each waterhole the Lizard Man drank from, each tree he cut a spear from, each cave he slept in, covering the whole long distance of the way.

— Bruce Chatwin, *The Songlines*

Peter said, "I've been searching through the Memory to find our common ancestors. Why can't I find them?"

Morwangu packed more pituri into his pipe and reached for a coal from the fire. "Giving the Memory to another, that's like pouring tea through a strainer."

"What do you mean?"

"Jus' leaves."

"You mean, uh, anything that doesn't fit into my own world I can't find?"

"Yeah. You got it."

Mokolé are descended from long chains of human and reptile ancestors. They carry the memories of these creatures as well as those of their true Mokolé ancestors.

Memories from human ancestors have clear views of scenes, and elements of the scene such as the social status or relationship of people present are more obvious. Language, if any is used, it a little easier to understand (the remembrancer gets the meaning of a speech if the ancestor understood what was being said), and the thoughts of the ancestor are more comprehensible in terms of analysis of the scene or event. Suchid ancestors think in much more sensory terms, in terms of patterns and textures or variations in scent. Animals, birds, plants and weather are familiar to the ancestor, though she may not know the names of them, and any implications such as a coming storm, are obvious. The suchid ancestor remembers sounds, including language but not what the words mean. Suchid awareness is much sharper than human. They can identify species and even individuals from a single footprint, and tell from the smell and taste of the water what is going on.

In terms of game mechanics, allow the guidelines above to govern how useful Mnesis will be. If the character is looking at a swamp through human eyes, she may see only water, trees and mud. A suchid looking at a war, however, sees only humans killing each other and does not see the meaning of the battle.

Mnesis Rapture

Mamu peered over the rise and sniffed. Lizard, plain as day. "It ends here, packmates. I do not know how these Wyrm-things lived when all the rest were dead. Maybe the Wyrm births them again to mock us." Restive growls arose from Talon and Kin alike, dingo bodies rippling and shifting as Rage boiled up. "We will camp here today and attack at nightfall. They are weakest at night." He looked Rage-In-The-Streets in the eye. "The thing that calls itself a Garou must die too. I do not know if it is a Black Spiral or something even worse, but it has betrayed us."

A scout returned. "Mamu. I have found a campsite of two-legs with food and bedding. I did not smell the Wyrm."

"They have found some evil way to hide their taint. We must strike as soon as the day is dead."

Rears-And-Rends spoke. "Mamu, should we attack the two-legs who were here first? They care for Mother Gaia as we do. If we do not smell the Wyrm, we may be in the wrong place. Remember Cracked Earth Pack, slain with silver because they took too many humans."

"Coward and traitor! Do you challenge me in wartime?' Mamu shapeshifted into Hispo, towering over the judge, and growled, eyes wild with Rage. Rears-and-Rends backed away, fled the battlefield.

The Talon settled head on paws and waited.

The Mokolé link to the past is profound. This is expressed not only through Mnesis trances but in daily life. Although spontaneous expression of Mnesis is rare, it does happen and can be a powerful Storyteller's device.

On infrequent occasions, a Mokolé may see an object or place that is also in Mnesis. When this happens, the Storyteller may allow an instant Mnesis roll. If the player gets one success, allow a vague sense of *déja vu*. Three successes allow the character to access the memories of what the ancestor saw. Five successes grant the "story" of what happened. If the roll botches, the character spasms with nightmares of bad Mnesis for a period of time. It's likely that the character will be enraptured for a number of hours equal to the number of successes; the Storyteller might allow the player to spend a Willpower point to avoid this.

Mnesis Rapture may introduce a story, a new theme, or even serve as a catalyst for a First Change.

The Wanderers

Mnesis is passed from parent to child — usually from mother to children. Mokolé are sedentary, usually requiring only small areas to survive by hunting, fishing and gardening. As the millennia have passed, this has led to Mnesis being extremely local. A clutch knows more of its own past than that of other clutches. To prevent the lines of memory from running apart and the Dragon Breed from being sundered into hostile "tribes," the office of Wanderer was brought into being long ago. There have been many, many famous Wanderers, from the Time of the Kings through the Age of Sleep and the Last Times. The Wars of Rage curtailed Wandering severely. The first Wanderer of the new era was Ornate Piers, followed by Seeks-The-Forgotten and others.

Wanderers are called "North Suns" in the Northern Hemisphere and "South Suns" in the Southern Hemisphere, because the Sun passes across the south sky for the Northern Hemisphere and the north sky for the Southern. They are also called "Hook-Suns" and "Cross-Suns" by tale-tellers, because at night the north sky is ruled by the Hook (Ursa Major) and the southern sky by the Southern Cross. In both cases, the image is of a sun outside the ecliptic. "Wayward Sun" is another old term for Wanderers. There are Rising and Setting Wanderers, Rising being younger ones and Setting Wanderers being old. Young Wanderers are usually male, while older ones can be either male or female. Clutches which meet them are obliged to provide them with food and shelter for at least one day and to hear their words within one day of their arrival. A visiting Wanderer usually stays "more than a day and less than a year."

Wanderers have three functions. First, they bring new stories and tales with them. These pass to the new clutch whom they visit either as they are told, or through Anamnesis, if anyone can perform the rite. Second, they breed when possible with fertile Kin, preventing inbreeding and giving new Mnesis to the clutch. Third, they forge alliances.

The Wanderers are ritually initiated into their office before they leave, and they may learn the Rite of Anamnesis before they go to allow them to spread Mnesis directly. They may also have the Rite of Anamnesis performed on them at clutches that they visit. Their journeys are arduous; many do not return home.

Player characters may be Wanderers, or their clutch may receive a Wanderer as a story seed (possibly with disturbing news and possibly being a disturbance herself). Many chronicles could be constructed around Wanderers and their hosts.

Sunbane

Peter returned from his prowl and shifted back to Homid. "Morwangu, wake up. We're in trouble."

The aged lizard lifted its head and spoke. "What is it, son?"

"I smell Garou. Talons. We have to go."

"Talons?"

"The Red Talons are the Garou who are all wolf. Uh, I mean 'dingo.' They hate humans, and hate Mokolé too, I guess. They probably brought a war pack." He hesitated. "They'll kill us all."

"They will do no such thing. Stay out of their way for now." The old one returned to contemplation, silent and still as the ancestor-stone where he sat.

Sun is not a vindictive or malign power, but offending Him is dangerous. Mokolé and Corax who advance the cause of darkness often suffer mysterious illnesses: disfiguring molts, horrible burns which destroy Appearance, skin cancer, even leprosy. These ailments are collectively called Sunbane and are greatly feared. It is up to the Storyteller to decide when Sun is offended enough to wreak such vengeance: this retribution should be used sparingly to emphasize its horrible nature. Note that skin diseases or molts can cause feathers to fall out, making some winged characters unable to fly, or may cause scale and plate armor to fall off, making the character defenseless until it regrows.

Camps

Morwangu arose and spoke with Jeffo for a long time. The two men then lit the fire and set some yams on to roast.

Finally, Peter shot to his feet. "How can you just sit here? They're coming, and they'll try to kill all of your mob, probably."

Jeffo answered without taking his eyes from the yams. "Well, man, first of all they're not killing anyone. Second of all, we can't outrun a dingo with a bee up his butt."

"So you're just going to sit here?"

"The mountains do the same. Maybe they know something."

Peter tasted guilt. Webby was nowhere to be found, and he knew why. It had sold him to the Talons in return for who-knows-what favor, and he had led the Talons to the Mokolé.

It was all his fault.

He could try to escape, reach the Umbra pathways to safety. But the Mokolé would die, and then the Talons would kill the aborigine mob too. He couldn't let that happen.

He couldn't stop it either. Not alone against however many berserk Talons.

He had to stand here and die. Nobody to tell the tale either, as if any Garou would even listen!

The yams were ready. Jeffo and Morwangu ate and then sat still once more.

The Army of the Aten

This war clutch of Mokolé, chiefly Rising Suns, spends most of its time in the Umbra warring to preserve Sun. Its members are required to prove themselves in battle and to know Gifts which allow Umbral passage. Fewer than a dozen Mokolé are members at any one time. Of these, at least two possess True Faith in Sun.

The Army of the Aten constantly prepares to fight a battle against the Dissolver and the forces of darkness. To prepare for it, they seek out ancient treasures hidden on Earth, the Near Realms, and the Dissolver Realms, and hoard them for their own use. They also seek out and destroy vampires and werewolves that seem to be servants of darkness. They are intolerant of those making deals with the Dissolver and will "correct" any Mokolé or Corax guilty of such a crime.

The Nomads of Time

This is not a "camp" so much as a society. The Nomads are Mokolé and a few Kin led by elders who know the Gift: Sleep of the Dragon and the Rite of the Sleeping Dragon. They hold a few wallows in the tropics, such as the swamps of Cameroon. Many are Zhong Lung.

The Nomads use the Sleep of the Dragon to wait out time. They sleep for a certain number of years while human Kin work to further their goals, then appear again as planned. Chosen Kin are put to sleep along with their Mokolé mates and children in order to perpetuate the Breed. Some Kin are encouraged to sleep until their proper mates are born. A few homids have recently invested money and then entered slumber, planning sleep until it is a huge fortune. Others use their long "lives" to pursue undead or to build strong wallows and clutches of Mokolé and Kin. A few have lived for thousands of years, although no Mokolé is known to be more than two thousand years old at the present.

Of course, the Nomads must keep their lairs secret even from other Mokolé lest the location be forced from them and the sleepers killed. No one knows how many Nomads remain asleep or where their lost fortresses may be. Given that they likely cache hoards of jewels, art treasures, and ancient manuscripts with them in order to have a "grubstake" when they wake, the location of these places would be most valuable.

Mokolé and Nagah

Why did it have to be snakes?

— Dr. Indiana Jones

The Nagah (weresnakes), the Judges of Gaia, are believed by most scholars to have been exterminated in the Wars of Rage. Mokolé, for the most part, agree with this and assume that the occasional "wereserpent" that they meet is simply another Mokolé. However, a few Mokolé know through Mnesis that the Nagah have survived into the modern period, and know the Nagah's secret. If you are playing a Mokolé, the Storyteller will inform you how much knowledge of the Nagah you may have. In most cases, you have none at all.

Mokolé who have learned the lore of the Nagah aren't necessarily friendly toward the Nagah and may even come into conflict with them in the course of the Nagah's frightening "mission." If the Storyteller decides to use the Nagah in his chronicle, he might allow a Mnesis roll against the Nagah's Willpower for any Mokolé to know who the Nagah really are. In addition, the Mokolé might have a chance of recognizing an apparently "fitting" death as in fact a very subtle execution; for instance, if a Mokolé came upon the remains of a notorious man-eating Bone Gnawer who had seemingly accidentally choked to death on a lump of meat. In such cases, the Storyteller may allow the Mokolé a Mnesis roll to realize that the Nagah are involved. Only do so, however, if you're interested in fully exploring the Nagah plotline — the Nagah have not survived by being careless about their secret, and would certainly notice if a Mokolé started spreading rumors. The Nagah are best used deliberately, never as filler.

Hope

The sun went down. Morwangu squatted motionless by the ashes of the fire. Jeffo stood beside him. Peter paced in Glabro. Leaving was cowardice. Staying was death.

How many Garou had died like this? He wondered for the first time about the Garou who had died in the Wars of Rage. How many had defended the other Breeds?

Was this just another battle in the Wars of Rage?

Mamu came over the rise and Peter's heart turned cold. The Talon was pony-sized, eyes burning with rage. Behind him came six other Garou and a dozen dingoes. Mamu glared at Peter and howled The Challenge. Peter spoke to him in return. "Mamu, we mean no harm. I am Peter Ward of the Taddle Creek Sept of the Glass Walkers. Our tribes are at peace. Let us continue so."

"Die, Wyrm lover! Die! Die!!" He advanced with open jaws.

The two Mokolé were still as death. Beneath the surface of his own mind Peter felt a current in the sea of memory. "Peter," came Jeffo's whisper, "your ancestors..." Cassie appeared in Peter's mind, laughing at some tale in moot. An older man in a suit, more he didn't know. What were they doing? The images came and went.

Mamu was on them. Peter could think of only one thing that might save them.

"I surrender, mighty Talon!" He shifted back to Homid and threw himself at the monster's feet.

Accept an Honorable Surrender. That had been the Law for untold eons. Mamu stopped. His pack gathered round, sniffed Peter for fear. A snout ran over his face, another at his crotch. "His action honorable," grated one voice, in Garou so accented with dingo that Peter could barely understand. "We not kill." The pack withdrew a few paces. Now Peter faced them, unable to stop shaking, while the two Gumagan stood still. At the edge of consciousness he felt men, women, wolves in forests, cities, battles, down mudbrick streets, across Ice Age meadows...

"NO! I am Alpha! I command! I say KILL!! KILL!!" Mamu roared. "KILL!!"

He lunged at Peter.

But he stopped short. Something was in the way.

It was a grey wolf. How could it be here? Peter looked closer, and so did the Talons. He heard it first from the almost-human one, Rage-In-The Streets. "The Ancestor."

It was not a wolf, but The Wolf. Peter knew in the depths of his soul that this was Him, the Progenitor of the Garou.

"First Of Us All, we...we greet you." It was Many Howls, the Talons' tale-teller. Mute, Mamu nodded, urged him on. "Your presence does us honor."

"I am honored that anyone remembers me. You are My Children."

"Father, we are of one Blood. What would you of us?" The ancient wolf gazed at each of them in turn.

"We are indeed of one Blood. All of us are the children of Mother Gaia. Her Peace be upon us all."

"Thank you, Progenitor Wolf. Why have you come here?"

"I come to end for all time the Wars of Rage. Today they pass into Memory forever. Heed my—" He was interrupted by howls.

"Good! Good! Kill lizard-things! Father say kill lizard things! KILL!! KILL!!" Mamu was ecstatic. "KILL NOW!! I—"

"Be silent, my child. Heed my words. You are no wolf, only dog. And the Dragon Breed are the Mother's firstborn. You will slay them no longer. They are the Mother's memory, and if you heed them, all that Was can be again. The Wars of Rage are over. Let the healing of Gaia begin." The shape shimmered, passed away.

"Brother Garou?" Peter blinked. It was Many Howls. "I...I almost cannot speak. You saw what we did?"

"Yes. Yes, I did." That had to be the right thing to say.

"That was the Ancestor. He spoke to us himself."

"We must do as he says." Peter tried to echo the awe and piety in the Talon's voice.

"These are the Dragons he spoke of?"

"Indeed so, and they call themselves Gumagan. Their names are—" He translated in his head for a moment— "Warmth In Darkness and Seeks-Other-Paths. They know many secrets."

Mamu growled low and long, shaking his head. At last, he rumbled out more broken words through his Hispo jaws. "This cannot be. I go. My pack, follow me."

None did.

"That settles the leadership issue," said Rage-In-The Streets. He shifted to Homid. "Wow, that feels good. He is one crazy sod. Your name's Peter?"

"Peter Ward, Taddle Creek Sept."

"Where's that?"

"Toronto. Canada."

"Long way to here, innit?"

"Yeah. Uh... yeah."

Jeffo came over to where the Garou were talking. "G'day. Say, did you ever hear what the Garou said to the Mokolé when he met him?"

Peter sighed. The wisdom of Gaia.

•••

Later, he sat by Morwangu as the Sun rose. "Father?"

"Yes, son?"

"Why did the Ancestor appear? You had something to do with that, didn't you?"

"No. You did. He isn't in my Memory. But he is in yours, all of yours."

"How did he speak to us? He isn't a ghost."

"No. He never died."

"What do you mean? Progenitor Wolf lived in...in the Ice Age!"

"He lives in you."

"But how...how could we see him?" Smell him? "How could he be, be real?"

"There is a rite. Memory may walk. Doesn't it always?"

"But— did you make him say that? To stop them?"

"I didn't make him say anything. It was all true."

"Thanks."

"Don't thank me! I was saving my own hide! Thank what is good in you. That's what made all the difference."

"I think we have a lot of talking to do with those Talons."

"Lot of remembering too."

Remember. The dragons live. Inside us.
— Peter Dickinson, *The Flight of Dragons*

Character Templates

Since time began, the Mokolé have loved their children. All the various Changing Breeds pay honor and respect to their ancestors and elders, but no Bête can boast of a greater parental love for their descendants than the love the Mokolé have for their young. Although Mokolé do not shelter their children, and do their best to ensure that their young ones are ready for the responsibilities of Mnesis, they remain very protective of their future generations.

This is exactly the reflex they need. Despite the Mokolé's religious reverence for the past, not all answers lie in the dawn of history. The key to sheltering and defending the Mother Cow lies in the generations yet being born, those who are inclined to look to the future as well as to the past. If the Dragon Breed are to endure and protect the Memory, they need the young ones, the young dragons.

Spring Sky: Military Diplomat

Quote: *Settle down there, big fella. White flag. Truce. You savvy? Good. I didn't come here looking for a fight — I can get those anywhere.*

Prelude: You were raised as a child of privilege and went to private school. Dad was a bigshot and Mom wasn't around much. Mom came to school when you were fourteen and took you out to the seashore dunes; there she told you to wait for her, and then left. You waited for days, till the visions came. Dragon's voice spoke between the waves of the sea, telling of life after life through ages of time. One morning of your vigil, as Sun showed his face, you became a dragon. Mom's clutch came to you then and taught you the Old Ways. You returned to school and to human society, slipping away now and then on clutch business.

Now you're a minor official in the national government, which gives you ample clearance to travel on "business." It's a good cover.

Concept: The elders found you, with your "human wiles," an excellent agent for Mokolé matters among the two-legs. The hardest missions are those to the other shapeshifters: you have made contacts among the Ravens, the Tigers, and the Makara. The Garou, now, that's another story. But someday, probably. If they're as bad news as Memory says, then maybe you should get them on your side.

Roleplaying Notes: Your fighting skills are formidable, even for a Mokolé, but you try to avoid renewing the old wars. Aware of the Mother's dire needs, you hope that the alliances you forge among your fellow Bête will prove potent against the Monster of the Deep Shadows. Your many Allies and Contacts are scattered all over the World of Darkness. You are young and inexperienced, though, and there are potent enemies that you know little about. Perhaps human shortsightedness is your most effective foe; it's certainly something that you're not readily prepared to fight.

Equipment: Passport, papers of office in your national government, Tec-9 pistol, dress uniform, credit cards.

Mokolé

Name:	Breed: Homid	Clutch:
Player:	Stream: Zhong Lung	Varna: Karna
Chronicle:	Auspice: Tung Chun	Concept: Military Diplomat

Attributes

Physical		Social		Mental	
Strength	●●●○○	Charisma	●●●●○	Perception	●●○○○
Dexterity	●●●○○	Manipulation	●●●○○	Intelligence	●●○○○
Stamina	●●○○○	Appearance	●●●○○	Wits	●●○○○

Abilities

Talents		Skills		Knowledges	
Alertness	●○○○○	Animal Ken	○○○○○	Computer	○○○○○
Athletics	○○○○○	Drive	●●○○○	Enigmas	○○○○○
Brawl	●●●○○	Etiquette	●●●○○	Investigation	○○○○○
Dodge	●●○○○	Firearms	●●○○○	Law	●●○○○
Empathy	●○○○○	Leadership	●●○○○	Linguistics	●●○○○
Expression	○○○○○	Melee	●●○○○	Medicine	○○○○○
Intimidation	●○○○○	Performance	●○○○○	Occult	○○○○○
Primal-Urge	○○○○○	Repair	○○○○○	Politics	●●●○○
Streetwise	●○○○○	Stealth	●○○○○	Rituals	○○○○○
Subterfuge	●○○○○	Survival	●○○○○	Science	●●○○○

Advantages

Backgrounds		Gifts	Gifts
Allies	●●●○○	Fatal Flaw	
Contacts	●●●●○	Bellow	
Mnesis	●○○○○		
	○○○○○		
	○○○○○		

Renown	Rage	Health
Glory	●●○○○○○○○○	Bruised ☐
●●○○○○○○○○	☐☐☐☐☐☐☐☐☐☐	Hurt -1 ☐
☐☐☐☐☐☐☐☐☐☐	**Gnosis**	Injured -1 ☐
Honor	●●○○○○○○○○	Wounded -2 ☐
●○○○○○○○○○	☐☐☐☐☐☐☐☐☐☐	Mauled -2 ☐
☐☐☐☐☐☐☐☐☐☐	**Willpower**	Crippled -5 ☐
Wisdom	●●●●●○○○○○	Incapacitated ☐
○○○○○○○○○○	☐☐☐☐☐☐☐☐☐☐	**Sun Dice**
☐☐☐☐☐☐☐☐☐☐		Gain an extra die to initiative dice pool.
Rank		

Noonday Sun: Lawspeaker Mystic

Quote: *Sun does not turn from his Path. You should have followed his example.*

Prelude: You hatched in the blazing noon of an Australian riverbank and headed for the water. The river was full of fish and you made yourself at home. Mom fussed over you more than the others, but you hardly noticed. Tough enough to survive out there; you never felt the many pairs of eyes on you.

The river began to taste bad one day, after the rains had come and gone. Filth made the fish die. Then two-legs came. Thunder from a blue sky, and Mom bleeding and still, same as the rest of the mob. Rage filled you for the first time, and the two-legs fled before a living Tyrannosaurus. They didn't flee far.

Human meat was better than fish any day.

As you bellowed triumph, the Crowning found you. The rites they taught you filled you with the wisdom of a thousand ancestors and the law of eons. Now you put that wisdom to work for you; it's the fire that floods your muscles when you set into motion. And you can move damnably quick when need be.

Concept: You serve your mob as a judge and lawspeaker. You are young for a judge; you have some knowledge of the Law but want to know more about it. You have already sat as judge at several Gathers, and your services are in demand among clutches, as good judges aren't easy to find. Your Gnosis helps keep you steady. Be harsh, as it's what the lawbreakers deserve, but fair. You can relax at Gather, though, and enjoy your clutchmates' company.

Roleplaying Notes: You speak slowly and deliberately; some would mistake it for a lack of intelligence, but it's a simple desire to say exactly what you feel. Speaking quickly garbles words. You are also relatively slow and measured in your movements — as you carefully observe the situation and watch for the precise point of action. When you actually choose to act, you're quicker than any snake.

Equipment: Body paint, favorite stones, staff of office.

Mokolé™

Name:	Breed: Suchid	Clutch:
Player:	Stream: Gumagan	Varna: Karna
Chronicle:	Auspice: Unshading	Concept: Lawspeaker Mystic

Attributes

Physical		Social		Mental	
Strength	●●●●○	Charisma	●●○○○	Perception	●●●○○
Dexterity	●●●○○	Manipulation	●●○○○	Intelligence	●●●○○
Stamina	●●●●○	Appearance	●●○○○	Wits	●●○○○

Abilities

Talents		Skills		Knowledges	
Alertness	●●●○○	Animal Ken	●●○○○	Computer	○○○○○
Athletics	●○○○○	Drive	○○○○○	Enigmas	○○○○○
Brawl	●○○○○	Etiquette	○○○○○	Investigation	●○○○○
Dodge	●○○○○	Firearms	○○○○○	Law	●○○○○
Empathy	○○○○○	Leadership	●●○○○	Linguistics	○○○○○
Expression	●○○○○	Melee	○○○○○	Medicine	○○○○○
Intimidation	●●○○○	Performance	●○○○○	Occult	●○○○○
Primal-Urge	●●●○○	Repair	○○○○○	Politics	○○○○○
Streetwise	○○○○○	Stealth	●○○○○	Rituals	●●●○○
Subterfuge	○○○○○	Survival	●●●○○	Science	○○○○○

Advantages

Backgrounds		Gifts	Gifts
Fetish	●●○○○	Speed of Thought	
Totem	●●●○○	Truth of Olodumare	
Wallow	●●●○○		
	○○○○○		
	○○○○○		

Renown

Glory
● ○ ○ ○ ○ ○ ○ ○ ○ ○
❑ ❑ ❑ ❑ ❑ ❑ ❑ ❑ ❑ ❑

Honor
● ○ ○ ○ ○ ○ ○ ○ ○ ○
❑ ❑ ❑ ❑ ❑ ❑ ❑ ❑ ❑ ❑

Wisdom
● ○ ○ ○ ○ ○ ○ ○ ○ ○
❑ ❑ ❑ ❑ ❑ ❑ ❑ ❑ ❑ ❑

Rank

Rage
● ● ● ● ● ○ ○ ○ ○ ○
❑ ❑ ❑ ❑ ❑ ❑ ❑ ❑ ❑ ❑

Gnosis
● ● ● ● ○ ○ ○ ○ ○ ○
❑ ❑ ❑ ❑ ❑ ❑ ❑ ❑ ❑ ❑

Willpower
● ● ● ● ● ○ ○ ○ ○ ○
❑ ❑ ❑ ❑ ❑ ❑ ❑ ❑ ❑ ❑

Health

Bruised		❑
Hurt	-1	❑
Injured	-1	❑
Wounded	-2	❑
Mauled	-2	❑
Crippled	-5	❑
Incapacitated		❑

Sun Dice

Subtract one die from dark-related foes' dice pool

Night: Lizardskin

Setting Sun: Social Worker

Quote: *Don't be getting in my face. I got something I gotta tell you.*

Prelude: You were born right here, far from the swampy South where Grandma spent her childhood pulling weeds and picking tomatoes. Later, she lived in the city, and she had her hands full raising you — Mama was spaced out on drugs and Dad long gone. Her tales of alligator-men, haints and other critters were just made up to entertain you, you thought.

One summer, though, the two of you rode the Greyhound down home, and an uncle you barely remembered took one look at you and started saying the same things. They hiked with you into the smelly, bug-filled swamp and you realized all of a sudden that you had been here before. Every tree, every creek, had a memory attached to it: slavery, flight, battle, freedom, work, play, and your own people. As the sun sank, you remembered more and more. By trail's end, it was a gator that accompanied your Kin.

You went to school on a scholarship (history was easy!) and decided that Dragon needed you more right here than somewhere you'd never been. At least you know the turf. Most of the worst kids on the streets give you some respect; those that don't, well, they learn to.

Concept: You are a social worker at a shelter on the dark streets of the big city. Your life hasn't been easy, and as a Mokolé, you feel threatened and cut off from Sun in this human realm of stone and concrete. However, the most precious resource in the world is here — new Mokolé. Unknowing Kinfolk from Southern farms and Third World warzones have settled here, and the clutch has sent you to find Dragon's Brood in the 'hood.

Roleplaying Notes: You need your high Gnosis to keep from exploding with Rage at the cruelty and stupidity of human society. Mokolé may eat human flesh, but they can't stand unnecessary suffering. You have been endlessly disappointed in your attempts to find and help lost hatchlings before the Garou or the Dissolver gets them. Each one you find, however, is a treasure beyond price. You have developed an awareness of the other Awakened on the dark city streets where you work, and have come to realize that it isn't practical to cull every Leech you meet. In fact, some of them are cultured and intelligent creatures with an enlightened self-interest in promoting the society of their human prey. Also, the telltales have twice led you to troubled kids who were Garou, not Mokolé.

You don't have much Mnesis, and you don't know as much about Mokolé life as you should — Grandma passed soon after you went to college. The one thing that you do know is that each and every one of Dragon's Kin is too precious for drive-bys, crack and gangs to get them.

Equipment: Dragon crystal, credentials, cellphone, van, apartment with spare bedroom.

Mokolé™

Name:	Breed: Homid	Clutch:
Player:	Stream: Mokolé-mbembe	Varna: Halpatee
Chronicle:	Auspice: Warding	Concept: Social Worker

Attributes

Physical		Social		Mental	
Strength	●●○○○	Charisma	●●●●○	Perception	●●●○○
Dexterity	●●○○○	Manipulation	●●●○○	Intelligence	●●○○○
Stamina	●●○○○	Appearance	●●●○○	Wits	●●●○○

Abilities

Talents		Skills		Knowledges	
Alertness	●●○○○	Animal Ken	○○○○○	Computer	○○○○○
Athletics	○○○○○	Drive	●○○○○	Enigmas	○○○○○
Brawl	●○○○○	Etiquette	○○○○○	Investigation	●●○○○
Dodge	●○○○○	Firearms	●●○○○	Law	●○○○○
Empathy	●●●○○	Leadership	●●○○○	Linguistics	●○○○○
Expression	○○○○○	Melee	●○○○○	Medicine	●○○○○
Intimidation	●○○○○	Performance	○○○○○	Occult	○○○○○
Primal-Urge	●○○○○	Repair	●●○○○	Politics	○○○○○
Streetwise	●●●○○	Stealth	●○○○○	Rituals	○○○○○
Subterfuge	●○○○○	Survival	○○○○○	Science	○○○○○

Advantages

Backgrounds		Gifts	Gifts
Allies	●○○○○	Falling Touch	
Contacts	●●○○○	Mother's Touch	
Mnesis	●○○○○	Talk	
Resources	●●○○○		
	○○○○○		

Renown	Rage	Health		
Glory	●●●●○○○○○○	Bruised		☐
●○○○○○○○○○	☐☐☐☐☐☐☐☐☐☐	Hurt	-1	☐
☐☐☐☐☐☐☐☐☐☐	**Gnosis**	Injured	-1	☐
Honor	●●●●●○○○○○	Wounded	-2	☐
●○○○○○○○○○	☐☐☐☐☐☐☐☐☐☐	Mauled	-2	☐
☐☐☐☐☐☐☐☐☐☐	**Willpower**	Crippled	-5	☐
Wisdom	●●●●●●○○○○	Incapacitated		☐
●○○○○○○○○○	☐☐☐☐☐☐☐☐☐☐	**Sun Dice**		
☐☐☐☐☐☐☐☐☐☐		+1 die to defend others, retreat or follow orders		
Rank				

Autumn Sky (Zarad): Rainforest Ethnobotanist

Quote: *No — breathe deeply, don't spit it out. Now feel its power. Strong stuff, eh?*

Prelude: Your parents died in a massacre in your war-torn nation. You grew up in refugee camps, then at a church orphanage where the kids were treated like zoo animals. The nuns were mean and the other kids were too, so you read as much as you could to escape. You learned that the world was a very big place, and that it was as troubled as you were. The botany texts were useful. Soon you were combing the nearby forests for your collection. Sister Mary got you a place at the conservation department, and you began working for a white scientist who studied your people and their ways, especially their use of the teacher plants. Soon you knew more than he. You enjoyed the altered states that the plant medicines brought, when the plants made you a lizard or a dragon.

One night you awoke to find yourself still a lizard. You were scared, but the hallucinations came back, stronger than ever-voices long dead, telling you who you truly were and what your destiny was.

You found other Mokolé, but it seemed that they cared for nothing but memory and the past. It was so obvious to you that now was the time to act, and that the life and lore of the rainforests had to be preserved before it vanished into past tense forever.

Concept: You are an indigenous helper to researchers who study the plant lore of the tropics. Obviously, many are corporate scientists who seek commercially exploitable products, while others are looking for the thrill of new hallucinogens. You do a lot of traveling and are in demand for trips. No one guesses that Mnesis makes you a perfect guide. In between trips, you are the ritemaster for two far-removed clutches, neither of whom has a Zarad of its own.

Roleplaying Notes: You know the local landscape like the back of your claw. You end up defending humans in word and deed: many of your fellow Mokolé don't see the point of cooperating with them at all. You need an easygoing nature to get along both with the pushy, demanding foreign scientists and the stuffy, hidebound crocodiles back at the wallow. You'd like to find a good Kinfolk mate, but the village men are lacking somehow. Maybe you'll meet someone on a journey.

Equipment: Khaki shorts, walking shoes, pouch of hallucinogenic plant specimens, smoking pipe.

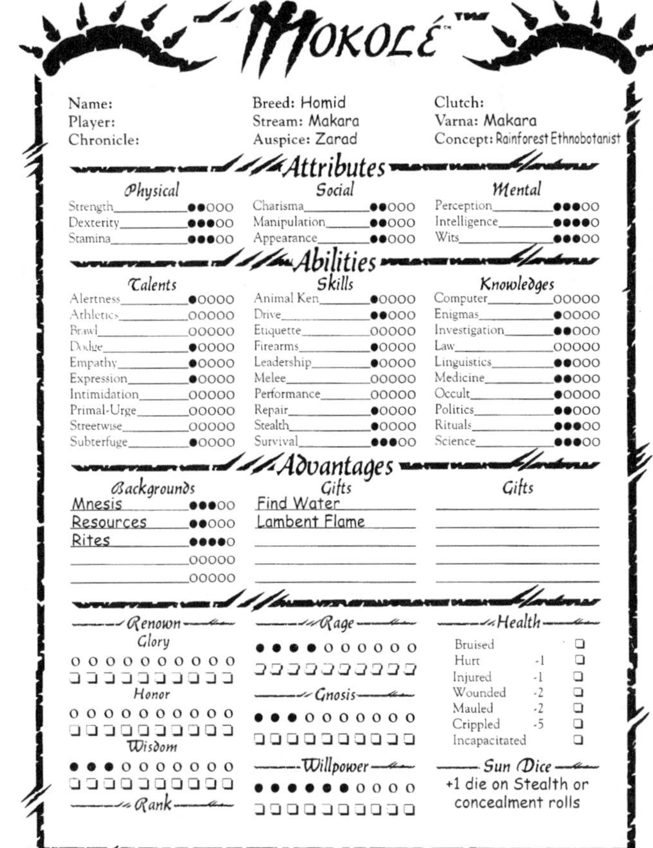

MOKOLÉ

Name:	Breed: Homid	Clutch:
Player:	Stream: Makara	Varna: Makara
Chronicle:	Auspice: Zarad	Concept: Rainforest Ethnobotanist

Attributes

Physical		Social		Mental	
Strength	●●○○○	Charisma	●●○○○	Perception	●●●○○
Dexterity	●●●○○	Manipulation	●●○○○	Intelligence	●●●●○
Stamina	●●●○○	Appearance	●●○○○	Wits	●●●○○

Abilities

Talents		Skills		Knowledges	
Alertness	●○○○○	Animal Ken	●○○○○	Computer	○○○○○
Athletics	○○○○○	Drive	●●○○○	Enigmas	●○○○○
Brawl	○○○○○	Etiquette	○○○○○	Investigation	●●○○○
Dodge	●○○○○	Firearms	●○○○○	Law	○○○○○
Empathy	●○○○○	Leadership	●○○○○	Linguistics	●●○○○
Expression	●○○○○	Melee	○○○○○	Medicine	●●○○○
Intimidation	○○○○○	Performance	○○○○○	Occult	●○○○○
Primal-Urge	○○○○○	Repair	●○○○○	Politics	●●○○○
Streetwise	○○○○○	Stealth	●○○○○	Rituals	●●●○○
Subterfuge	●○○○○	Survival	●●●○○	Science	●●●○○

Advantages

Backgrounds		Gifts	Gifts
Mnesis	●●●○○	Find Water	
Resources	●●○○○	Lambent Flame	
Rites	●●●●○		
	○○○○○		
	○○○○○		

Renown	Rage	Health	
Glory	●●●●○○○○○○	Bruised	❑
○○○○○○○○○○	❑❑❑❑❑❑❑❑❑❑	Hurt -1	❑
❑❑❑❑❑❑❑❑❑❑	**Gnosis**	Injured -1	❑
Honor	●●●○○○○○○○	Wounded -2	❑
○○○○○○○○○○	❑❑❑❑❑❑❑❑❑❑	Mauled -2	❑
❑❑❑❑❑❑❑❑❑❑	**Willpower**	Crippled -5	❑
Wisdom	●●●●●●○○○○	Incapacitated	❑
●●●○○○○○○○	❑❑❑❑❑❑❑❑❑❑	**Sun Dice**	
❑❑❑❑❑❑❑❑❑❑		+1 die on Stealth or concealment rolls	
Rank			

Midnight Sun: Triceratops Poet

Quote: *Petals fall, and so do we. But what is Within, we pass on.*

Prelude: You were hatched a lizard in the deserts of the American Southwest. Sun, sand and chomping rats were your world, until one night a gigantic creature began chasing you instead. It had two legs and smelled very bad. You fought madly, and you began to change shape, shifted until you were big as a sand dune and bellowed Rage from your beak, brandishing horns at the two-legs.

He smiled and laughed. Then he hissed at you, words that you suddenly knew. He was your friend, he said, a shapechanger, descended like you from the lost Kings whose shape you wore beneath the ten thousands suns of the midnight desert. He told you the lore and legends of the Mokolé, and of your own sun sign, the crazy backwards Midnight Suns.

You met a local clutch soon after, and tried walking as a two-legs into the small town nearby. It was too noisy and smelly. Even the "reservation" where human Kin lived was a nasty place. The desert had more to say.

Mokolé

Name:	Breed: Suchid	Clutch:
Player:	Stream: Mokolé-mbembe	Varna: Unktehi
Chronicle:	Auspice: Shining	Concept: Triceratops Poet

Attributes

Physical		Social		Mental	
Strength	●●○○○	Charisma	●●○○○	Perception	●●●●○
Dexterity	●●●●○	Manipulation	●●○○○	Intelligence	●●●○○
Stamina	●●●●○	Appearance	●●○○○	Wits	●●●○○

Abilities

Talents		Skills		Knowledges	
Alertness	●●○○○	Animal Ken	●●○○○	Computer	○○○○○
Athletics	○○○○○	Drive	○○○○○	Enigmas	●●●○○
Brawl	●○○○○	Etiquette	●○○○○	Investigation	○○○○○
Dodge	●●○○○	Firearms	○○○○○	Law	○○○○○
Empathy	●○○○○	Leadership	○○○○○	Linguistics	●○○○○
Expression	●●●○○	Melee	○○○○○	Medicine	○○○○○
Intimidation	○○○○○	Performance	●●●○○	Occult	○○○○○
Primal-Urge	●●○○○	Repair	○○○○○	Politics	○○○○○
Streetwise	○○○○○	Stealth	●○○○○	Rituals	●●○○○
Subterfuge	○○○○○	Survival	●●●○○	Science	○○○○○

Advantages

Backgrounds		Gifts	Gifts
Allies	●○○○○	Shed	
Mnesis	●○○○○	Spirits of Laughter	
Rites	●●○○○		
Wallow	●●○○○		
	○○○○○		

Renown

Glory: ●○○○○○○○○○ / ☐☐☐☐☐☐☐☐☐☐

Honor: ●○○○○○○○○○ / ☐☐☐☐☐☐☐☐☐☐

Wisdom: ●○○○○○○○○○ / ☐☐☐☐☐☐☐☐☐☐

Rank

Rage: ●●●●●○○○○○ / ☐☐☐☐☐☐☐☐☐☐

Gnosis: ●●●●○○○○○○ / ☐☐☐☐☐☐☐☐☐☐

Willpower: ●●●●○○○○○○ / ☐☐☐☐☐☐☐☐☐☐

Health

Bruised		☐
Hurt	-1	☐
Injured	-1	☐
Wounded	-2	☐
Mauled	-2	☐
Crippled	-5	☐
Incapacitated		☐

Sun Dice

+1 die when faced with hopeless odds

Concept: In your human shape, you are a drifter who lurks about the fringes of a small town. As a Gila monster, you are a careful and efficient hunter in an inhospitable environment. As a Mokolé, you are a star watcher, an amateur astronomer, a poet and a storyteller. Flowers are not only beautiful — but they taste pretty good after a day of cropping sage.

Roleplaying Notes: You tell tales of Mokolé and the Kings to your clutch and their Kin, and teach the young ones their great heritage. You mix Mnesis and your own imagination. After all, if you make it up, it's still a Mokolé tale, isn't it? If they can tell what's true and what's false, they'll have learned to think for themselves.

You are peaceful and quiet most of the time, sunning, hunting, grazing, and watching the Many Suns. When roused to action, you're a hard hitter but a little slow.

Equipment: Sunny rock outcrop, burrow, bunch of flowers, human clothes (cached in burrow), necklace of native beads.

Summer Sky: Seeker of Mnesis Lore

Quote: *You talk like Kasyapa. Who was he? King over the land, a thousand and some years back. What do you mean, how do I know?*

Prelude: You were hatched a crocodile on the banks of the Madras River, but even as a hatchling, you knew more than you should have. Your sunny naps were filled with dreams wherein you walked like a man and wielded a golden spear, or quested across jungles and stormy mountains in the shape of a great dragon warrior. When the Change came, you were more than ready. Your clutch gathered round you and listened enraptured to the tale of your Mnesis vision. The elders consecrated you a Wanderer. Then you set to work at your great task: reuniting the Mokolé of the world though Mnesis.

Concept: You know how much the Mokolé know and how much they have lost. You wander from clutch to clutch, or from clutch to rumors of a clutch, seeking to find all the Mokolé remaining on the Mother's Face and learn Mnesis lore from any and all. There is no stick hard enough to drive you away when you can learn something (though many have tried). When you can, you teach what you have learned. When you cannot, you remember it. You have even learned the two-legs' writing to store your knowledge: anthropologists and historians would kill to get hold of your journal.

Roleplaying Notes: You are cheerful, friendly, and easy to get to know. People of all species like you. If you don't like them, they never find out. You are insatiably curious and are sometimes reproached for acting like the Proudest Monkey.

You have Allies and Contacts in many wallows round the world, who help you get from place to place when you can't walk (in human form) or swim (as a crocodile). You take messages, parcels, and greetings from wallow to wallow, do people favors and help get things under control. Many clutches lack a Gathering and ask you to stay. Maybe someday...

Equipment: Sandals, Dedicated backpack with enormous notebook written in your variant of the Dragon's Tongue, letters in six different languages, and lunch.

Mokolé

Name:	Breed: Suchid	Clutch:
Player:	Stream: Makara	Varna: Karna
Chronicle:	Auspice: Grisma	Concept: Seeker of Mnesis Lore

Attributes

Physical		Social		Mental	
Strength	●●○○○	Charisma	●●●○○	Perception	●●○○○
Dexterity	●●●●○	Manipulation	●●●○○	Intelligence	●●○○○
Stamina	●●●●○	Appearance	●●○○○	Wits	●●○○○

Abilities

Talents		Skills		Knowledges	
Alertness	●●●○○	Animal Ken	●○○○○	Computer	○○○○○
Athletics	●●●○○	Drive	○○○○○	Enigmas	●●○○○
Brawl	●○○○○	Etiquette	○○○○○	Investigation	●●○○○
Dodge	●●○○○	Firearms	○○○○○	Law	○○○○○
Empathy	●○○○○	Leadership	●○○○○	Linguistics	●●●●○
Expression	●○○○○	Melee	○○○○○	Medicine	○○○○○
Intimidation	○○○○○	Performance	●●○○○	Occult	○○○○○
Primal-Urge	○○○○○	Repair	○○○○○	Politics	●○○○○
Streetwise	○○○○○	Stealth	●●●○○	Rituals	●○○○○
Subterfuge	●●○○○	Survival	●●○○○	Science	○○○○○

Advantages

Backgrounds		Gifts	Gifts
Allies	●●●○○	Speed of Thought	
Contacts	●●●○○	Pilot Snake	
Mnesis	●●○○○		
	○○○○○		
	○○○○○		

Renown	Rage	Health
Glory	●●○○○○○○○○	Bruised ❑
○○○○○○○○○○	❑❑❑❑❑❑❑❑❑❑	Hurt -1 ❑
❑❑❑❑❑❑❑❑❑❑	**Gnosis**	Injured -1 ❑
Honor	●●●●○○○○○○	Wounded -2 ❑
●●●○○○○○○○	❑❑❑❑❑❑❑❑❑❑	Mauled -2 ❑
❑❑❑❑❑❑❑❑❑❑	**Willpower**	Crippled -5 ❑
Wisdom	●●●●●●○○○○	Incapacitated ❑
○○○○○○○○○○	❑❑❑❑❑❑❑❑❑❑	**Sun Dice**
❑❑❑❑❑❑❑❑❑❑		+1 die when acting collectively to benefit Mokolé
Rank		

Eclipsed Sun: Native-rights Guerrilla

Quote: *Land and liberty!* (rattle of machine-gun fire)

Prelude: You were born to Kinfolk parents, a chief among The People and her husband. You'd be a chief too someday, they said. But the tall strangers had taken your people's land, killed the animals, cut down the trees and flowers. Your people worked for the new masters, drank liquor, or did nothing at all.

The old men had their eyes on you, though, and one day when you were tall enough to work, they told you that you were more than you knew. Born as the corona flickered amidst the noonday stars, you were destined for greatness, the first Dragon Chief that The People had seen in a hundred years. Then the Ancestors within you showed you how to take the Dragon shape and wield the Gifts of Sun.

The "landlord" came after that and evicted The People, told them the land had metal on it, so it wasn't yours. When your mother led a protest, she was jailed and beaten to death. Survivors fled the village and the only home they'd ever known. Huddled in slums and refugee camps, The People needed a hero.

That's you.

Concept: You are the leader of a native-rights guerrilla movement. Despite your youth, you have scored several coups on the landlords who made your tribe homeless: maybe the courts and the judges will listen. If they don't, they can argue with Dragon's Fire. Leading your team of Kin, you have brought justice to the men who killed your mother. Now it's the landlord's turn.

Your tribe of Kinfolk relies on you and almost worships you; you have two lovers among the Kinfolk and would like to have a child when the time is right. You worry about what would happen to them if you weren't there. It may be time to seek allies in this struggle.

Roleplaying Notes: You are a Crowning, tough, confident, and beloved by The People. That and 75 bhat will get you a cup of coffee. You want a peaceful solution to the problems you face, but no one seems to care. You are a king, but your kingdom is a few thousand people in a shantytown, and things aren't getting much better. Despite being an Eclipsed Sun, you are going to have to play some serious politics, and fast.

You are a good fighter, but all of your actions have been against humans. If other Awakened beings oppose you, you won't stand long. Your Archid form is ideal for jungle warfare, but you are the only Mokolé you know. There must be others, and they might be friendly.

Equipment: AK-47, fatigues, explosives, binoculars, jungle knife.

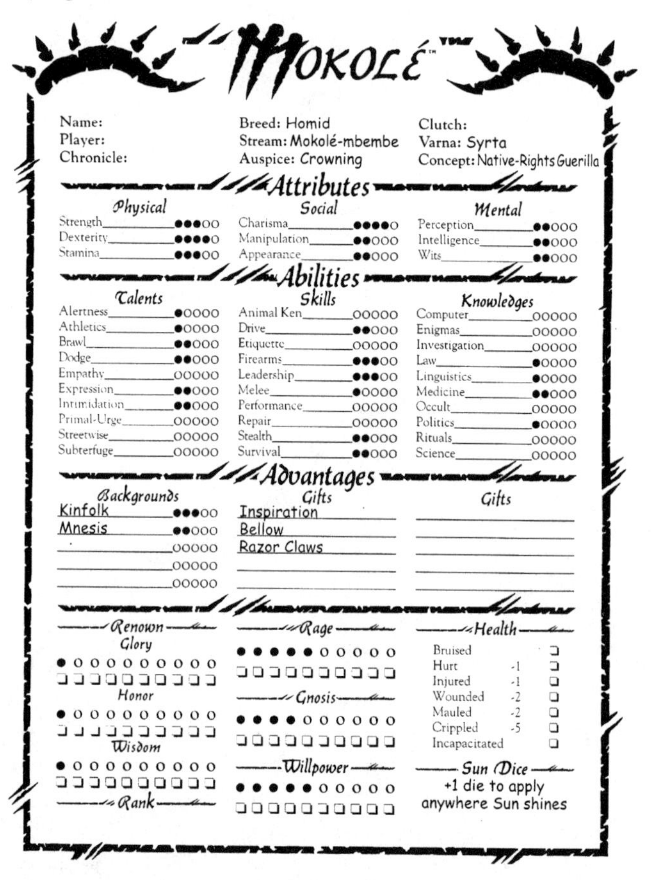

Mokolé™

Name:	Breed: Homid	Clutch:
Player:	Stream: Mokolé-mbembe	Varna: Syrta
Chronicle:	Auspice: Crowning	Concept: Native-Rights Guerilla

Attributes

Physical		Social		Mental	
Strength	●●●○○	Charisma	●●●●○	Perception	●●○○○
Dexterity	●●●●○	Manipulation	●●○○○	Intelligence	●●○○○
Stamina	●●●○○	Appearance	●●○○○	Wits	●●○○○

Abilities

Talents		Skills		Knowledges	
Alertness	●○○○○	Animal Ken	○○○○○	Computer	○○○○○
Athletics	●○○○○	Drive	●●○○○	Enigmas	○○○○○
Brawl	●●○○○	Etiquette	○○○○○	Investigation	○○○○○
Dodge	●●○○○	Firearms	●●●○○	Law	●○○○○
Empathy	○○○○○	Leadership	●●●○○	Linguistics	●○○○○
Expression	●●○○○	Melee	●○○○○	Medicine	●●○○○
Intimidation	●●○○○	Performance	○○○○○	Occult	○○○○○
Primal-Urge	○○○○○	Repair	○○○○○	Politics	●○○○○
Streetwise	○○○○○	Stealth	●●○○○	Rituals	○○○○○
Subterfuge	○○○○○	Survival	●●○○○	Science	○○○○○

Advantages

Backgrounds		Gifts	Gifts
Kinfolk	●●●○○	Inspiration	
Mnesis	●●○○○	Bellow	
	○○○○○	Razor Claws	
	○○○○○		
	○○○○○		

Renown	Rage	Health		
Glory	●●●●●○○○○○	Bruised		❑
●○○○○○○○○○	❑❑❑❑❑❑❑❑❑❑	Hurt	-1	❑
❑❑❑❑❑❑❑❑❑❑	Gnosis	Injured	-1	❑
Honor	●●●●○○○○○○	Wounded	-2	❑
●○○○○○○○○○	❑❑❑❑❑❑❑❑❑❑	Mauled	-2	❑
❑❑❑❑❑❑❑❑❑❑	Willpower	Crippled	-5	❑
Wisdom	●●●●●○○○○○	Incapacitated		❑
●○○○○○○○○○	❑❑❑❑❑❑❑❑❑❑	Sun Dice		
❑❑❑❑❑❑❑❑❑❑		+1 die to apply anywhere Sun shines		
Rank				

Famous Mokolé

Sal-Afsan, Far-Seer, Concealing the Clutch of the Land's Heart

The Kings ruled for endless ages, their ideas and beliefs changing as slowly as the continents drifted. Afsan was different. A bright young reptile, he hatched under a cloudy sky and was therefore assumed to be a mystic by his Gaia-worshipping clutch. He showed promise at counting the stars and was set to be trained as a sky-watcher. During a long sea trip, he observed the celestial bodies closely and devised a new device to make them appear more clearly — the "far-seer" or telescope. With this instrument, he concocted the idea that the planets circled the sun, rather than Gaia. He was accused of heresy by Gaia-worshippers and the Noonday Suns gave true meaning to his sun auspice — Afsan was blinded in punishment. The evidence for his theory became impossible to ignore, however, and within his lifetime he was vindicated. Afsan was single-handedly responsible for knowledge of the structure of the Solar System among Mokolé. He had eight Mokolé children, two of whom became noted scholars. His instrument, the "far-seer," became standard equipment until the WonderWork. Tragically, although the Mokolé still remember the story of Sal-Afsan, the humans had to learn the same lesson all over again.

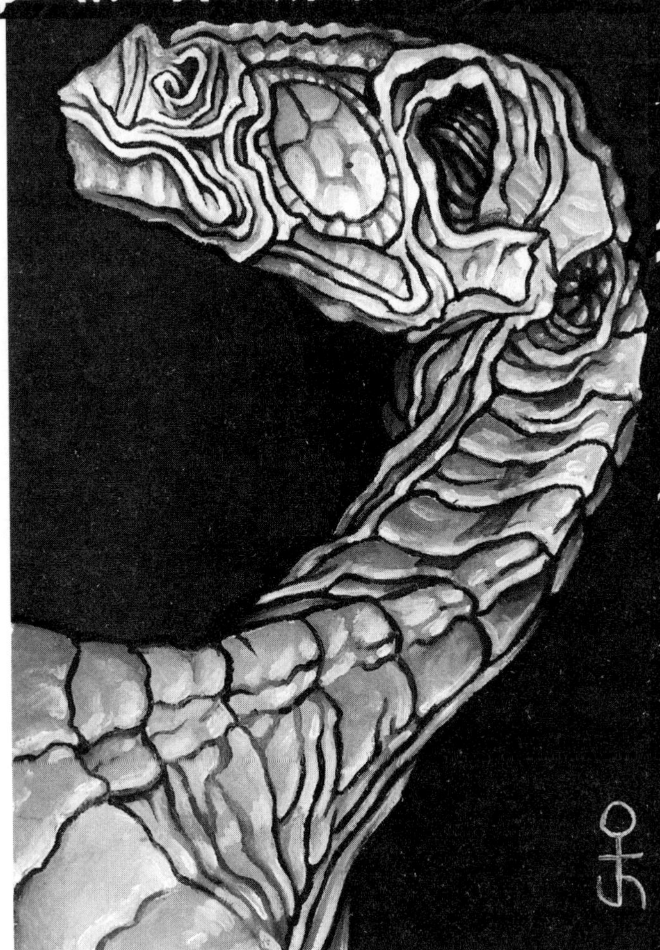

Joy-Hunter, Striking For the Clutch Of The Golden Beaches

The Kings loved the climate of what would someday be the American Southeast. One of their cities was The Golden Beaches, located in today's Florida. Joy-Hunter was hatched in the middle Cretaceous. Her mother was a powerful Crowning and her Kinfolk father a soldier. She was famous even in her time for her fearless pursuit of dangerous animals, of whom the Cretaceous had plenty. Her Archid form was a raptor, but she loved to hunt in Drachid form, carrying weapons of her own creation, relishing the challenge. She even hunted the new creatures, mammals, as they were pests in the Kings' cities.

Joy-Hunter laid seven clutches of eggs, two of which contained true Mokolé, and many living Mokolé carry her Mnesis. The Shining Wave-Without-A-Shore jokes that he regrets that Joy-Hunter did not kill any more mammals than she did.

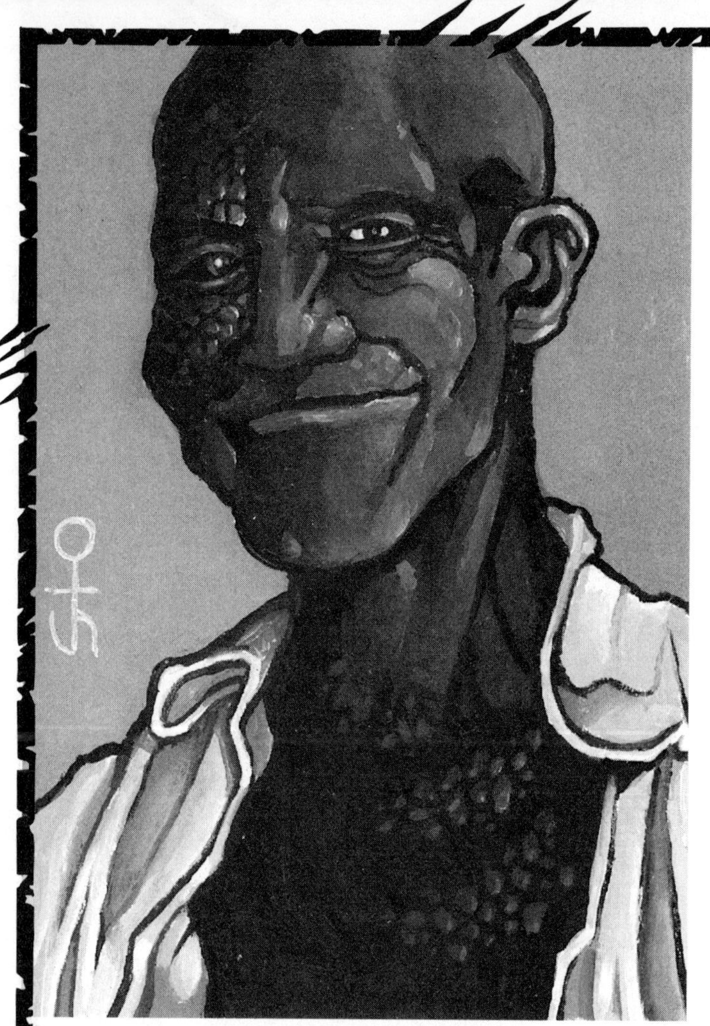

Morwangu

Morwangu was born after the Great War, when the Dreamtime shook to the death screams of the Bunyip and the lands of the Dead convulsed with a war of their own. Clouds darkened the sky as the greatstorm poured rain on the land. His legal name was Abraham Miller, but to the Alligator River Mob he was Morwangu. Ulungan (Arnhem Land) was his home, in the dryland of Australia's north coast. The old women, who recognized the signs, knew soon enough that he was Gumagan. At his man-making, he received the sacred scars and entered the dreaming, where he took the shape of a crested, beaked Dreamtime beast and walked with Perenty Man under the moon.

Morwangu showed that he was much more than a shapeshifter. He spent many years sitting with the old men of Ulungan's mobs, sifting through tales and dreamings to reconstruct lore that white invaders had hoped was lost forever. His powerful Mnesis enabled him to reach back to a time before whitefella came, but always one memory eluded him — the fate of Wolaru and the clutch of Scales of Many Colors. He sought among one corroborree after another for some clue to her fate. In the process, he became a master of Koori rites and lore. He even went so far as to seek the Bunyip, but they were long gone.

Morwangu realized when he heard of the War of Tears that the Garou would slaughter the Gumagan if they found them, and so cast powerful magics to prevent this. His work has so confused the Garou that several have met Morwangu without knowing that he was anything but an old Koori.

Uncle Monday the Great Alligator Conjure Man of the Everglades, Concealing the Clutch of the River of Grass

The Seminoles, descendants of Muskogee Indians who had fled into the Florida swamps, welcomed runaway slaves into their midst. Uncle Monday, named for the day of his birth, was an African-born Mokolé who had gone across the ocean to protect his people. When the United States government forced the "Treaty" of Payne's Landing on the Seminoles in 1835, the Kinfolk chief Osceola led resistance, aided by the Garou Micanopy of the Uktena and Jumper of the Wendigo. They led Major Francis Dade's forces into the Everglades, although the white man's Dissolver-weapons killed many of the Seminoles. When the Garou had cut off Dade's retreat, Uncle Monday shapeshifted into a huge alligator and called hundreds of scaly Kin to his aid. Of Dade's 108-man detachment only one man was allowed to return. Uncle Monday was a homid Rising Sun from the Clutch of the Congo, and bore the scars of the Congo nation. He and his fellow Mokolé, sometimes allied with Garou in this time of need, held off the federal troops until 1842, when the government called off the removal effort. His clutch, the River of Grass, still holds an ancient wallow site in the depths of the swamps. Uncle Monday himself entered the Sleep of the Dragon long ago, and the River of Grass claims that they know how to wake him should he be needed.

Morwangu was in his fifties when his daughter had a true Mokolé son, Jeffrey Miller, or "Jeffo." He took the boy in hand, but soon realized that Jeffo took nothing seriously at all. Jeffo held that the Koori had better laugh or they would do nothing but cry.

Morwangu and Jeffo realized when a Wanderer brought news of the Amazon War that the war could bring peace between Garou and Mokolé — or at least, that was Jeffo's typical backward reasoning. Sun led Peter to them and them to Peter and Peter's remarkable education was the result.

Hei Lungren, Tung Chun of the Clutch of Seven Pearls

Chinese alligator suchids are thoughtful creatures; the near extinction of their varna has made them reluctant soldiers and deep thinkers. Hei Lungren hatched in an alligator nest along the Yangtze basin and immediately began fighting for her life — early on, a quick snap convinced a "collector" this specimen wasn't worth the trouble. She grew to maturity hunting in the river's mud and keeping out of sight: the warlords' era was unsafe for anyone.

Her First Change came during World War II, when the nearby village was massacred by Kuomintang soldiers and the few survivors hid in the swamps. Hearing their prayers to the Great Mother, Hei Lungren went into a Mnesis trance and emerged as a horned, crested dragon who guided the peasants to safety in a hidden valley that she remembered from ages ago. When Mao became an even more tyrannical ruler, she sought a nearby clutch, at the Spring of Seven Pearls, and with the help of clever Kin, had the entire area organized as a commune with Kinfolk for members. Her Mnesis of ancient Zhong Guo was a tactical advantage as she battled Kuei-jin, technomages intent on draining the dragon nest of chi, and the Rage-demons who fattened on violence and fear. The Kuei-jin, who fed endlessly on corpses from the death camps and grew mighty, were a terrible menace. She remains extremely intolerant of any vampires today and the mere mention of the undead can send her into killing rage.

At the death of Mao she entered the Sleep of the Dragon and did not wake until a few years ago, preferring to leave clutch business to the Kin and the other dragons of the clutch. The recent menace posed by dams to the Yangtze's natural energy flows was a serious enough problem for her Kin to wake her.

In her human form she is a small, fortyish woman with her hair in a bun and traditional peasant blouse and pants. In her alligator form she is also small, but agile and quick. In her Archid form she is a huge chi'lung with a royal crest, long claws, and a fiery, blazing pearl on her forehead. She sometimes wanders Asia, and might be found fighting evil creatures, seeking justice for her people, or exploring long-forgotten mountain trails and swamp passages.

Sun's Hand, Grisma of the Clutch of Kanpur

The Makara are the Stream of the Folk, the diplomats and go-betweens of the Mokolé. Sun's Hand is remarkable even

among his own people for his energy and successful maneuvering in the complex field of human-Makara interactions.

Hatched to a Gharial clutch near Kanpur, India, Sun's Hand saw the swamp vanish as the two-legs drained more and more for their beanfields. The elders of the clutch knew early on that he would be a forceful leader when they saw him lurking to scare away villagers, then slip off before retaliation could arrive. On the day of his Change, he assumed the form of a great three-headed Sun-lizard, a living embodiment of the Makara of legend. His Mnesis was not strong, but his wish for justice was. His human form, in which he entered the nearby villages as a holy beggar or *sadhu*, served well as he gathered information about who and what was really behind the despoiling of his land. Memos on the desk of the mayor proved that Magadon wanted the land for a drug manufacturing plant, and planned to stage an "accident" that would render the land valueless. Sun's Hand vowed to bring justice to them.

He has worked with human and gavial as well as the Dragon Breed and his methods have been as subtle as distributing comic books to the village children (the hero was a brave gavial) and as blatant as extorting money from the crooked mayor to buy land for a "gavial breeding farm" which has become a showpiece for ecodiversity proponents.

Now in his sixties, Sun's Hand is referred to as "Crowning" by Mokolé-mbembe, even though he is nothing of the kind. He is one of the most prestigious Judges in all India, and petitioners come to him from the many clutches of the land. In his gavial form, he is a large, very old Gharial with a prominent red lump on his snout. In his Archid form, he has three heads, scaly armor and huge, tearing claws. This battle-form has allowed him to thwart fomor "enforcers" and gangs of Magadon thugs who still seek to wrest his home from him. His human form is an elderly, bearded man, usually in loincloth and begging bowl, who "wanders," listening to people's talk and occasionally offering oracles or preaching a sermon. He uses the name Vijay Suryadatti when in human form.

Sun's Hand has sought alliances with other clutches and streams, although in the present they are more and more difficult to locate. He recently contacted Towers-Above-The-Kings and learned of their troubles. He has offered them refuge on his land, but they are unable to travel so far.

Braney, Shining without a clutch

I love you
You love me
Let's perform atrocity....
— Braney

For the past several years, an immensely popular children's TV show created by two Texas "housewives" has aired on OmniTV, Pentex's mega-television network. The show features a cheerful crowd of children abandoned at a daycare child-barn, who are endlessly entertained by a happy purple dinosaur. Movies, ice shows, and a large line of toys and clothing perpetuate this character, "Braney," owned by Tygers Group, one of Pentex's smallest and least-known subsidiaries.

Braney is actually Deep Purple Dark, a No-Sun Mokolé raised on a Louisiana gator farm. His search for power led him to the Atrocity Realm, where he operates a torture pit. Child-spirits are lured into the realm and burned, raped, flayed and eventually eaten by the devil-dinosaur. Pentex's Black Spiral camera crews tape the scenes and draw up scripts for the TV show, in which Braney appears to be a harmless toy who comes to "life." However, tapes of the Atrocity Realm sessions are hot items at the very highest-level Pentex corporate parties; Benjamin Rushing has personally approved funding for the show for so long as the "creative muse" remains with its star.

A few homid Mokolé have become aware of Braney's hideous actions and want to do something about him, but they aren't sure what. Access to the Atrocity Realm isn't easy, and simply killing this creature would probably not stop the demand for the tapes — Pentex could well find another star and another venue, one that would be better-hidden next time. The real solution may be more difficult.

Sister Rae, Bearing the Clutch of the River of Grass

Kinfolk are accorded honor among the Mokolé, but rarely is there anyone as extraordinary as Sister Rae. Born to

the human Kin who dwell in the Everglades near the River of Grass wallow, she chose See-How-He-Shines, the clutch's Rising Sun, as her mate and bore him two children, one a true Mokolé. She then developed True Faith in Sun, which she expressed in music, and several years ago left the clutch to found the Church of the New Sun in a storefront in Tallahassee. The Church has spread, with revivals and prayer concerts featuring Sister and the gospel choir, whose CDs have become popular among a small circle of admirers. She preaches that God's love is for all, and her faith has taken her to the sinister byways of the World of Darkness — she even hopes to someday find one of the mythical "vampire clubs" and sing there, to urge the dead that Sun shines for them. Elders have warned Sister Rae and even forbidden her to preach to other Awakened, but her outreach has made connections in many strange places, and a motley crowd of Awakened show up for her concerts and church services, drawn by her compelling preaching style and beautiful music.

Suchids and Their Kind

Waving Flags finished piling soil on the tall flowers that were her namesake and slid her long body back into the water. Sun was hot this day, and a swim was in order. Refreshed, she headed downriver to where the two-legs came to play. She knew the Law: leave them alone when other meat was ready to her jaws. But a fool could be culled. She puzzled how the two-legs themselves didn't seem to know this.

Not much meat on a two-legs hatchling anyway.

Waving Flags tasted the change before she saw it. The pond was gone, with a stone hill instead, a two-legs' burrow. Bitter oil tainted the water. She saw two-legs running a metal thing that killed trees and tore the earth. The gator headed back to the wallow. The Wise needed waking. Trouble was on its way.

Alligators, crocodiles, and monitor lizards are fascinating creatures, much more intelligent than humans suspect, and as close as any of us can get to seeing the dinosaurs. Roleplaying a reptile can be a wonderful exercise in imagination. The following information can help. The details here concern crocodilians and monitor lizards, the two largest groups. Mnesis records other kinds of Mokolé, but none are known to have lived through the Wars of Rage. There are no Mokolé still alive whose Suchid forms are turtles or small lizards; such bloodlines did not survive in the extermination attacks of the egg-smashers.

Alligators and Crocodiles

The World of Darkness has twenty-three species of crocodilians and one species of wolf. The Mokolé varna are thus extremely diverse, even before including the monitors and Gilas.

An adult American alligator is up to 19 feet long, living in watercourses in the South. They feed on fish, mammals and birds and nest on the banks. They also dig waterholes deeper and pile up earth, triggering the growth of "alligator flags," a flowering grass. This is how a wallow is created; it's an essential skill for suchids. Alligators are slow-moving, but capable of sudden bursts of speed. They are ambush hunters, lurking to take prey by surprise. Hunting is usually by taste and smell, rather than sight. Gators can dive and swim underwater for up to one hour. They pass winter hibernating in burrows or shelters, and cannot tolerate freezing weather.

The number of alligators in any given watercourse varies, but up to 75 can live in a five-mile stream. In any area, one adult will dominate all the others, although there is not a complex hierarchy. Alligators are not strongly territorial, but will defend themselves if threatened. Mating is once a year in April-May and eggs are laid in June. Courtship is highly elaborate among ordinary gators; it's doubly so between suchids and their Kin. Eggs are laid every 2-4 years among older alligators. The mother lays 20-70 eggs in a nest near water. She watches them carefully for the nine weeks that they incubate and packs vegetation round them to warm them; this instinct is what led to the creation of the Rite of the Nesting Mound. If the eggs are not kept warm, they can still hatch, but will take until September or October to do so. The entire wallow guards them, but the mother stands over the nest personally and guards the hatchlings as well; older gators think nothing of breakfasting on a hatchling. Hatchlings are nine inches long and have sharp teeth. They are able to breed when five years old. Small alligators (smaller than humans) can climb trees and even sleep there. An eight-year-old can be up to 8' long and is fully mature, although growth can continue for many more years. The American alligator was threatened earlier in the twentieth century, but has been protected for some time thanks to lobbying by Kinfolk. Alligator farms operated by Kin and Homids have been a key step in this process, and true Mokolé are born there.

The Chinese alligator (Lung) is similar, although smaller. This animal inhabits the Yangtze river basin in Anhwei and Kiangsi Provinces and is unknown elsewhere. Few grow to more than 5' in length, although ancient Zhong Lung were 10' or more long. Like the American alligator, it feeds on fish, turtles and mammal prey and digs dens in riverbanks. It is almost extinct, leading to fear among the Zhong Lung of China that they will "lose the dragon" and no longer be able to shapeshift.

South Florida and the Caribbean are home to the rare American crocodile, which is up to 15' in length. It eats mammal and fish prey. This creature lives on seacoasts and will dig out depressions for sleeping and shelter. Thirty to seventy crocodiles can live in one area. Mating is in March, April and May. Its huge nests are 10-12 feet across and contain 50-75 eggs which hatch in July and August. The Orinoco crocodile, found throughout the Orinoco river basin, is similar, as are the Cuban and Morelet's crocodiles. The Orinoco crocodile buries its eggs in the sand to avoid detection, rather than making a nest. The Cuban crocodile, near extinction, preys on fowl, pigs, and dogs and is very aggressive. Cuban crocodiles are heavily armored, especially on their legs, but are rarely more than 7' long. Though poor at swimming in the sea, these crocodilians are commonly carried long distances on rafts of floating vegetation. Therefore, they have been able to colonize islands and seacoasts far from their usual range.

The Gumagan whose varna was the Johnston's crocodile, a harmless species native to Australian rivers, are now extinct. This has caused many Garou to believe that the Gumagan are completely gone, but some do remain. The New Guinea crocodile is similar to the saltwater crocodile, but smaller. It reaches a length of 5-9 feet and nests on the banks of rivers in New Guinea. New Guinea crocodiles are territorial and are good swimmers. The Mindoro and Thai crocodiles are similar.

Please note that of the world's crocodilians, only the American alligator is not endangered. Even the Nile crocodile of Africa is extinct throughout much of its range, particularly with the Dissolver's efforts to hunt down Mokolé and Kin.

The Indo-Pacific, or saltwater crocodile, inhabits the coastal waters of Zhong Guo, westward to India. This mighty creature is possibly the largest living reptile on Earth, known to grow to a length of 23 feet and weigh 2,000 pounds. Unconfirmed reports of these crocs indicate that they may grow up to 30 feet, though certainly such sightings may be Delirium-fed rumors. Saltwater crocodiles also inhabit places as far away as China and Malaysia. Indian saltwater crocodile-born Mokolé call themselves the Karna, after a spirit of the waves. As great travelers amongst the Mokolé, they are renowned amongst Indian Mokolé for bearing memories of lost Pacific cultures and outsiders. Inland Makara often seek them out for ritual exchanges of memories. The coastal Karna also act as a sort of first defense for the Indian lands against unwanted taint. The Karna see themselves generally as the Makara meant to follow the Trimurti of the Creator, known amongst Hindu homids as Brahma. They know that life came from the sea and consider themselves its protector. Karna clutches are active in trying to save marine life and in efforts to eliminate damage to coastal environments. It is said that the Karna try to coax the Creator into blessing the earth with new species; they remember evolution with particular nostalgia. They can swim 600 miles across the sea, and once wiped out a whole company of Japanese soldiers during World War II. They prey fearlessly on humans who defile the wild. Nests are large piles of vegetation up to 5 feet wide and contain 25-75 eggs. Hatchlings are known to grow 18-20" per year. Salties hunt well and cover their prey with stacks of grass to hide it for later consumption. They sunbathe less than other varna and are less gregarious. "Buaya," an insulting term, is derived from a Malay word for the sex-crazed male crocodiles. Today it means any sex-crazed male, especially a salty.

The true leaders amongst the Mokolé of India are descended from the mugger crocodiles. Indeed, it is from the Sanskrit "Water Monster" that the mugger's name originates, reformed as Magar in Hindi from Makara, and changed to "mugger" by the English. Of course, the unforgetting Mokolé of this line still refer to themselves as the Makara. Mugger suchids and their homid relatives rule the swamps of India. They have powerful ties to religious sects stemming from ages spent serving as temple crocodiles. Those who know of their true nature alternately regard them as demons or avatars of the gods. The Makara are the kings amongst the Mokolé of India, masters of mystical secrets and seekers of truth. The Makara seek to preserve all of India against the Destroyer, whom they see as the Dissolver-corrupted. The true accomplishment of the Makara is found in their relations with humanity. No other Mokolé have more Kinfolk or more influence in the mortal realm. From their hidden swamp wallows, the clutches of the Makara have ensured that India has absorbed invader after invader and contained them all, preserving religions and ideas that might have otherwise perished. They see mankind as a worthy child of the earth-mother, Jya, and court the monkey-children carefully.

A third suchid breed is fairly common in India, as the subcontinent is home to the gavials. Gavials are crocodilians, not true crocodiles. They grow to be 21 feet in length and possess long, narrow snouts. The gavials live in India's rivers and eat fish. The gavial suchid breed is found along four rivers in Asia. The Brahmaputra, Ganges and Mahamadi Rivers in India are home to the gavial, as is the Koladon River of southeast Asia. It is certain that the species was on the way to extinction until it was declared an endangered species and extensive repopulating programs were begun. Gavials are timid crocodilians, but are held to be sacred by a number of Hindu sects. The Gharials, as gavial-born Mokolé call themselves, are not as combative as most Mokolé. In part this is due to their weaker jaws. It also comes from their perceived roles as protectors of the sacred rivers and watchers of the dead. Male Gharials are marked by the strange red fleshy lumps that are found between their snout nostrils. Indeed it is these lumps that give them their names, as "ghar" means "pot" in Hindi. They are reputed to be bear the secrets of fertility and to wield great respect from Gaia for their role. Gharials are possibly the only Mokolé in the world amongst which males accorded such a potent Matre-like position. The Gharials serve the Dissolver-Uncorrupted, the Trimurti of the Dissolver. This strange relationship explains their simultaneous connection with death and sexuality. The great river Ganga is said by the Hindus to have been sent to the Earth by Shiva, and the gavials are its rulers. They watch the dead who are reverently placed in the river, and are said to occasionally Dissolve those who need to die for the better protection of Jya. An unusual feature of gavial life is that the animals are right-or left-handed, just like humans. They nest in sand, laying 20-40 eggs which hatch in April.

Caimans are alligator-like crocodilians native to Central and South America. Caimans are 10-13' long at most (many are very small, only 4-6' long) and feed on fish and mammal prey. Some will eat plant foods when they are hungry or ill. They are shy and do not group into wallows easily: many live alone. Often they hunt by night and sleep by day. There are several species, the most common being the spectacled caiman. They nest like American alligators, but lay only 25-30 eggs. Many caimans have a color-changing ability like that of the chameleon. Some also have rough, scaly backs. The caiman Mokolé of South America are very few in number. They are believed to have only two wallows left in the Orinoco basin. This varna are the keepers of the land, the knowers of its secrets and the guardians of the deepest Mnesis. They know more about the Bird Kings and Pouch Kings than any other beings on Gaia's face. They are the most devoted parents of any varna. Females will guard their eggs and hatchlings communally and carry the young to safety.

All crocodilians are meat and fish eaters, but can live on very little food. Seven crocodiles each weighing 100lbs. can live on the same amount of food as one 95-lb. wolf. Thus crocodilians and Mokolé can survive in smaller areas than running packs of wolves and Garou.

There are fossil remains of many more species of crocodilians unlike any extant today, including sea crocodiles which bore their young alive, duckbilled fish-eaters, gigantic 60' dragon-like crocodiles, land-dwelling runner crocodiles and many more. The Storyteller may include such creatures in the game through Mnesis.

Monitor Lizards: The Ora

'Ho! Ho!' he said. 'That one a Big One. A Walk One. A Perenty One.'

— Bruce Chatwin, *The Songlines*

Species of monitors are found throughout the tropics of the Old World, from the Nile eastward to Australia. The largest species, the Komodo dragon, is a good example. The Ora, the Komodo dragon varna of Mokolé, are rare, but very prestigious. Only four clutches of Ora are known to exist.

The Komodo dragon evolved in the Miocene period in Southeast Asia and is related to the monitor lizards of Africa, India, and Asia. When Mokolé spread across the world after the Age of Sleep, Komodo Island became a center for Mokolé. Komodo dragons are found along with their Mokolé relatives on the islands of Flores, Padar, Rintja and Komodo itself. These small island refuges are dry savanna with patches of forest: the Komodo dragon is the largest predator, as lions are in Africa. They grow up to 12 feet long, weighing 550 lbs, and live on land eating deer, buffalo, and other game. Humans are not eaten unless they provoke the dragons or break the Duties. They are ambush hunters, striking quickly, and can reduce a 70-lb. animal to hair and hooves (they eat the bones) in seventeen minutes. Cooperative hunting is rare, but seems to take place on occasion. They eat up to 80% of their own body weight in a single meal. They also eat carrion and can smell a carcass more than 6 miles away. This adaptation allows them to survive on small islands. The lizards can go for more than 45 days without eating or drinking. They are the most intelligent reptiles in the world, and have a consistent body temperature because of their large mass (they are technically "cold-blooded" but in fact maintain a uniform temperature). The dragons can dive and swim up to half a mile, or further when swept by wind and storms from island to island. They dig burrows for shelter and as hunting blinds and can dig three feet in an hour. All monitor lizards have wide fields of vision, over 240°, with the central 60° being binocular. They see in full color and often hunt by sight.

Komodo dragons mate in June, July and August and incubate a clutch of up to 28 eggs for eight months. Courtship often takes place at a kill site or near a carcass, and a bull may court a cow for many months before she agrees to mate: some devoted bulls court throughout the year. To compete for a female, males may "joust" by walking on their hind legs (to honor the Kings, the Mokolé say) and wrestling until one surrenders. Mating is often for many years, even for life. Eggs are laid once a year at most and some females lay eggs only once every two or three years. Cows can store seed for up to one year before laying eggs. The mother lizard does not care for the young, who eat insects and small animals. Three or four males are found for each female. Females are able to mate at age five or six; Komodo dragons may live for two decades more. Starting in September, the dragons molt, shedding skin, and any who have suffered Dissolver-taint can avail themselves of the Rite of Shedding, which cleanses them. Usually all Komodo dragons bathe in ponds, streams or the sea when done molting.

The clutch on Towers-Above-The-Kings, or Komodo Island, had four Mokolé and several hundred Komodo relatives. Human Kin, exiled to the island by the sultan of Bima on Flores in the nineteenth century, number about five hundred. The early voyages of the Chinese ("Bajini") brought merchants and sailors to the Sunda Islands, including Wanderers from the Yangtze River clutches of Zhong Lung. They rejoiced to find the Dragon Breed thriving in this far land. Malesi, the last matriarch of the clutch, was born at this time and has slept for many centuries.

In 1912 the Komodo Dragon was "discovered" by the scientists of Europe. Kinfolk on the island made sure that the "giant lizards" were a worldwide sensation, nixing any attempt to exterminate them, and got the Sultan to declare that killing a lizard was a sin against Allah. The Komodo dragon was thus one of the first protected species in the world. Reports of 23-foot monster reptiles on the island, starting when two Dutch fishermen saw the Mokolé in Archid form, were quashed when scientists came and tourists followed. The cash flow kept the Mokolé solvent and ensured that the island would stay a wild preserve.

The Australian supercontinent, including Tasmania and New Guinea, was home to many species of the Kings, ending with the 23-foot lizard Megalania, weighing over 1500 lbs. Perenties, the eight-foot gigantic lace monitors of Australia, are similar to Komodo dragons and are closely related to them. An adult perenty can weigh up to 35 lbs. They live in desert and scrub areas and prey on mammals (including kangaroos) and smaller reptiles. These lizards have excellent color vision and can see a human 1000 feet away. Their lifespan can be over 20 years. Many are Kin to the Gumagan. They are excellent diggers and excavate 20-30 foot caverns to hide from heat and cold. They can also climb trees. Perenties hibernate from May to August, often with their mates. They do not like water. Two clutches of perenty Gumagan are known to exist. Frightened by the War of Tears, their Kin and allies went to the Australian government and had the monitor lizards protected. It is now illegal to hunt them or remove the from Australia unless for a legitimate zoo.

Unktehi — The Desert Dragons

The Kings in Laurasia left few relics behind, but the venomous lizard species of the Southwest have persisted for more than one hundred million years. The native varna of the American Southwest and Mexico is also the smallest known: Gila monsters and Mexican beaded lizards. They refer to themselves as the Unktehi, a name passed to their Kin among the Native Americans. These animals are up to 3 1/2 ft in length and live on bird eggs and small mammals, usually swallowing their prey whole. They are colored and marked in order to hide in the desert sands. Their venom acts slowly but is as deadly as cobra venom. Humans usually do not die from it, but their bite is exceedingly painful. These varna store fat in their tails and can live for more than a year without food. They run slowly and can swim only in emergencies. Mating occurs in summer and eggs come in July or August. The eggs incubate from one to four months. Gila monsters figure prominently in local folklore. They are supposed to be able to control the weather and the cycles of women's' bodies, and their private parts were at one time eaten as an aphrodisiac. Only two clutches, one in Mexico and one in Nevada, are known of these strange Mokolé-mbembe. Unless a character's Archid form includes the characteristic "Huge Size," he will be only as large as his Homid form when in Archid, as the Suchid forms of the Unktehi are so small.

Antagonists

Mokolé and Vampires

Mokolé hate vampires because they are creatures of darkness, forever barred from Sun's glory. The Mokolé greeting "Sun sees you" is never given to a vampire, as Sun's light destroys them (obvious proof that vampires are forever damned). Mokolé ferociously attack any Leech, unless forcibly prevented from doing so or forewarned that they are fatally outmatched. Mokolé know little about vampiric society, and what they know disgusts them; their belief is that the only moral action for a vampire is to destroy himself in the hope of Sun's forgiveness. Most vampires barely know that the Mokolé exist, save for the Followers of Set, who know them all too well. When they meet, the result is catastrophic for the Kindred, as none but the mightiest of the Damned can stand against the Dragon Breed in combat.

Vampire thralls ("halfdeads") are seen as pathetic, and may be spared if they do not threaten Mokolé. Any thrall who is Mokolé Kinfolk will be the target of "rescue" attacks from her Mokolé relatives, who will not spare life or property to get her back (willingly or unwillingly). One cell of the ghoul-sect called the Unmastered was destroyed when Giant Footsteps, a Mokolé from Bayou Têche, got word that his sister was at their hideout.

Mokolé cannot be Embraced — Sun prevents this. If a vampire tries to Embrace a Mokolé, the werecrocodile is allowed the standard Gnosis roll. The Mokolé may succeed, in which case she dies and enters the Memory of Gaia. She may fail, in which case she dies slowly and in great pain. If she botches, she becomes an Abomination and instantly enters a berserker frenzy, during which she will likely slay her "sire" and anyone else nearby, as well as uprooting trees, leveling buildings and diverting rivers. It's said that Leeches, on seeing the raging Archid "Abomination," have died the Final Death from sheer fright. The undead Archid certainly inspires the Delirium in vampires (Rötschreck checks if using **Vampire: The Masquerade** rules; at the Storyteller's option, botching this roll can even inflict damage on the luckless vampire as Sun enfleshed rages before him). The frenzy lasts till sunrise, when the Mokolé burns up, releasing the final shards of her spirit. Should the pseudo-vampire Mokolé be prevented from rushing into sunlight, she will die at the next sunset; without Sun, there is no life nor unlife. Mokolé Kin can be Embraced, but any Kin with Gnosis may make a Gnosis roll as above to return to Gaia. Should Mokolé learn that a Kinsman has been Embraced, they will almost certainly try to destroy him at once, as well as his "sire" and any other Leeches they see.

The Mokolé who drinks vitae (a vampire's blood), should roll Gnosis, difficulty 7. For each success, one blood point is vomited up or lost through explosive diarrhea. The taste of vitae ensures that no Mokolé will drink it willingly, although it might be given as an enema or injected. If given vitae through trickery, a Mokolé might well go into frenzy. Vomiting and diarrhea continue until all the vitae is gone; if the Mokolé botches, she will have the vitae in her system until sunrise, when one point of vitae will disappear. One more point will disappear with every sunrise. Mokolé cannot ever learn vampiric Disciplines, other than the automatic one point of Potence that comes with successful ghouling. In addition, Mokolé may suffer from bad Mnesis while the vampire-filth spreads through their bodies.

Vampires who know of the Mokolé and have managed to feed on them usually have no desire to repeat the experience. Kindred who feed on them will often desire only to bask in moonlight or may go into torpor. The exception are the Followers of Set, who preserve tales of the wonderful elixir that is Mokolé blood. They say that it gives them "serpent power." The truth of this is unknown.

The Haunters of Mnesis

Dream Hunters

Jeffo closed his eyes and imagined Ulungan before whitefella: grass tall and green with the hills of Dreamtime in the distance, a scent of smoke as Perenty Mob burned the wattle trees. He would walkabout into Memory and watch his ancestors work the rite: they had insights he needed badly. He walked within, in his ancestor's footsteps. Sun was sinking as he neared the meeting pool. With surprise he noticed a wallaby drinking. As he came closer, it rose to meet him. Willing game? The ancestor-hand lifted a spear. It was wise to take what the spirits offered.

The wallaby grew, impossibly, and hopped toward him with hand-long claws. It ripped his chest open while he struggled to raise his arm for a spear cast. He shapeshifted... and so did this monster, into a pouch-lion. The Gumagan yelled and bit at the thing, losing blood fast.

Jeffo opened his eyes, gasping, and clutched at his chest. No rites for him today.

Dream Hunters are memories so compelling that one place or time within Mnesis cannot hold them. They break free when recalled and roam the corridors of time and memory. They are usually hostile to the Mokolé who goes within, seeking to subdue or possess him.

Rage 8, Willpower 7, Gnosis 5, Power 40

Charms: Dream Warp*, Possession, Materialize, Shapeshift (the Dream Hunter can take any shape which exists in the scene that the Mokolé remembers. For example, if the Mokolé was remembering ancient Dahomey, it could appear as a lion, soldier or messenger).

***Dream Warp** — The spirit can pervert a dream it enters by rolling its Gnosis versus the victim's Willpower. Only one success is needed, and the Power cost is 1.

Image: The Dream Hunters are shapeshifters and appear as part of the scene they invade. They are clever and will seem to be a rock, tree, animal, human — whatever is necessary.

Background: Dream Hunters migrate from memory to memory and even from Mokolé to Mokolé. They are apparently immortal and are very hard to kill: it is possible to destroy them entirely by erasing the memory that they come from or with certain Rites.

They will try to drive Mokolé out of Mnesis, making them afraid to go within, so that the Dream Hunters can control the Memory. They can also possess the Mokolé who remembers them and control his actions. The Storyteller should keep in mind that the Dream Hunters are not Umbral beings, but creatures of pure memory.

Smrtihara (Eaters of Memory)

Skandadasa spread spirit wings and caught a thermal of dreamfire. The astral winds were cool on his not-body. He strained his eyes to the limit — there it was, the memory of his ancestor's pilgrimage to the source of the river. If he could only find it and bring it back to Bhatta Ma, the route would be clear.

With strong wingbeats he soared closer. What was that shape clinging to the outside of the memory? He could make out insect legs, a swollen abdomen. He glided near to the memory-form and the thing raised its head and looked at him. Skandadasa gasped at the hole it had eaten.

He had to fight it off. He landed on the memory-sphere and gripped the surface firmly. The Eater of Memory ticked and clacked toward him. It was a huge creature, and fear gripped him. He held still as it sniffed. What did a Makara taste like to something that ate the past?

Pretty good, it seemed! It opened a mouth to bite, and the young seeker clamped jaws onto its body. Ichor spewed over him, the rot of time. The two struggled on. Skandadasa worried: even if he could defeat this thing, what was left of the memory that it had stolen?

Smrtihara are Umbral creatures who roam the Astral Realm and consume memory, feeding off it. They are creations of the Wyrm and their original purpose was to prevent Gaia's mind from cluttering with trivia. But with the corruption of the Dissolver, they have become vicious predators who attack Mokolé travelers and the memories they seek.

Rage 10, Willpower 10, Gnosis 8, Power 40

Charms: Airt Sense, Reform, Incite Frenzy, Eat Mnesis*

* **Eat Mnesis** — The Smrtihara can bite into a memory; its current Gnosis is opposed to the Gnosis of the Mokolé who guards the memory, or they may engage in combat directly in the Umbra. The Smrtihara must accumulate as many successes as the level of Mnesis of the memory in order to devour it entirely. For each level of Mnesis it eats, it gains a corresponding number of Power points.

Image: The Smrtihara look like huge tomato hornworms or potato-bug larvae, with insect legs, arthropod jaws and mandibles, and big compound eyes. They are colored weird shades of neon green and blaze orange with black spots along their flanks. To travel in the astral "sky" they wriggle like swimming worms.

Background: The Dissolver-Uncorrupted whelped the Eaters of Memory as janitors for Gaia's Mind, erasing unneeded memories to prevent madness. They fell with their maker and became menaces to the Memory. They roam the High Umbra doing damage and looking for trouble. They have no social organization and will gladly eat each other: when one reaches twice the Power listed above, it splits into two smaller Eaters of Memory. They seek out travelers with lots of memories and try to kill and eat them. They are unintelligent but have all the knowledge from the memories that they have eaten: for example, they certainly know what Mokolé are.

Pratigata: the Vanished Memories

Skandadasa held his not-breath, fearing to disturb the weird creature. How did you say hello to a forgotten dream? He decided to be bold.

"Namaste, sri Pratigata. I am Skandadasa Carries-the Sign."

"Oh? I am... I am... I forget." The ancient was a thin thing, the stars and gas sheets of the Astral Realm visible through its form. Its crest and scales bespoke the Time of the Kings. "It has been too long."

"Revered one, could you be the Sutra of Dragon's Eye? I have searched long for you."

"The... what?"

"The Sutra of Dragon's Eye, revered one. For long the Makara of Ganga thought you lost. You are the greatest of wisdoms."

"I do not feel very wise."

"You are that sutra!"

"If you say so. I am tired."

The Pratigata are the lost memories: many Mokolé spend years or centuries on Mnesis and Umbral quests to find them and the teaching that they contain. The Pratigata are quixotic, alien and often more trouble than they are worth. But the hope of finding treasure in the wrecks of time lures Mokolé to this day.

Rage 2, Willpower 4, Gnosis 5, Power 5

Image: An ancient Mokolé whose form is hard to see. Usually they will appear as someone who might remember the memory which the seeker is looking for.

Background: The Pratigata are wraiths: the Restless Dead of memory. They originate when the last holder of Mnesis dies or when a memory is forgotten or erased. They are usually unaware of their own role or importance and appear and disappear at random. They often refuse to cooperate with a seeker and are capricious and unpredictable — not unlike a demented old professor with Alzheimer's.

Roleplaying Notes for the Past

The married woman hunts the kangaroo and wallaby
The emu runs in the forest
The boomer runs in the forest...
The dog-faced opossum [runs in the forest]
— Fanny Cochrane Smith, Tasmanian aborigine

The Kings

The Storyteller must create the world of the Kings for himself, based on maps of the world in the Mesozoic. The Kings were an intelligent toolmaker species, or group of similar species, who flourished in the Jurassic and Cretaceous periods. They were Kin to the Mokolé. They had humanlike technology, the level of which varied according to the place and time (most typically Bronze Age or the equivalent). The information given below is for the cities of Laurasia's coast in the middle Cretaceous.

Attitudes toward Mokolé varied in the Mesozoic: in some cities, they were rulers, priests and so on; at other times and places, they were shunned as dangerous creatures by all

but their own Kin. However, the Dragon Breed lived out in the open; there was no need to hide during this time.

Mokolé in this era have three forms: Suchid, Archid, and Drachid.

• **Suchid:** The Suchid form is a crocodilian or monitor lizard. Statistics are the same as for the modern period.

• **Archid:** Use the list of Archid form characteristics. The result will usually be more dinosaur-like than dragon-like. The Rite of Passage is the same and so are character attributes.

• **Drachid:** The Drachid form resembles a bipedal dinosaur with opposable thumbs and a large brain. This was also the form of the Drachid Kin: statistics are below.

Character creation for the Kinfolk is similar to that for humans, although some Skills and Knowledges will be different. The following assumes a low technological level, but of course, higher technologies are possible. The Kings did not usually wear clothes but would protect themselves from the cold. Their society was hierarchical, even in their equivalent of the Stone Age, and rank was as important to them as to the true Mokolé (assume that characters start at Rank 1). Their tools and weapons were often "grown" by living creatures instead of being "made" from stones, etc. For example, vats of algae were kept which could secrete gold or iron from seawater. The algae could then be burnt to extract the metal. Living creatures were bred which could serve as tools. For example, a soft, warm-blooded creature would be kept as a cloak.

Attributes 8/6/3, Abilities 21/12/7, Backgrounds 6, Willpower 5

Suggested Attributes: Assume ratings of 2, with physical being 3 or 4 for hunters and warriors, social 3 or 4 for traders/rulers and mental 3 or 4 for scholars.

Suggested Abilities: Alertness, Athletics, Brawl, Dodge, Melee, Thrown Weapons, Leadership, Stealth, Expression, Primal-Urge, Survival, Enigmas, Medicine, Rituals.

Equipment: Spear, bow and arrows, tool pouch, medicinal herbs, warm cloak, ceremonial headdress, devices.

There is no Gauntlet in this time; the worlds of spirit and flesh are one. The Delirium and the Veil do not exist

Disclaimer

Some among you might be offended by the very thought of a pre-human civilization, particularly one that left no artifacts behind, WonderWork or no. Well, there's a very simple solution to this: Ignore the idea.

Yes, that's right. Ignore the idea.

After all, you can easily presume that Mnesis has been corrupted, potentially by the WonderWork, and that there was never any such era. You can even ignore references to the Time of the Kings, and simply say that such a time never was and the Mokolé don't remember any such thing. It's your game. You have the power.

unless they are inventions of the Dissolver or Designer. Dinosaurs are very common, of course. The Dissolver seems to have become deranged in the Cretaceous, leading to the WonderWork. The extent of this isn't clear, but the Storyteller may create monstrous Dissolver-things as she sees fit.

Bird Kings and Pouch Kings

The Kings failed, but they did not die. The WonderWork killed the dinosaurs, but enough reptile Kin remained that Mokolé could survive. But alligators and crocodiles weren't the only heirs of the Dinosaur Kings. As old Gondwanaland broke up (broken-hearted at the WonderWork, sages say), upon her fragments lived the Bird Kings and the Pouch Kings. The Bird Kings, giant flightless strutters and hunters, strode the plains and savannas of the southern continents like the dinosaurs that they had been; the marsupials ruled Bandaiyan and Ambalosokei (Australia and South America) without challenge. Birds and marsupials are warm-blooded, of course, but their close relationship to reptiles means that the Mokolé counted Diatryma(the great running hunter-bird) and Thylacoleo (a marsupial "lion") as Kin. The last of these great lineages live on into our own time, and Mokolé all round the Indian Ocean sing the Adventures of Greatpouch and the Song of the Dodo to this day.

Something like the reign of the Bird Kings is portrayed in Piers Anthony's novel *Orn*. Orn is a Mokolé-like sentient bird with Mnesis, and the book could be a chronicle all by itself. The Bird Kings and the Pouch Kings present many possibilities for adventure: they could search through Mnesis for the lore of the dinosaurs, investigate ruined cities and lost Dissolver-hives, and travel through the realms of the Umbra, which was a very different place in the early Cenozoic. The Pouch Kings and Bird Kings present the Storyteller with the theme of "possible worlds." If the southern continents' marsupials instead of the North's placentals had ended up prevailing when the continents collided, what would our world be like today? What about a world in which mass extinctions never happened, or where the other phyla (bizarre creatures) developed sentience? Would Gaia be the "great mother" to a world of intelligent trilobites? The imaginable consequences are summed up in Stephen Jay Gould's *Wonderful Life*.

In the World of Darkness, possibilities multiply, divide and converge. The Umbra contains memories and fragments of these un-places, and a visit to such a tiny realm would be very interesting. The Mokolé Shrouded Suns have often sought for another realm ruled by the Kings, and some claim to have been there.

The Last Times

A chronicle set in the Last Times could be very interesting. The Garou and Mokolé could fight side by side against Dissolver creatures, explore new lands, probe the depths of Mnesis, or travel in the Umbra. Characters could be Mokolé, humans, or other Changing Breeds, including the lost Grondr and Camazotz (for whom the Storyteller must invent rules). The Gauntlet would be almost nonexistent: 2 or 3, most likely. There would be no Innocents, making travel in the Umbra easy. High Mnesis and Pure Breed would be very common: to reflect this, the Storyteller could allow them to be purchased for half price or give them to characters automatically.

Most Mokolé would be suchid: as the period ended, homids comprised perhaps a tenth of the Dragon Breed. It is possible that sterile suchids or homids could be born from a union of two Mokolé, although they would not be true "metis." If such an event took place, Mnesis does not record it. Some Kinfolk could also be Kin to the Garou, connecting the two Breeds by ties of blood.

The coming of the Dissolver's corruption awakened a sense of foreboding in the Mokolé, as they recalled the WonderWork that destroyed the Kings. Their apprehension was not understandable to the Garou. The most poignant use of the Last Times is as an inwitting story for Mokolé who are alive today; they can feel the grief and loss more sharply if they know the glory that went before.

The Wars of Rage

The Wars of Rage provide many ideas to the Storyteller. The players could be defending against Garou onslaughts, counterattacking against Garou who slew their Kin or clutchmates, seeking refuge by flight into wilderness or across the oceans, or questing for better weapons and tactics. The Mokolé, in their desperation, could seek allies among the Bête; some might even listen to the false promises of power held out by the Dissolver. As the Grondr, Apis, Camazotz and Khara died off one by one, the Mokolé would try to preserve any lore or memories of them that existed: Mokolé fought in the sounder of Brazentusk when he fell brandishing the Sword of the Boar, and the memory remains to this day of the Grondr's heroism.

They could also be trying to end the War (it never ended; the Garou simply assumed that the Mokolé were extinct). Perhaps a third party such as the Corax could help with negotiations. Could human Kin who are related to both Changing Breeds be caught in the middle?

Another story could involve the present day, as Mokolé journey back to the Wars of Rage to begin a healing process with the Garou slaughterers. The Garou could learn through Past Life what atrocities they committed. The Mokolé could learn through Mnesis that the Garou were not the only ones to do wrong.

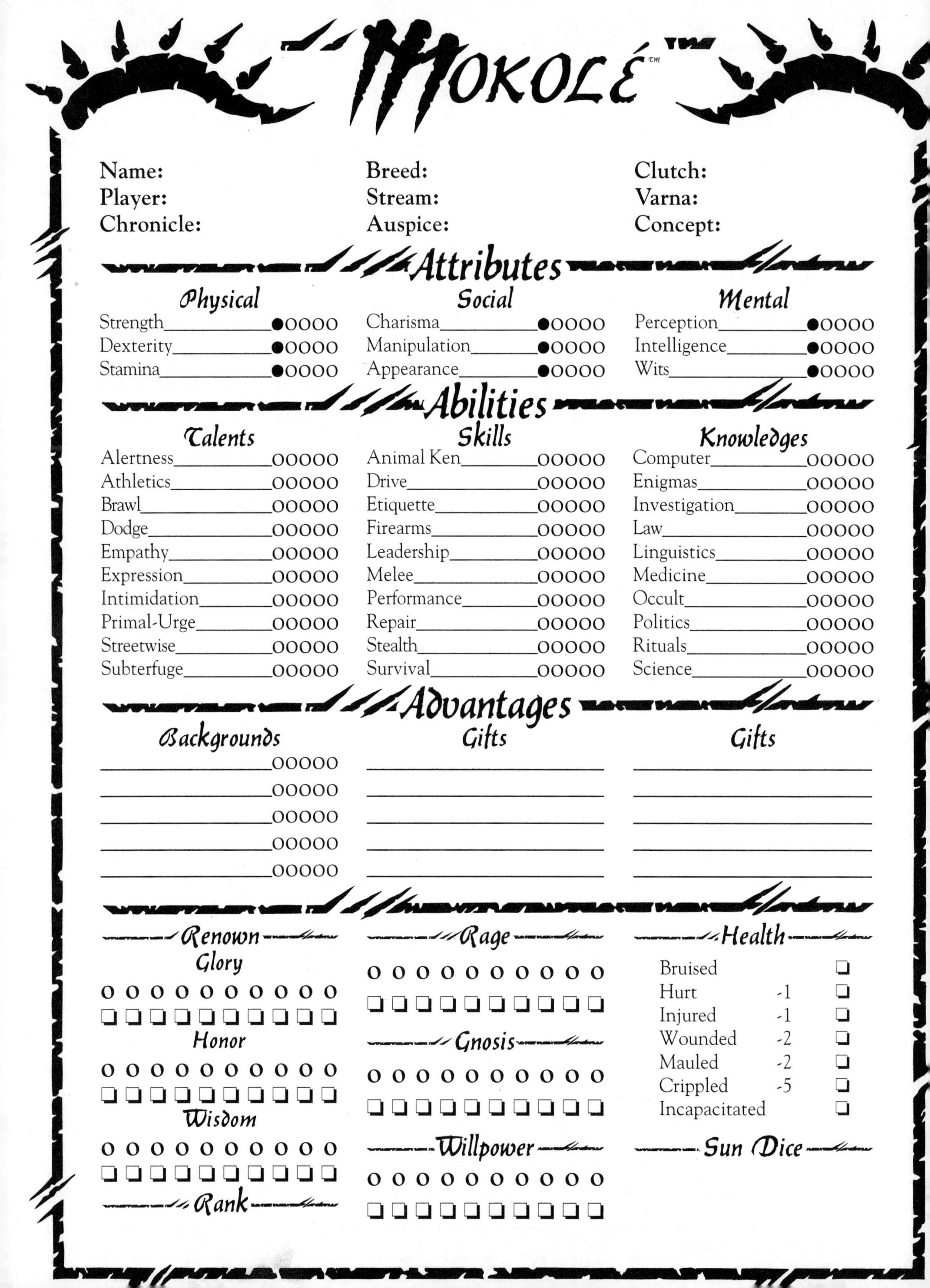

Mokolé™

Name:	Breed:	Clutch:
Player:	Stream:	Varna:
Chronicle:	Auspice:	Concept:

Attributes

Physical		Social		Mental	
Strength	●0000	Charisma	●0000	Perception	●0000
Dexterity	●0000	Manipulation	●0000	Intelligence	●0000
Stamina	●0000	Appearance	●0000	Wits	●0000

Abilities

Talents		Skills		Knowledges	
Alertness	00000	Animal Ken	00000	Computer	00000
Athletics	00000	Drive	00000	Enigmas	00000
Brawl	00000	Etiquette	00000	Investigation	00000
Dodge	00000	Firearms	00000	Law	00000
Empathy	00000	Leadership	00000	Linguistics	00000
Expression	00000	Melee	00000	Medicine	00000
Intimidation	00000	Performance	00000	Occult	00000
Primal-Urge	00000	Repair	00000	Politics	00000
Streetwise	00000	Stealth	00000	Rituals	00000
Subterfuge	00000	Survival	00000	Science	00000

Advantages

Backgrounds		Gifts	Gifts
________	00000	________	________
________	00000	________	________
________	00000	________	________
________	00000	________	________
________	00000	________	________

Renown

Glory

0 0 0 0 0 0 0 0 0 0

❑ ❑ ❑ ❑ ❑ ❑ ❑ ❑ ❑ ❑

Honor

0 0 0 0 0 0 0 0 0 0

❑ ❑ ❑ ❑ ❑ ❑ ❑ ❑ ❑ ❑

Wisdom

0 0 0 0 0 0 0 0 0 0

❑ ❑ ❑ ❑ ❑ ❑ ❑ ❑ ❑ ❑

Rank

Rage

0 0 0 0 0 0 0 0 0 0

❑ ❑ ❑ ❑ ❑ ❑ ❑ ❑ ❑ ❑

Gnosis

0 0 0 0 0 0 0 0 0 0

❑ ❑ ❑ ❑ ❑ ❑ ❑ ❑ ❑ ❑

Willpower

0 0 0 0 0 0 0 0 0 0

❑ ❑ ❑ ❑ ❑ ❑ ❑ ❑ ❑ ❑

Health

Bruised		❑
Hurt	-1	❑
Injured	-1	❑
Wounded	-2	❑
Mauled	-2	❑
Crippled	-5	❑
Incapacitated		❑

Sun Dice

Mokolé™

Homid

No Change

Difficulty: 6

Archid

Strength (+4)____
Dexterity (-1)____
Stamina (+4)____
Manipulation(-3)____
Appearance: 0

Difficulty: 6

CAUSES DELIRIUM IN HUMANS

Suchid

Strength (___)____
Dexterity(___)____
Stamina(___)____
Manipulation(___)____

Difficulty: 6

Archid Traits

____
____
____
____
____
____
____

Other Traits

________________________OOOOO
________________________OOOOO
________________________OOOOO
________________________OOOOO
________________________OOOOO
________________________OOOOO
________________________OOOOO

Fetishes

Item:________________ ❑Dedicated Level____ Gnosis____
Power:________________________________

Item:________________ ❑Dedicated Level____ Gnosis____
Power:________________________________

Item:________________ ❑Dedicated Level____ Gnosis____
Power:________________________________

Rites

____
____
____
____
____
____
____
____

Combat

Maneuver/Weapon	Roll	Difficulty	Damage	Range	Rate	Clip

Brawling Chart

Maneuver	Roll	Diff	Damage
Bite	Dex+Brawl	5	Strength+1†
Body Slam	Dex+Brawl	7	Special
Claw	Dex+Brawl	6	Strength+2†
Grapple	Dex+Brawl	6	Strength
Kick	Dex+Brawl	7	Strength+1
Punch	Dex+Brawl	6	Strength

†These maneuvers do aggravated damage.

Armor:________________

Nature: ______ Demeanor: ______

Merits & Flaws

Merit	Type	Cost	Flaw	Type	Bonus

Expanded Background

Allies

Mnesis

Contacts

Resources

Kinfolk

Totem

Possessions

Gear (Carried): ______

Equipment (Owned): ______

Wallow

Size: ______

Location: ______

Experience

TOTAL: ______

Gained From: ______

TOTAL SPENT: ______

Spent On: ______

Mokolé™

History

Prelude

Description

Age:
Hair:
Eyes:
Race:
Nationality:
Sex:

	Height	Weight
Homid:		
Archid:		
Suchid:		

Battle Scars:

Visuals

Clutch Chart

Character Sketch